Henry Toole Clark

Henry Toole Clark

Civil War Governor of North Carolina

R. MATTHEW POTEAT

Foreword by Joe A. Mobley

McFarland & Company, Inc., Publishers
Jefferson, North Carolina, and London

LIBRARY OF CONGRESS CATALOGUING-IN-PUBLICATION DATA

Poteat, R. Matthew, 1969–
Henry Toole Clark : Civil War governor of North Carolina /
R. Matthew Poteat ; foreword by Joe A. Mobley.
p. cm.
Includes bibliographical references and index.

ISBN 978-0-7864-3728-3
softcover : 50# alkaline paper ∞

1. Clark, Henry T. (Henry Toole), 1808–1874.
2. Governors — North Carolina — Biography.
3. North Carolina — Politics and government — 1861–1865.
4. North Carolina — Politics and government — 1775–1865.
5. North Carolina — Biography. I. Title.

F258.C58P68 2009   975.6'03092 — dc22 [B]   2008053641

British Library cataloguing data are available

©2009 R. Matthew Poteat. All rights reserved

*No part of this book may be reproduced or transmitted in any form
or by any means, electronic or mechanical, including photocopying
or recording, or by any information storage and retrieval system,
without permission in writing from the publisher.*

On the cover: Henry T. Clark, ca. 1850. This original oil painting
of Clark hangs in the home of the Governor's great-grandson,
Dr. Henry T. Clark, Jr., and his wife Blanche, of Chapel Hill.
The portrait was probably completed shortly after Clark's marriage
to his cousin, Mary Weeks Parker (photograph by the author).

Manufactured in the United States of America

*McFarland & Company, Inc., Publishers
Box 611, Jefferson, North Carolina 28640
www.mcfarlandpub.com*

For Katherine, and
my many friends and family
who made this possible

Contents

Acknowledgments ix
Foreword by Joe A. Mobley 1
Chronology 3
Introduction 5

1. Frontier Aristocrats 15
2. Coming Into His Own 38
3. "We rely upon his honesty" 70
4. "North Carolina has been neglected" 90
5. "With no man to protect us" 104
6. "That Odious Constitution" 119

Epilogue 145
Appendix A. The James West Clark Letters (1822–1827) 153
Appendix B. "On the English Character," Clark's University Oration 166
Appendix C. A Poem Describing Members of the North Carolina Senate, 1861 169
Appendix D. Maps 172
Chapter Notes 177
Bibliography 193
Index 203

Acknowledgments

Reading a book's acknowledgments section is revealing. Writing one is an exercise in humility. Acknowledgements are a form of genealogy through which the reader can trace the author's "academic family" (Clark would be proud). As a young author I stand humbled before them. My family, both academic and real, has grown over the four years I've spent with "the Governor" and along the way I've picked up many new friends and built on existing relationships.

This book would not have been possible without the influence of my teachers. Phyllis Creech first encouraged me to pursue a career in history. The enthusiasm of Professors Charles Taylor and Robert Gowen proved to me how important a smile and a kind word can be to a young undergraduate. Nancy Mitchell gave me the chance to prove myself as an academic and a leader. John David Smith did as much as anyone to show me the craft of history. His professionalism and work ethic are ever before me as an example of both what a professor and a historian should be. Joe A. Mobley took me under his wing and pointed the way to this project. He read its earliest drafts and I am in his debt both professionally and personally.

There are many other people to whom I am indebted. Bill Mitchell spent many long hours with my work. His keen eye and bracing comments made me work harder and dig deeper to make the text more muscular. His friendship over the years has been invaluable. Chris Meekins at the State Archives in Raleigh answered several frantic SOS calls for research and provided top-notch advice. Monika S. Fleming answered many nagging questions. She spent hours digging in the recesses and dark corners of Edgecombe County history and contacting Clark family members for valuable information.

Others deserving of recognition are Patrick Reddick, a great-great-great grandson of the governor, who granted permission to print several images; Shelia Blackmon Limerick of the Julia Tutwiler Library, University of West Alabama; and the staffs at the Special Collections Library, Duke University, and the Blount-Bridgers House in Tarboro.

The North Caroliniana Society provided me an Archie K. Davis research grant that allowed me to travel to Alabama. I am also grateful to the *North Carolina Historical Review* for granting me permission to reprint parts of my two articles on Clark.

Several individuals read part of the manuscript or provided lucid commentary: Monika

Acknowledgments

S. Fleming; Lorri Glover of the University of Tennessee; David H. McGee, my colleague and friend at Central Virginia Community College; Sidney Bland of James Madison University; Ann Miller, editor of *The North Carolina Historical Review*; and my dear friend, Harriet Hanger. Chriss Hardison, a long-time friend, drove me around Bertie County taking pictures and searching for Clark artifacts. I am fortunate to have friends who live near archives: Christin Noble did some invaluable research for me at Princeton University, as did Wendy Carter at the National Archives in Washington, D.C.

The book could not have been written without the assistance of Dr. and Mrs. Henry T. Clark, Jr. Hank and Blanche supported and encouraged me from the first day I contacted them about this project. The Clarks have kept family records and memories intact for future generations and they graciously opened their home, and their hearts, to me. Sadly, Hank died in September 2008, only a few days shy of his ninety-first birthday. He deserves a biography in his own right and in no small way, this book serves as a memorial to him. Blanche continues to soldier on. She has an amazing memory and a gracious heart, and she helped me untangle the Clark family bloodlines that made this book possible.

My parents, of course, deserve special recognition. Dad has always been an excellent travel partner on our tours of Civil War battlefields and sites. He helped me in the archives at Livingston, Alabama, and he became particularly interested in Clark's agent, James Hair. He unearthed a few pearls of information about him but unfortunately not all of it could fit into the book. His love of history and intellectual curiosity continue to inspire me. My mother's patience with us both continues to overwhelm me.

Finally, writing a book with small children in the house is no easy task. Fortunately, my wife, Katherine, was there to help. She has an extraordinary ability to deal with the kids — Sophie and Julian — but her intellectual insight, editorial skills, and loving companionship made this whole thing bearable. Katherine has shown the patience of Job during the lifetime of this project, especially as she has been working on a book of her own. Hopefully she will no longer need to refer to herself as the "biographer's widow."

Foreword by Joe A. Mobley

Students of the American Civil War often overlook the important role played by Southern governors in the war effort of the Confederate States of America. But it is doubtful that the Confederate government could have sustained itself and fought a devastating war, lasting four long years, without the cooperation and support of the state governors.

Perhaps the Confederate governor most neglected in Civil War historiography is Henry Toole Clark of North Carolina, who served as chief executive of the Tar Heel State from July 1861 to September 1862. Historians of America's great sectional conflict generally treat superficially Clark's role in the South's struggle to establish an independent nation. After acknowledging the defiance of the secessionist governor John W. Ellis, who led North Carolina out of the Union before his death in early July 1861, scholars usually move quickly to the career of the well-known and bombastic Zebulon B. Vance, who guided wartime North Carolina from September 1862 until the Confederate surrender in April 1865.

However, Clark, a wealthy and aristocratic planter from Edgecombe County, played a vital role during the thirteen months he held sway as his state's commander in chief. As speaker of the North Carolina Senate, he ascended to the office of governor upon the death of Ellis, because at the time the state constitution did not provide for a lieutenant governor. Clark took up his new responsibilities at a crucial period, as the newly formed Confederate States of America labored to establish a viable government and put a formidable army in the field. It fell to him to organize and equip local troops for service in the Confederate army, to provide for the protection of the state from Union attack, and to otherwise place North Carolina on a wartime footing. Simultaneously, Clark had to deal with such home front challenges as shortages of supplies, dissension from Unionists and peace advocates, and resistance to conscription (the draft) and other new and objectionable measures levied on the Tar Heel populace by the Confederate government.

After years of neglect, Clark's life and career have now been thoroughly explored in R. Matthew Poteat's book. Not only has Poteat judiciously evaluated Clark's performance as governor, but he also has described in detail Clark's political and social roles as a member of the "planter elite," both before and after the war, including the Edgecombe County planter's stance on Federal reconstruction. Through rigorous research, the author has explained fully for the first time the constitutional crisis that brought Clark to power, the nature and management of his slaveholdings, and the circumstances surrounding his Federal pardon. Anyone interested in the history of the nineteenth-century South, especially the Civil War, will find this work fresh and enlightening.

Joe A. Mobley is author of *"War Governor of the South": North Carolina's Zeb Vance in the Confederacy.*

Chronology

ca. 1760–1764	Christopher Clark leaves England and arrives in Edenton, North Carolina.
1779	James West Clark is born at Elmwood in Bertie County.
1803–1804	James West Clark marries Arabella Toole, moves to Edgecombe County and establishes a plantation at Walnut Creek.
1808	Henry Toole Clark is born on February 7 at Walnut Creek.
1812–1814	War of 1812, Maj. James West Clark serves in the local militia, is elected to the U.S. Congress, and serves as an elector to the Madison ticket.
1822	Henry T. Clark begins study at the University of North Carolina.
1826	Graduates "honor man" from UNC, earns his A.B. degree.
1831	Nat Turner's rebellion in Virginia.
1832–1833	Earns A.M. degree from UNC, reads law under his uncle William Haywood, admitted to the North Carolina bar. Moves to Tarboro.
1835	Thirty-one of the Clark family slaves relocated to Sumter County, Alabama, for hire; North Carolina's constitution amended to allow for the popular election of governor.
1843	Clark's father dies at home on December 20.
1850	Clark marries Mary Weeks Parker, is elected to the state Senate and serves for the next ten years. He buys his own plantation. Congress passes the "Compromise of 1850."
1858–1861	Serves as speaker of the state senate. North Carolina secedes on May 20, 1861.
July 1861–Sept 1862	Serves as governor of North Carolina.
July 1863	Union troops raid his home and burn Tarboro.
1864–1867	Serves as Edgecombe County justice of the peace, chairman of the county courts.

Chronology

1866–1867	Serves as state senator from Edgecombe County.
1868	North Carolina ratifies new constitution. Clark elected Edgecombe county commissioner.
1869–1873	Local politician, Calvary Episcopal church leader, works on genealogy and history projects.
1874	Dies at home on April 14, age 66.

Introduction

On the morning of July 8, 1861, only seven weeks after North Carolina had seceded from the United States, a telegram arrived at the Department of Military Affairs in Raleigh informing the state that Governor John W. Ellis was dead. Ellis was a popular leader who had led North Carolina out of the Union and into the Southern Confederacy. Unfortunately, he was a sickly man. Though only forty-one, he suffered from the ravages of tuberculosis. In a last-ditch effort to restore his health he had traveled on June 21 to Red Sulphur Springs, Virginia, seeking a remedy from its curative fountains. The resort's healing waters did nothing, however, to combat his "rapid consumption," and he died just two weeks after his arrival. An unusual aspect of North Carolina's government, established by the state constitution of 1776, was that there was no popularly elected successor should a governor die in office — there was no lieutenant governor. Instead, the duties of the chief executive were conferred on the Speaker of the Senate, a man who had been chosen by the other senators, and one who had no popular mandate to lead the state. That man was Henry Toole Clark, a Tarboro planter and secessionist Democrat.[1]

Clark is a little-understood subject of Civil War scholarship, and his governorship is neglected in the period's historiography. Any discussion of North Carolina and its chief executive during the Civil War is usually framed within the context of governors Ellis and Zebulon B. Vance, prominent men of that time. Indeed, much of the historical record begins with Ellis's brusque rebuff of President Abraham Lincoln's request for troops, and then leaps forward into the conspicuous and generally popular Vance administration.

Clark served as governor from July 1861 to September 1862, a crucial time as North Carolina established itself as a constituent member of the Confederate States and first suffered the hardships of war. He led the state during that formative period, providing for its defense and mobilizing troops in support of the war effort. No other state sacrificed more of its men to the Confederate cause than did North Carolina.[2] Yet historians today have generally ignored Clark's vital role during these perilous times.

In his day, however, Clark was well respected as a planter and a politician. Important men sought his counsel on a variety of topics ranging from politics and law to farming and history. Family members included Revolutionary-era heroes, congressmen, and clergymen, and like them he distinguished himself as a state party leader, planter, and businessman before rising to the governorship of North Carolina. He occupied a prominent position in the social, economic, and political life of Edgecombe County — a county whose powerful Democratic constituency played an active role in the state's political dramas of the 1840s and '50s, which culminated in the Civil War. The local planter elite controlled this "Edgecombe Democracy" and, with the support of white yeoman farmers, lobbied for the protection of slavery and eventually for secession, to protect their interests in land and slaves. When this antebellum coalition of small farmers and planters collapsed under the strains of the Civil War, Clark, like most members of his elite class, worked to reestablish the old political order.[3]

Clark is representative of that class of antebellum planters who dominated politics and society in North Carolina, a social class that became the nearest thing to aristocracy that can be found in American history. Membership in this "aristocracy," however, was a relatively recent development for the Clark family. His grandfather, Christopher, was an immigrant merchant from England who worked his way into the South's social elite though land and slave investments during the late eighteenth century — investments his son and grandson would continue to develop. Slave-owning families like the Clarks created great wealth for themselves, and this wealth permitted them entry into the political life of North Carolina.

An advantageous marriage by Clark's father, James West Clark, cemented the family's connection to wealth and power. He moved to Edgecombe County and was the first Clark to hold elected office. He served in both houses of North Carolina's General Assembly (1802–1803, 1811–1814), was a presidential elector on the Madison ticket in 1812, and was elected as a Democratic-Republican to the Fourteenth Congress (1815–1817). From 1829 to 1831, he served in President Andrew Jackson's administration as chief clerk of the Navy Department. Yet very little is known about him today. His influence and public example, however, are important to a proper understanding of his son, and their lives mirrored each other in many ways: both men were politically active, "strong churchmen," officers in the state militia, and regarded as leaders in the community. And both retired abruptly from public service, giving little public reason why.

Old South planters like the Clarks were generally a homogenous group. Members of this master class dominated the region's economic and political life and usually owned dozens of slaves and thousands of acres of land. They often ran the local stores and grist mills, and extended credit or loaned supplies to small farmers and laborers. They controlled the marketplace, the courthouse, and all political offices. They took care, however, not to offend their social inferiors. As Wayne Durrill points out, planters deferred to "lesser white men when it cost them nothing." In a culture obsessed with honor and appearance, these elites made a point to "salute any small farmer" because not to do so would give "mortal offence." In addition, planters "intervened on behalf of poor people in court, and they mediated relations between poor whites and slaves who could not adjudicate their disputes in a court of law."[4]

The term "planter" is usually applied to those who owned twenty or more slaves, but though Clark owned as many as fifty-five, he was not strictly a planter in a monolithic understanding of the term. Whereas some planters of the Old South may have "raised cotton to buy Negroes, and bought Negroes to raise cotton," Clark generally raised grain and row crops. Most of his slaves were hired out to others for profit rather than worked gang-style on his home plantation. His "plantation" was urban, a four-hundred-acre farm located one mile from Tarboro's Town Common. He was a well diversified businessman whose interests stretched from New York to North Carolina, Alabama, and Tennessee, involving slave hire, real estate, shipping, banking, and the operation of a local grist mill.[5]

But he was very much like his planter peers in other ways. Like them, Clark was a university graduate and read law. He enjoyed a standard of living far above that of most North Carolinians. He defended slavery and white supremacy. He held public office, raised a large family, and performed his role as patriarch at home and in his community. Two books in particular shed light on Clark and that class of men that shared his values: Bertram Wyatt-Brown's *Southern Honor: Ethics and Behavior in the Old South* (1982) and Lorri Glover's *Southern Sons: Becoming Men in the New Nation* (2007).[6] These scholars have shown how men of Clark's station acted according to an elaborate and compelling code of honor. From childhood, these men faced a series of "tests" before society would recognize them as "men" worthy to shoulder great responsibility. As Glover points out, "Successful boys devoted themselves to family, distinguished themselves in society, and [shone] as ornaments in the young Republic."[7] They had to acquire a classical education and enter into a socially acceptable marriage before tackling more difficult tests of manhood, such as holding political office and successfully exercising authority as slave masters in their own right. Clark, as this book will demonstrate, passed these tests and joined the South's elite planter class.

Like all successful businessmen, Clark possessed considerable administrative ability and intelligence. He was widely read and subscribed to many, varied newspapers from throughout the country. For twenty-five years he ran a prosperous plantation and slave-hire operation. Clark also notched up over twenty years of service with the Democratic Party as a platform writer, local party chairman, state and national delegate, and eventually an elected official, serving over ten years in the North Carolina Senate, and rising to the speakership of that body.

As a state senator, Clark generally promoted state-funded internal improvement projects, though he was suspicious of any extension of government authority. He considered himself as belonging to the school of states rights and state remedies and he distrusted Henry Clay-Whigs, Northern men, and the federal government. As a strict constructionist, he was committed to small government, low taxes, and debt avoidance. He voted against ad valorem taxation of slaves and opposed federal subsidies for public projects. On national issues he supported the Mexican War and Southern rights, and he considered slaves to be private property protected by the U.S. Constitution. Thus he supported slavery's expansion to the territories. He advocated state-funded colonization of free blacks to Africa. He thought secession was a legal right held by the states, but he was never a fire-eater. During the critical decade of the 1850s, he warmed to the thought that separation from the Union would be the only way to protect slavery, but took a cautious approach to the winter seces-

Introduction

sion crisis of 1860–1861. He believed Lincoln's election an inadequate excuse for leaving the Union and publicly supported secession only after the firing on Fort Sumter.

As war governor, he was a Confederate nationalist, rigidly enforcing such unpopular Confederate policies as conscription. He believed in a southern slaveholding confederacy — a confederacy of strong states governed by a virtuous white male democracy with members of the planter master class at its head. When this vision was shattered at Appomattox, Clark re-entered politics and was re-elected to the state senate in 1866. He backed President Andrew Johnson's lenient Reconstruction plan. He joined the newly formed Conservative Party, comprised of Democrats and former Whigs, to oppose the Republicans and North Carolina's 1868 constitution, which modernized the state's antebellum government and granted certain rights to the newly freed slaves. He resisted "radical" Congressional Reconstruction and as a state senator voted against ratification of the Fourteenth Amendment to the U.S. Constitution, which provides equal protection under the law to all persons.

Clark was an active participant in these turbulent, interesting and perilous times, yet surprisingly he warrants little scholarly treatment of his life and political career. In his master's thesis of 1965,[8] Gary Mercer examines the planter's tenure as governor and concludes that he was a mediocre executive. Mercer argues that "Clark was not an outstanding governor. He possessed neither the necessary qualities of political leadership nor the desire to be governor. He was a man of high character rather than distinguished talent."[9]

Other references to Clark are buried in the texts of peripheral works, and what little is written of him is often negative. In these scant references, he is regarded as an ineffective "fill-in" who left little mark on the office, a weak leader who retired from public service after a short, unremarkable tenure. Historian Glenn Tucker dismisses him as "devoted to routine."[10] These previous accounts fail to place Clark in the context of his social class. None discusses his family history or responsibilities, background, education, ideology, or his attitudes towards politics in any depth. Without such an analysis his political failures cannot be explained, and neither can his underacknowledged successes as an administrator.

Presenting Clark as a victim of his own inabilities, Mercer contends that Clark's "lack of ambition" lay behind his not seeking another term: "The demand of the state for more forceful leadership combined with his own lack of political ambition resulted in Clark's retirement from political life after only one year in the executive chair." Mercer views the governor as feeble and ineffective, but a man of "strong character," personal worth, and indomitable work ethic. Acknowledging that he "did achieve a certain amount of success" in raising, equipping, and mobilizing the state's troops, Mercer concludes that Clark ultimately failed to lead North Carolinians through the first year of the war.[11]

Mercer also asserts that the governor was "sensitive to criticism" and that he "tried to remain aloof from politics and please all factions as far as his conscience would allow."[12] Clark's actions suggest that he did indeed possess an aversion to political factionalism. The claim, however, that he tried to "please all factions" or that he was "sensitive to criticism" is incorrect. Clark was neither timid nor sycophantic. His honesty and forthrightness in the political arena had earned the respect of both Democrats and Whigs in the state Senate, a coalition of whom twice elected him the presiding officer of that body.

The historian John G. Barrett re-examined Clark briefly in a chapter in *The Confederate Governors* (1985), edited by W. Buck Yearns. Barrett somewhat revises Mercer's negative interpretation and concludes that "Henry Toole Clark was a capable individual devoted both to his state and to the southern cause. He performed his duties as war governor faithfully. Yet he was never able to lead forcefully the people of North Carolina in time of civil crisis."[13] Barrett blames Clark's failures less on his personal traits and more on the Confederate government. The Richmond authorities siphoned the best men and resources for service on the Virginia front, leaving Clark in a "most difficult position" in defending North Carolina.[14] As Union troops consolidated their hold on portions of eastern North Carolina, the governor could do little but press the need for more arms and troops from the Confederate government.

Though Barrett makes Richmond authorities complicit in Confederate blunders in eastern North Carolina, he does not absolve Clark of what he sees as the governor's failure to lead. Barrett undoubtedly views the governor as a man unequal to the task set before him. He believes that Clark's "partial term" limited his ability to mobilize public opinion and that he did not have enough time to form an effective policy to meet the demands placed upon him. He was simply unable "to come to grips with the monumental problems associated with guiding an independent-minded state through a bitter and devastating civil war."[15] Glenn Tucker, a Vance biographer, expressed similar sentiments twenty years earlier and devoted less than a paragraph to Clark's tenure, claiming that "[Vance's] task was well near Herculean because the preceding governors, Ellis and Clark, served only partial terms and neither had sufficient opportunity — even had they possessed the capability — to come to grips with the stupendous task of organizing and conducting a populous and independent minded state through the [Civil War]." Vance's most recent biographer, Gordon McKinney, claims that Clark's administration was completely ineffective, contending that Clark's "sudden elevation did little to improve the performance of the state's government."[16]

Many historians see Vance as a redeemer of sorts, a political leader of commanding presence and skill who single-handedly transformed the state's ability to wage war. Barrett claims, "A majority of North Carolina's war measures consequently are attributable to Vance. Either their inception or their effective implementation can be traced directly to him." Another historian says that "North Carolina's role in the Civil War and its relations with the Confederate government bore most clearly the imprint of the character of one man — Zebulon Baird Vance."[17]

Vance's abilities and accomplishments as governor are well known. He was, and has remained, one of the most compelling figures of North Carolina and Civil War history. Vance did, without question, transform the executive branch with his dynamic, forceful style. In many respects, he was the first modern governor in North Carolina history. He engaged the public with his many speeches and cultivated an image as an executive who protected the interests of North Carolina's citizens. To suggest, however, that the state was devoid of leadership at the beginning of the war, or that Vance's success can be attributed to his skill alone, is an oversimplification and inaccurate.

I contend that Clark was a much more influential administrator than previous historians have suggested. Indeed, Clark left the executive department with positive achievements for Vance to build upon. At the outset of the war, with the help of North Carolina Adjutant General James G. Martin, Clark succeeded in equipping the state's troops; though not as well equipped as some would have liked, they were able to fight effectively at least during the first half of the war. It was Clark who first suggested the state buy a blockade runner to bring in supplies and much-needed equipment from overseas sources. In addition, he established the first, and only, Confederate prison in North Carolina, arranged the production of salt for the war effort, inaugurated trade with England, and built a successful and important gunpowder mill — all notable administrative achievements.

It is true, however, that Clark failed as a political leader. The party did not offer him, nor did he seek, the nomination in 1862 for another term as governor. Military defeats in eastern North Carolina created disaffection among the state's citizens. The increasing scarcity of goods, rising prices, and resentment over conscription all combined to create a difficult political situation that Clark failed to manage effectively. Growing pockets of Unionist sentiment in western portions of the state and in the Quaker Belt of the Piedmont region deepened his troubles. Unlike Vance, Clark made no effort to unite in the common cause of Southern independence the state's two contending political factions — the Secessionist Democrats and the Conservatives, a coalition of former Whigs and Union Democrats.[18]

Though Clark did not overcome these difficulties, it is hard to imagine any governor at the time who could effectively manage such a situation, given the limits placed upon the office by the state's constitution. Except in his role as commander in chief of the state militia, the governor's power to intervene directly in the domestic affairs of citizens was constrained. Though popularly elected to a two-year term of office, North Carolina's chief executive could not veto legislation, grant pardons without the consent of the legislature, or authorize direct relief assistance to the public. These constitutional limitations, combined with a traditional suspicion of a powerful executive authority, constrained the role of the governor. Moreover, antebellum citizens did not look for the same level of government intervention in society that most Americans expect today. They tended to view the government as a necessary evil, and saw its principal purpose as the protection of life, liberty, property, and the public order. The hardships inflicted by the Civil War, however, caused North Carolina's people to rethink the role of the government and its chief executive. One of the reasons for Clark's political failure was his refusal to adjust his conservative antebellum approach to government and push energetically for expansion of the governor's authority.[19]

Vance was a more skilled politician and — at least publicly — showed more energy in empowering the office of governor to do more for the state's citizens. He faced many of the same problems as Clark — hostility to conscription, confiscation of goods, labor shortages on farms and in all other areas of production, and growing disaffection with the Confederate cause — and he dealt with them in similar ways. Both governors were wary of the increasing centralization of Confederate power, but generally cooperated with directives from Richmond. Both men enforced Confederate conscription. Both questioned certain hegemonic Confederate policies and bristled at any real or perceived slight to North Carolina, and they especially questioned the Confederacy's decision to defend Virginia at the cost of North Carolina. Though Clark would assert states' rights in defense of the individual, especially in cases of impressment of arms and goods, like Vance he was committed to a Confederate victory. Contrary to historian Frank Owsley's contention that Confederate governors hindered the war effort, Clark and Vance usually supported the laws and policies as dictated by the Confederate Congress and President Jefferson Davis. Vance's call to "fight the Yankees and fuss with the Confederates" might also have been Clark's policy, except in one important way — Clark fussed with the Confederates privately and never publicly aired his grievances. His refusal to do so greatly damaged him politically.[20]

Though Clark displayed administrative skill, his failure as a political leader can be partly explained by his conservative ideology and his vision of a "pure" Confederate republic — a republic supported by a white-male democracy and the slave economy. He was opposed to what he believed were the corrupting influences of factionalism and strove for a strong and unified Democratic Party, believing it was the best means to preserve slavery, national unity, and constitutional government. In many respects, he was an idealist, a man who envisioned America as a modern Roman republic, ruled by enlightened, benevolent paternalists. Like many southerners, he was attracted to Jefferson's agrarian, democratic ideal and supported a government of strong states and limited federal powers.[21]

Clark inherited the ideological traditions of the anti–Federalists. His major intellectual influences derived from the political philosophies of Nathaniel Macon and Willie Jones, two conservative antebellum firebrands from the northeastern region of North Carolina. Macon and Jones, like Clark, adhered to fundamental principles of strict economy and avoidance of debt. Each desired a government conducted with honesty, transparency, simplicity, virtue, and maximum liberty for the white individual, for the community, and for the state. As the historian Drew McCoy states, such men "assumed that a healthy republican government demanded an economic and social order that would encourage the shaping of a virtuous citizenry."[22]

In *The Confederate Republic* (1994), historian George Rable describes men like Clark as ideological Confederate leaders dedicated to preserving the conservative principles of America's founders. Rable argues that the architects of the Confederacy sought to rescue the republican values of their Revolutionary War forebears from a modernizing, dominating, and increasingly politicized federal Union. More than a few Southern leaders rejected partisan politics in favor of unity, believing themselves the inheritors of the founders' revolutionary tradition. Such men envisioned a "pure" republic, free from the corrupting stain of politics, and wedded to the idea of a limited government dedicated to the protection of "life, liberty, and property."[23]

Although Clark eventually failed as a political leader, his performance as the state's military commander was adequate to the task. He had earned military experience as an adjutant and a colonel in the state militia and was competent in military affairs, frequently issuing clear, sensible orders to subordinates, and offering sound advice to Confederate authorities—advice that they generally ignored.[24] He was not blind to North Carolina's military needs. He worked diligently to acquire more money, men and weapons, but he simply did not receive sufficient support from Confederate authorities to perform his job as North Carolina's commander in chief. Given the Herculean responsibility placed upon him, Clark did as well as any southern governor could have done in preparing his state to wage war.

The purpose of this book, therefore, is twofold. Firstly, it aims to show that Clark must be viewed as an important historical figure in his own right, and a man of significant accomplishments. As the governor, he had to pick up the burden of leading the state's war effort, a burden that has fallen on few men. At the same time, it fell to him to develop the relations between North Carolina and the Confederacy, relations that his successor, Vance, was then able to build upon. As historian Michael Albert Powell has shown, Confederate governors negotiated a "cooperative federalism" with Richmond, "as each sought whatever resources were available to survive."[25] Clark was directly responsible for finding and making use of whatever resources North Carolina could provide for the Confederacy. His great success was in providing soldiers to fight in its armies, but that very success led to his political undoing, as the drain of men from North Carolina to Virginia allowed Union forces to capture strategic locations on the Outer Banks and in the east. The public unfairly condemned him for these losses, and Clark never sought to defend or apologize for his decision.

Secondly, this book considers Clark within the context of his time and place, by examining his life as a member of that generation of elite southern men first raised to conceive of themselves as Americans, who nevertheless led the South toward sectionalism and Civil War. Chapter One surveys his family history. It begins with his grandfather's emigration to America, his father's marriage and subsequent move to Tarboro, and continues though Clark's student years at Chapel Hill. Chapter Two examines his entry into southern manhood as a businessman, planter, and politician, and looks in detail at his slave-hire operations in Alabama. Chapters Three though Five describe the most consequential two years of his life—his role as North Carolina's Civil War governor. The concluding chapter looks at his later years, detailing his struggle to obtain a presidential pardon, his final term in the state senate after the war, and his efforts to resist Congressional Reconstruction.

Careful readers will notice that women are generally silent in this account. This work is chiefly an examination of a public figure, and nineteenth-century southern women often occupied a private, domestic space, playing virtually no role in the public sphere, which was dominated by white male elites. However, women played an important role in Clark's life. His mother and two sisters were central figures in his formative years and he cared for them deeply, becoming their guardians at his father's death. He fathered three daughters who adored him. His wife, Mary, was a dutiful "plantation mistress." She ran the household while he, as southern society expected, supervised the family and tended to his public duties. Written evidence of their affection for each other is thin and what few letters survive say little of their day-to-day life or her thoughts of her husband's travails as governor. It is a paradox that while family is often the most important part of life, there is often little evidence of the daily interaction of its members. Regrettably, then, the Clark women can only remain in the background of this study.

However spare the written evidence, Clark's ambition and sense of duty as an antebellum patriarch often guided his decisions and led him to seek public office. It is on his public role as planter and politician that this book is centered. I contend that Governor Clark was typical of that class of men, one of hundreds of mid-level politicians who led the South during the antebellum period and brought it into a devastating civil war. As historians Donald Butts and Ralph Wooster have noted, members of the planter class made up a small percentage of North Carolina's white population, yet held over a third of all legislative seats. A survey of the 1850 North Carolina legislature reveals that more than 80 percent of its members were slave owners, the highest ratio in any southern state. Clark was part of that antebellum order of slaveholders who, as the historian Drew Gilpin Faust points out, "successfully dominated the [South] through their ability to elicit the consent and cooperation of the largely enfranchised masses of the nonslaveholding whites."[26]

The Civil War, however, disrupted the traditional ruling equilibrium. The planters were no longer able to exert hegemony over the yeoman class. The mastery they had held over their slaves and their former political allies disappeared. A new political reality came into being in which all the old "complex rules, bargains, and limits" had changed.[27] Clark was unable to maneuver in the new environment. As governor, he had neither formulated a compelling vision for the future, nor rallied public opinion to support his efforts; instead, he had striven to maintain the conservative values of the Old South in his conservative way. The ironies of his story are that he led the state into the war that destroyed many of those values: later, although slavery ended and the planters' hegemony was crippled for a time, the values that Clark helped to shape in North Carolina continued to resonate. In fact, they continued to determine political life well into the next century.

1

Frontier Aristocrats

The Clarks were members of that elite planter class which dominated social and political thought in eastern North Carolina during the antebellum period. Henry Toole Clark's grandfather and father both owned thousands of acres of land and dozens of slaves, and census records from 1860 for Henry Clark and his family list an inventory of thirty-three slaves, with personal and real property valued at over seventy thousand dollars.[1] The family's wealth was first acquired through shipping and trading and later expanded into land and slave investments. Though not exactly affluent by South Carolina low country standards, the Clarks enjoyed a lifestyle far above that of the average North Carolinian.

Henry's paternal grandfather, Christopher Clark, established the family's fortunes in the late eighteenth century. He was born in the north of England sometime around 1740 and immigrated to Edenton, North Carolina, perhaps as early as 1760. Given his rapid rise in the shipping business, he probably arrived in North Carolina with some money of his own and quite possibly his own sloop.

The Edenton he discovered was a lovely and prosperous port village, the trading and mercantile center for the Albemarle region of northeastern North Carolina. It had become one of the principal settlements in the colony as more people migrated out of Virginia and into the Albemarle in the 1660s. There they encountered significant settlements of Chowanoke Indians, who died from European diseases or were quickly pushed off their lands.

The Albemarle was a proprietary holding of a larger province of "Carolina" until 1689, and in 1712 the colony was divided into two halves. North Carolina expanded slowly, however. Though settled by whites relatively early, South Carolina's northern neighbor attracted few settlers until the mid–1700s. Its first town, Bath, wasn't founded until 1705 — nearly a century after Jamestown, Virginia. Its geography limited all but the most intrepid from settling the region. Thick swamps covered many parts of its eastern interior. The Outer Banks, a long chain of sandy barrier islands, prevented the entry of most ocean-going vessels and made navigation of its shallow inland waterways treacherous. Only one river, the Cape Fear, emptied directly into the Atlantic Ocean. As a result, most early colonists chose to live in other less remote parts of North America where more reliable communication systems provided more lucrative opportunities. Compared to Virginia, South Carolina,

New England and the Middle Colonies, the hardscrabble life that North Carolina offered early in its history simply wasn't attractive. The colony remained poor and isolated for many years.

As demand for land increased, however, more colonists took a second look at North Carolina. By the mid-eighteenth century, it was one of the few remaining frontier areas in English North America where land was cheap and readily available. The English had clung to the eastern seaboard of that continent for decades, confronted by the French to the north and west and the Spanish to the south in Florida. In addition, significant populations of Native Americans made westward settlement over the rugged Appalachian Mountains a dangerous prospect. As more and more colonists arrived on these shores and as its natural population increased, the colonists searched for new farm land, and many of them found it in North Carolina.

The town of Edenton was incorporated in 1722 and soon became important to the young colony as a shipping and mercantile center. The growing village was selected as the seat of North Carolina's colonial government and remained so until 1766. In 1748 the Carolina Proprietor Lord Granville established his land office in Edenton. He had retained his ownership of a sixty-mile-wide strip of land adjoining the Virginia border, and over two million acres of land from this strip were sold to settlers between 1748 and 1763.

Edenton would have been a good place to set up shop for an enterprising young shipper expecting to meet the demands of a small but steadily growing population. Though a newcomer, Clark quickly established himself in the community and became a well-known figure. He befriended many, and "he conducted his business with the best men in that section, acting as their agent and [trade] representative."[2] A great deal of his business involved trade and passenger service between London and Edenton, though he did additional business in the Caribbean, New York, and continental Europe. His sloop, *William*, often plied the warm waters from Edenton to the Barbados and then to London and back, carrying passengers and trade goods such as cotton, whiskey and wool cloth. Mahogany was a favorite luxury item to be found in his cargo holds. Clark's customers may well have included James Iredell, the state attorney general and future United States Supreme Court justice, who purchased an extraordinary amount of mahogany to decorate his Edenton home, which still stands today.[3]

Other cargoes could be more exotic. For example, his ship the *General Washington* brought in on one load "tea, lemons, oranges, muslin, salt, wine, and port" from Lisbon, Portugal, valued at over two thousand dollars. Portugal was a favorite trading partner of the colonies and early republic, eager for American grain products such as wheat and flour and offering in exchange exotic "East India goods" from Portuguese holdings in the Pacific, and large quantities of the highly desirable Portuguese ports and Madeira wines.[4]

Thomas Jefferson would have approved of Captain Clark's Lisbon cargo. Writing in 1783 from Paris to future president John Adams in London, Jefferson described the need for more open trade with Portugal. Ever the oenophile, he observed that "the strength of the wines of Portugal will give them always an almost exclusive possession of a country where

1. Frontier Aristocrats

The view of Salmon Creek at Elmwood in Bertie County, facing north. This deep creek empties into the Chowan River, less than a mile from this spot. Capt. Clark would have loaded and unloaded his goods and received passengers and mail here. (Photograph by the author.)

the summers are so hot as in America. The present demand for [Portuguese wines] will be very great.... If they consider the extent and rapid population of the United States they must see that the time is not distant when they will not be able to make enough for us." Christopher Clark was doing his part to supply that demand in eastern North Carolina.[5]

Captain Clark was also a farmer. He owned property on Salmon Creek in Bertie County as early as 1767 and there began building his home, Elmwood. Lying only a few miles west of Edenton, some of this land had been cleared and settled by whites perhaps as early as 1658, and Elmwood stood on land owned a century earlier by the infamous proprietor-era governor of Carolina, Seth Sothel.[6] It remains today a fine example of a Georgian style plantation home and is furnished with the mahogany and other products Clark acquired as an importer.

This home and its location served him well. It was situated on a small hill about one hundred and fifty yards from Salmon Creek, a relatively wide and deep tributary of the Chowan River. The creek was lined by sturdy cypress trees and oaks that protected the home

Elmwood, Captain Christopher Clark's eighteenth century home. Much of the original house is intact and has been fully restored and modernized. It is an outstanding example of a Georgian plantation home. (Photograph by the author.)

and his docks from the brisk gales that often cut across the open expanses of the much larger Chowan. Access to this great river facilitated travel and trade, and given its location to the Albemarle Sound and the Atlantic shipping lanes, his business did well. Supplies and cargoes could be loaded and unloaded with ease and mail and news packets delivered more quickly. In addition, the spacious home (over three thousand square feet) likely served as a comfortable inn where passengers on Clark's ships could spend the night before embarking on future voyages abroad or traveling inland to the interior.[7]

Elmwood was also home for a growing family. Captain Clark, like many southerners who braved the wet, malarial lowlands of the Virginia-Carolina tidewater, married more than once. Of his first wife, Elizabeth, nothing is now known except that she bore him three daughters — Elizabeth, in 1765, Sarah, in 1767, and Mary, in 1770 — and died some time before or during the year 1778. That year, he married a local woman, Hannah Turner, the daughter of Thomas Turner of Bertie County. She was to become the mother of Clark's only son, James West, born in 1779.

While the family and business grew during the 1770s, other events were making trade with the mother country increasingly difficult. Clark's adopted hometown, Edenton, had always been a center for revolutionary activity, and protests against British imperial policy were becoming more vocal and demonstrative. In October 1774, fifty-one Edenton women held a "tea party" and declared their support of the American boycott of British goods. (The protest was even noted in London and made famous in vulgar satire.) Though members of Clark's family were probably not present, scenes such as these suggest that everyone, even those in small communities like Edenton, was affected by global events. Indeed, families throughout the American colonies at this time were being forced to choose sides, and such a choice may have fallen particularly hard on Clark, a newcomer only recently arrived in North Carolina.

Early in the conflict with Great Britain, Clark probably dreaded the prospect of war, simply because it would be bad for business. And when British frigates began patrolling the shipping lanes and closing ports of call in the Caribbean, legal commerce became difficult and dangerous. Aspersions may well have been cast on Clark's loyalties.

It is difficult to gauge the level of Loyalist sentiment in eastern North Carolina, but after the British defeat at Moore's Creek Bridge in February 1776 and the subsequent departure of the British royal governor Josiah Martin, anyone who harbored Loyalist sentiments in the Tar Heel state either joined the British cause and moved away, or made peace with his neighbors. The historian William Nelson has noted that "almost all the Loyalists were, in one way or another, more afraid of America than they were of Britain."[8]

It is not known if Clark harbored or even flirted with Loyalist sympathies, though several of his friends and neighbors did. William Duckenfield was a wealthy Loyalist whose 6,842 acres bordered Clark's property. Duckenfield's lands were confiscated and sold when he fled America for England during the war. Another friend and a colleague of Clark's, Colin Clark (no relation) of Scotland, was a fellow ship captain and trader who left behind four small children to be cared for by his dead wife's family in Edenton. Unlike these men, Christopher Clark remained in Bertie County. Indeed, the fact that he remained suggests that he had little to fear from the country that had made him a rich man.

It seems in fact that Clark served the Patriot cause and may have used his shipping business to support the war effort. One family story claims Clark was a privateer in the war, and owning a ship named the *General Washington* strongly suggests that he was a patriot, or at least wanted to end any speculation among his neighbors that he was anything other than an American. In 1788, after the war was over, the North Carolina General Assembly appointed Captain Clark one of fourteen commissioners charged with "opening a navigable passage into the ocean" from the Albemarle Sound to Roanoke Island and "into the ocean." That same year, Clark's sloop, the *William*, brought the news that New York had ratified the constitution of the United States. Given this evidence, it's hard to imagine that Clark was ever anything but a committed Patriot.[9]

During this period, Clark began investing in land and slaves. Between 1767 and 1780, Clark bought over six hundred acres of land, most of it adjoining his property on Salmon Creek, and much of it land previously owned by his neighbor, William Duckenfield. In addition to his Bertie County lands, he owned, along with a Swiss-born ship captain living in Edenton named William Borrits (or Borritz) two tracts of land in Georgia totaling 1,500 acres. Although we know he was a trader and slave owner, it is not clear whether Clark profited directly from the transport of African slaves to America. His ships, not being "slavers," probably carried only passengers and trade goods.

We do know, though, that Clark had purchased twenty-six slaves by 1790—fifty-nine other planters in Bertie County at that time owned more than twenty—and by 1800, Clark owned thirty-two. The family enlisted the medical services of Dr. James Norcom to care not only for themselves but also for their slaves. Receipts from Dr. Norcom to Captain Clark request payment for "tending slaves and bleedings." Norcom would become infamous years later to readers of Harriet Jacobs' book *Incidents in the Life of a Slave Girl* (1861). His charge for "bleedings" suggests that he attended Clark on his death bed in late 1801. That year, Christopher Clark died at Elmwood of causes unknown, leaving most of his property, including the home and ten of his thirty-two slaves, to his son, James West.[10]

James West Clark was born at Elmwood. He was named in honor of his father's "worthey friend" and the executor of his will, Captain George West, who would later marry James's sister Mary. Nothing is known of James West's childhood, but he was sent to the College of New Jersey (Princeton) as a teenager and graduated in 1797 aged eighteen. A Princeton education was attractive to wealthy southern families of the early republic. Its Presbyterian heritage was in contrast to the Puritan roots of Harvard and Yale, and given its location outside of Yankee Massachusetts, Princeton was relatively tolerant toward the institution of slavery. The proportion of southerners at Princeton rarely fell below forty percent before the 1850s.[11]

James West enjoyed his studies and was active in the American Whig Society—a political, literary, and debating society that played an important role in the development of the college and also the intellectual and social development of its students. Such student societies were popular in American universities of the eighteenth and early nineteenth centuries. Founded in 1769, the American Whig Society at Princeton had nothing to do with the American political party of the same name; rather, the titles "Whig Society" or "Plain Dealing Club" "signified adherence to ancient principles of British political and religious dissent, principles that later found concrete form in the Revolution and in the founding of the American Republic."[12]

James West was a learned man who valued hard work, discipline, and attention to one's duty, and he required the same of his son, Henry Toole. Speaking of his own student years, he told young Henry, "The two years I spent at college I was never absent from prayers after the first week." "I entreat you," he advised, "attend strictly to every part of your prescribed duties, confine yourself strictly and closely to your room during such hours as you are required to be there."[13] He had probably followed his own advice as a student. As the valedictorian of his graduating class, he had the honor of giving the student commencement address. His topic, "emulation," perhaps related the evils of ambitious or envious rivalry to the detriment of one's "republican" character.[14]

1. Frontier Aristocrats

James West later earned a master's degree (A.M.) from Princeton, but since two devastating fires at Nassau Hall in the mid-nineteenth century destroyed many of the college's older records, it is difficult to fix an exact date for that degree. Some sources suggest 1844 when, a year after his death, Princeton awarded him an honorary master of arts degree, while others suggest he earned his A.M. shortly after his graduation in 1797. If so, he may have served as a tutor to undergraduates, or studied law, or both, in the interim years before his marriage.[15]

In 1802, five years after earning his A.B., James married Arabella Toole, the daughter of Colonel Henry Irwin Toole and Elizabeth Haywood of Edgecombe County. The Toole family had settled in Edgecombe after arriving from Virginia in the early 1700s and were involved in the founding of Tarboro in 1760. Located at the inland-most point of navigation on the Tar River, the town had prospered and was set to become an influential community in North Carolina history. The legislature considered relocating the state capital there after the American Revolution, but instead chose Raleigh.

The Tooles had become a prominent eastern North Carolina family, and several mem-

James West Clark, ca. 1800–1820. Clark served three one-year terms in the North Carolina House of Commons in 1802, 1803, and 1811; and a term in the state Senate from 1812–1814. In 1812 he served as a presidential elector on the Madison ticket. From 1829 to 1831 he was Chief Clerk of the Navy Department during President Andrew Jackson's first administration. He died in 1843. (Courtesy Patrick Reddick Family Papers & Photos collection.)

bers had served in various local, state, and national offices, as did members of Arabella's maternal family, the Haywoods. Her grandfather, William Haywood, had served in the 1776 Provincial Congress at Halifax and helped write the original North Carolina Constitution, and several members of both the Haywood and Toole families had served with distinction in the Continental army.

In early 1804, James and Arabella Clark left Bertie County for a new life in Edgecombe. They sold Elmwood and purchased five hundred acres of land from Lewis Fort for "£625 sterling" on the "south side of the Tarr river at the branches of Walnut Creek," adjoining "George Anderson and Judge Haywood's land" where the new couple made their home "eight or ten miles above Tarborough." This land lies almost directly west of the town, halfway between Tarboro and Rocky Mount. There the Clarks maintained numerous slaves and raised their four children: Henry Toole, Laura, Maria, and Mary.[16]

The move to Tarboro made economic and political sense. Much of the state's political power was held by eastern planters, and this power was shifting from the Albemarle toward the south and central areas of eastern North Carolina following the expanding cotton economy. From 1800 to 1850, Edgecombe County's population grew from about ten thousand to over seventeen thousand. Tarboro was the county's most important town, its population doubling from five hundred to over one thousand in the same period. Though small, it remained an important farming and mercantile center for the region. Its politics, as in virtually all antebellum southern communities, were controlled by a small, landed planter elite, and Clark's marriage into the influential Haywood and Toole families opened the door to political service and greater business opportunities. His family connections were enhanced further when his sister-in-law, Mary Toole, married Theophilus Parker — a wealthy planter and merchant, and later, in the War of 1812, part owner in the famous privateer *Snap Dragon*, captained by Otway Burns. James West bought a small lot in town from his father-in-law, Henry Irwin Toole, in February 1807 and made it his office. Located on Main Street next to the courthouse, the lot was a prime and visible location from which to conduct business.[17]

In addition to buying Walnut Creek and smaller lots in Tarboro, he bought farms in other parts of Edgecombe County. In 1820, he purchased two parcels of land on "Conetoe Pocoson, one for 150 acres and the other 200 acres for a total of $3048." He also invested in lands to the west. At some point in the early 1820s, he bought five thousand acres of land in Dyer County, Tennessee, and another 3,800 acres in Obion County, Tennessee. Some of the funds need to purchase these lands may have come from the sale of his father's land in Georgia.[18]

As a member of the local elite, James Clark became an active member of the Edgecombe community, and his moral and civic example would deeply mark his son. Indeed, their lives mirrored each other in many ways. Henry was often compared to his father, as both had similar manners and were noted for their "pleasant ways." Both were highly literate party men for the Democrats and worked behind the scenes writing speeches and platform literature. Both father and son eventually held elected office, and each would retire abruptly from the larger public view. Both were businessmen and planters, investing in new technologies and agricultural production methods. They bought lands, traded in slaves, and invested in a local canal enterprise. Like most wealthy southerners James West served as an officer in the local militia. As Henry would do, his father served as a trustee on a local school board and sought to improve the educational opportunities for his children. In 1821, James West was appointed a trustee to the University of North Carolina, serving alongside some of North Carolina's leading lights for the next twenty years. A loving husband and father, he was well read and erudite, and he frequently attended and served as a leader in the local Episcopal church.[19]

As a civic leader, James West often gave orations at local events and festivals. Before leaving Bertie County he was asked by the Committee of Arrangement, a local board of prominent citizens that managed community events, to give an oration on February 22, 1800, commemorating the birthday of the recently deceased president George Washington. Emphasizing the "reluctance with which I enter the execution of my gratitude," he nevertheless proceeded to give a moving speech that encouraged his fellow Americans to "learn from lessons like [the example of Washington's life], and guard and prize [the] liberty and Independence of your country."[20]

James West consistently sought to cultivate the arts and sciences, and he advocated internal improvements for the betterment of trade, commerce, and agriculture. He was a founding member of the Edgecombe Agricultural Society — one of the first such organizations of its kind in the state. It met each quarter and offered prizes for livestock improvement and high crop yield and boasted about thirty members. In an address to the Edgecombe Agricultural Society in 1811, he declared that "if we wish to promote agriculture, if we desire to raise the latent energies of our fellow citizens and call into action all their enterprise and industry, we can not do it more effectively than by improving and extending the navigations of our rivers and creeks." In 1823 he petitioned for a canal to go through his property to connect to the Tar River, and he became a major investor in a canal project to improve navigation along the Tar River in the 1830s.[21]

The term "internal improvements" was a loaded word in the early nineteenth century. Essentially the term connotes "public works," but given the national debate over federal-state relations in those days, it often carried a deeper political meaning. Supporting internal improvement schemes could be seen as compromising one's loyalty to party, state and country. The Federalists, and later the Whigs, made federal improvement projects a central part of their party's platform. For Jeffersonian, and later Jacksonian, Democrats, any improvement to the nation's banking systems, roads, canals, and lighthouses should be carried out at the state level. For some very strict republicans, public improvements shouldn't be carried out at all, except by the individual citizen or private business.

As the historian Alan D. Watson has argued, however, political parties in antebellum North Carolina "were not monolithic" and "both Democrats and Whigs advocated elements of internal improvements and opposed others."[22] James Clark's record accords with Watson's observation. Clark tended to be more practical and centrist in these matters, and he generally supported strengthening the nation's infrastructure. As the national debate over slavery became more rancorous in the 1820s and '30s, however, James Clark, like his son Henry, became increasingly suspicious of federal internal improvement projects, believing that if the federal government involved itself too deeply in the affairs of the states, it would soon be meddling in another, more sensitive, state affair — slavery.

James Clark was an active Jeffersonian Democrat, and Edgecombe County was the most Democratic county of any in the state. It consistently voted for conservative, state rights' candidates who toed the party line. James was respected by the local party elites as a successful businessman and cool, level-headed leader. He served three one-year terms in the state House of Commons (1802, 1803, and 1811) and one two-year term in the state Senate from 1812 to 1814. In 1812, he served as a presidential elector on the Madison ticket. He was generous to his supporters and, as was the custom, provided plenty of whiskey to his electorate each August during the election season.[23]

He supported the War of 1812, and after the remaining Federalists who had opposed that war were discredited by its successful outcome, he became more prominent in the Democratic Party. He was elected to the U.S. Congress in 1814, but he never adjusted to life in Washington and only served one term as a congressional representative. He preferred being at home, supervising his plantations and business interests in Edgecombe County, but he returned to Washington to serve as a cabinet official in President Andrew Jackson's first administration. In 1829, he was appointed chief clerk of the Navy Department by his friend and fellow North Carolinian John Branch, the Navy secretary and future Whig politician. This appointment meant that James had to remain in Washington for much of the year with few opportunities to visit home, a prospect he did not relish. He hated living in Washington, and he hated the political squabbling and scandal he witnessed there. As a cabinet official, he would see firsthand the intense bickering and destructive political infighting that plagued Jackson's inner circle of advisors. Few scandals were as destructive as the Peggy Eaton Affair.

The Eaton Affair, or "Petticoat Affair," was a sex scandal that involved rumors of infidelity, a suicide, and political intrigue, resulting in a permanent rift between Jackson and his vice-president, John C. Calhoun, and increasing sectional tensions within the Democratic Party. Margaret "Peggy" O'Neale was a handsome and charming woman of lowly origins. The daughter of a Washington tavern keeper, she worked as a barmaid and served a variety of customers that included powerful politicians and Washington insiders. At a young age she had married a navy purser, John Timberlake, who suffered from debt and depression and was often away on long sea voyages. In 1818, Mrs. Timberlake met the widowed senator from Tennessee (and close personal friend to President Jackson) John H. Eaton while he was lodged at her father's tavern. Eaton befriended her and became her escort while her husband was serving at sea. He and Peggy were soon suspected of having an affair. When word came in 1828 that her husband had committed suicide, Eaton determined to make Peggy an "honest woman" and proposed marriage. Ignoring the social convention which required widows to remain in mourning and not remarry for at least a year, the couple was married in a few short months.

Senator Eaton's appointment in 1829 to President Jackson's cabinet was not met with approval by Washington society. Vice President Calhoun's wife, Floride, objected to the appointment and snubbed the Eatons. Peggy, as a "fallen woman," became the subject of much gossip, and the couple was black-listed. President Jackson was livid. He recalled the rude treatment he and his wife had received years earlier because of their own controversial relationship and he rushed to Peggy's defense, publicly proclaiming her "chaste as a virgin." His secretary of state, Martin Van Buren (a widower), lavished attention on her in an attempt to cure the "Eaton malaria" and bring some semblance of harmony to the cabinet.

The wives of Jackson's cabinet members, however, were unmoved, and the chilly treatment continued. Jackson blamed Calhoun in what he believed was a conspiracy against Peggy, drawing ever closer to Van Buren. When Van Buren announced his resignation from the cabinet, Eaton, too, decided to leave. Seeing an opportunity to rid himself of Calhoun's partisans, the president asked for the remaining cabinet members' resignations. Jackson then nominated a new cabinet beholden to him. Jackson and Calhoun remained bitter enemies thereafter, while Van Buren, who was later appointed minister to Great Britain, became Jackson's Democratic Party successor. Secretary Branch accused Van Buren of exercising a "malign influence" over the president.[24]

Though a Jackson supporter, James West tired of Washington and its intrigues. He supported the president and, like Branch and many other southern Democrats, he resented Van Buren's influence in the party. He wrote frequently to his wife lamenting his solitary existence, bereft of her support during these difficult times. In one particularly moving letter to Arabella in 1829, James West wrote, "You ask if 'I am tired of writing to you.' Ara, this is too cruel. No, my wife. The only consolation I have in this cruel separation from my family is to commune with them in this [letter writing]. Deprive me of this resource and my time here would be intolerable. I live in hope of hearing from you again in the course of a week. This expectation keeps me alive."[25] To bide the time, he immersed himself in his duties, yet his wife and children were never far from his mind. He found little that interested him in Washington and complained of the dirty, bustling streets, the threat of epidemic and "fevers," and the ambitious sycophants who crowded the city in search of advancement. "Here," he wrote, "there is nothing that for one moment engages my attention except my business. This great city, with all its pomp and vanities is to me a great solitude." To compensate, he would loose himself in the affairs before him, but sadly, he said, "The evening returns and with it I return to my cheerless apartment. No wife or children to greet my return, or any person to provide the nameless conveniences which home affords."[26]

He instead thought often of the time when he could return to Tarboro, and entertained thoughts of quitting his post, though "duty" demanded otherwise. He believed he could do the same job from Raleigh, and thought of asking Branch to relocate him there as a clerk, but he never did. Thinking of the summer season when the business of government often shut down in fear of yellow fever, he wrote, "I hope to return to my home before nine months are gone with the means of remaining there the balance of my days."[27]

While James West may not have enjoyed the political life of Washington, he did make some interesting comments on its society. He described for Arabella the weather, the latest fashions, and social events. "This day and night," one such letter began, "are by far the coldest we have had this winter." He hoped that Arabella "had a comfortable wood fire" because, as he lamented, "mine is coal." James West's nights, while often cold, were not always as empty as many of his letters suggested. He socialized and attended parties, however reluctantly, where the movers and shakers of Washington life were in attendance. "These fetes," he groused, "go on uninterruptedly. I have been to three this week." One such party held at the home of Attorney General John M. Berrien was "large and crowded [and] literally impossible to move."[28]

But not all social events were unpleasant. The most enjoyable, he wrote, was a party given by "Mr. [Secretary] John Branch" with about "100 present," some of whom were probably other North Carolinians and southerners Clark knew. He commented thankfully that the party "was very agreeable and had room sufficient for the Belles to display their steps and finery." Noting the fashions worn by the party-goers, Clark described for his wife the guests' dress and deportment, and made comments on their hem lines, hair and manners, saying wittily of one lady from Boston, "her hair appeared to me drawn up so high that she could not shut her mouth for it was mostly open."[29]

His comments on Washington society ended with his resignation on May 12, 1831—the same day as the resignation of Navy Secretary John Branch. Commenting on his resignation, James West, perhaps foretelling a similar event in the future political life of his son, said very little publicly about his reasons for leaving the cabinet, only that he had resigned "not for political purposes, but from motives purely of a private nature."[30] Though protocol demanded he leave the Navy department because Jackson had asked for Branch's resignation, thus requiring him to go the way of his superior, his motives of "private nature" were most likely his deep desire to return home to his family.

James West never regretted leaving Washington. His resignation allowed him to personally attend to his many business affairs. In 1831 he bought "lot 42" on the corner of Church and St. Patrick streets in Tarboro and moved the family into town, where he built a fine two-story federal-style home which still stands today. The Clarks maintained their plantations at Walnut Creek and Conetoe, in addition to the several lots in Tarboro; and like his father Christopher, James West engaged in shipping and trading. According to receipts, he owned at least one ship, the schooner *Sally*, a thirty-six ton, two-masted vessel over forty-eight feet in length. James West was a diversified investor, having interests in shipping, real estate, slaves, and farming.

The Edgecombe County lands were often rented out, though Clark grew a few cash crops and grains on the land he retained. His lands in Dyer County, Tennessee, were cleared and the timber harvested. Dyer County, in northwestern Tennessee, was bordered by the Mississippi River. Situated about seventy-five miles north of Memphis, it was an attractive location for small farmers looking to grow grains and cotton.

Plots were surveyed and leased. The land was rented at between two and four dollars

1. Frontier Aristocrats

The James West Clark home, ca. 1832. James West Clark built this home in Tarboro as his business affairs expanded into slave hiring and land rentals. He kept his Walnut Creek and Conetoe plantations, but relocated to this house shortly after returning from Washington, D.C., to be nearer to his downtown office and civic duties. The home has been completely restored and modernized. It is owned by Mr. and Mrs. Bob Nicolosi. (Photograph by the author.)

an acre for a term of seven to ten years, and it provided the Clarks with a steady income. By the late 1840s, James West was under pressure from his Tennessee agent, Daniel E. Parker, to sell more of his lands to meet the growing demand, but he only occasionally sold property. Henry, however, would later sell these holdings in the 1850s.[31]

Sections of these Tennessee lands were valuable and said to "far exceed any lands in N[orth] Carolina for fertility." The lands also abounded in a wide variety of desirable hardwood trees such as ash, poplar, hickory and black oak. Other sections of land were rated "2nd and 3rd rate," though Clark's agents claimed that even the poorest of his lands would "make from 8 to 10 barrels of corn to the acre and from 12[00] to 1500 [pounds] of [seed] cotton."[32] A barrel of corn in the 1830s measured five bushels, so Clark would expect this land to produce forty to fifty bushels to the acre, a profitable yield for corn farmers in the 1830s. Indeed, these predicted yields exceeded what other farmers were receiving from the poorer, worn out lands on eastern farms, where twenty to forty bushels per acre was the norm.[33]

The Clarks' principal land agent, Daniel Parker, was hired in the 1840s and he proved a faithful steward. Parker is an interesting side note to America's expansionist story. He was one of many thousands of white Americans who moved west over the Appalachians and onto the much-coveted Indian lands. A successful farmer and livestock trader from Virginia, he immigrated to Dyer County, Tennessee, in 1826, buying over one thousand acres of land and building "a cabin as a temporary barracks and protection from the wild beasts." He became famous for ridding the area of dangerous bears and wildcats. As a county magistrate and trustee, he was connected to all Dyer County land transactions and its real estate market. Upon his death in 1856, he was the wealthiest man in Dyer County, owning over six thousand acres of land.[34]

Like most men of Parker's time and social class, he had but limited formal education, and his letters to the Clarks often contained misspellings and grammatical errors, though his handwriting is good and his meaning is easily understood. He wrote often to the Clarks, but for some reason Henry Clark (who had largely taken over the family business by the 1830s) rarely replied. In one letter Parker reminded him, "I have written you this the fifth time since February [1847] and no answer yet." "I am," he continued, "perfectly astonish[ed] at your silence. There must certainly be some thing rong. Are you dead? You can not be," he said, "because your people would have told me." Perhaps Clark didn't reply often because many of the letters he received were requests to sell the lands, or were of an anecdotal nature. More likely it was because Henry T. Clark hated writing letters.[35]

Henry Toole Clark, James and Arabella's only son, was born February 7, 1808, on the family's Walnut Creek plantation. Little else is known of his childhood. Early references list his full name as Henry Irwin Toole Clark, but he dropped the Irwin sometime during his student years at Chapel Hill. His first memories, he liked to say, were of his father in uniform.

James West was a major in the state militia and during the War of 1812, when young Henry was only five or six years old. There was apprehension and fear throughout the United States as the British threatened numerous coastal ports and ransacked towns and villages in the Chesapeake and northwest regions. Rumors of British atrocities filled the newspapers and many people believed the British would attack their community at any moment. Defensive preparations were made in each state, and local militias were called up for muster. Henry recalled riding with his father on horseback to the muster grounds located on Tarboro's Town Common. Major Clark, in an outstanding example of the military fashion of the day, was bedecked in a full-dress uniform of his own purchase—epaulets, gold braid, and plumes. On one occasion, the Clarks inadvertently surprised a neighbor who was walking to muster: gobsmacked at the sight of Major Clark in his dazzling uniform, the man fled into the woods. Major Clark called to the man by name, who then recognized him and his young son, confessing, "I thought it was Bonaparte!"[36]

Clark adored his father (he referred to him as "Pa") and rode horseback with him often, checking on the livestock or having a look at the crops. Records suggest that Henry enjoyed reading, especially poetry and history — activities he carried into adulthood. He also enjoyed riding and racing horses. As the eldest child and only son, Henry Clark was raised a gentleman and classically educated at a private academy in Tarboro, gaining an education befitting a young plantation aristocrat.

Clark's father served as a trustee of the Academy of Tarborough, established in 1814. An academy was essentially a college preparatory school, and a cut above the subscription education which consisted of a basic reading, writing and arithmetic curriculum. Academy students, by contrast, were instructed in Greek, Latin and advanced mathematics. Tuition for the Tarboro Academy ranged from sixteen to twenty-two dollars a term, a handsome sum, and school enrollment averaged seventy students a year, all male, who came from several surrounding counties.[37]

The school, and Clark's father, prepared him well. Though James West served as a trustee to the University of North Carolina from 1822 until his death in 1843, his son would still have had to meet certain academic requirements for admission, including proficiency in Greek and Latin. Clark was enrolled at UNC in the autumn of 1822 at age fourteen and graduated four years later.

It is not known exactly why Clark's father sent him to Chapel Hill rather than to Princeton. State pride was certainly a factor, but given the rising tide of sectionalism, southern boys of the early republic were increasingly being sent to southern universities where they were less likely to encounter northern influences such as abolitionism. Southern states established their own colleges in the late eighteenth and early nineteenth centuries (North Carolina in 1789) and quickly began promoting a more assertive pro-southern and pro-slavery agenda. Northern students were extremely rare on southern campuses.

Chapel Hill's antebellum student body was composed almost entirely of North Carolinians or other southerners. Of the twenty-one members of Clark's graduating class of 1826, only three hailed from out of state — one from Virginia, and two others, Erasmus Darwin North and Oliver Wolcott Treadwell, from Connecticut; of the 122 students who graduated during Clark's four years at Chapel Hill, North and Treadwell were the only northerners Clark encountered. In fact, those two were the first northerners to graduate from the University of North Carolina, and the only non-southerners to do so until 1855.[38]

While a pro-southern political climate existed on southern campuses, the high tuition charged by these colleges also contributed to the dearth of northern students in the region. North Carolina charged more than any northern school save Harvard, and remained the most expensive southern college until 1840, when the University of Virginia earned that distinction. Minimum annual expenses at Harvard in 1825 were estimated at $176, not including the fifty dollar tuition, while tuition at the University of Georgia was about twenty dollars. The average annual tuition of thirty dollars to attend UNC did not include expenses; books, room and board, and supplies such as paper and postage could push the yearly cost of attending college well over one hundred dollars, at a time when the average income for most families was less than three hundred dollars a year.

Northern colleges were slowly modernizing their curriculums while those of the South retained a classical approach.[39] As historian Eugene Genovese describes, they focused heavily on the classics: "History, ancient and medieval as well as American, fascinated educated southerners. College students got large doses of Greek and Roman history as well as literature, and many retained a lifelong interest."[40] It was believed that a classical education prepared men for leadership roles as statesmen, judges, legislators and community leaders. The example of Greek and Roman history reinforced wealthy southerners' notions of virtue and honor, and the ancients' reliance on slave labor provided the planters' justification, however strained, for their own dependence on African slavery. In addition, long hours of Latin and Greek translation and recitation prepared these students not for any practical vocation but rather for membership in an elite club, marking them as different from the middle ranks of society. A leading South Carolina thinker of that time, William J. Grayson, declared, "The end of education is to improve the manners, morals and mind of the student." The historian Lorri Glover argues that while universities in the North and in parts of Europe began modernizing their curriculum to emphasize "scientific and practical instruction," institutions in the South continued to stress "classics and oratory [which] affirmed the southern conviction that education should be less practical than ornamental; for elites classical training marked a man's elegance and respectability."[41]

Chapel Hill students were also steeped in mathematics. Of the 125 credit hours required to earn a bachelor's degree, fifty were dedicated to a wide variety of mathematical subjects. Some students complained of the three to five hours required per week in algebra, geometry, and trigonometry, though six hours a week for nineteen weeks were spent on "Surveying, Mensuration and Navigation."[42]

Languages, however, filled the bulk of the class schedule. Latin and Greek were required for all students in each year of studies, with the addition of French for juniors and seniors. Whereas sophomore students might take a natural history class for two hours a week for two weeks, Latin and Greek were served up for four hours a week for thirty-seven weeks. Students attended classes on average about fifteen hours a week, including a Bible recitation on Sundays. Junior and senior classmen sat for lectures, which were either written or delivered, and all students gave weekly recitations, in addition to their classwork and lectures, to their professors. Most instruction, however, came from textbook work.[43]

Students began arriving in Chapel Hill in late July to find housing and take entrance exams if needed. Classes began in August. The day started early with the ringing of the campus bell, and underclassmen gave their first recitation before breakfast. The next class began at nine. Each professor heard about ten recitations a week and gave several lectures in that time. The academic year was divided by a long Christmas break beginning about the first week of December and ending in mid–January. Classes ended in late May with week-long festivities, culminating with a graduation ceremony in June.

Occasionally the college would close in response to some great event or extraordinary occurrence. One such occasion happened in 1825 — Clark's junior year — when Gen. Marquis de Lafayette, the French hero who served under Washington during the American

Revolution, arrived in North Carolina on his famed tour of the United States. The university closed for six days to allow its students the opportunity to see this living legend. Clark was doubtless among the many students who "were so anxious to go [to Raleigh] that some of them walked in the rain, and others rode in wagons." The Raleigh *Register* reported "some of the Faculty and a greater part of the Collegians from the University, came here 28 miles, most of them walking, to see Lafayette. We honor the motive which actuated, and the spirit which carried into effect the patriotic curiosity of the students." The paper commented (rather prophetically) that "Should the time ever recur, similar to those, 'which tried men's souls,' we predict that this juvenile Band [of students] will not be the last to assert their country's rights, and to defend that independence which Lafayette fought to establish."[44]

Henry Toole Clark, ca. 1820. This painting on stone is considered by some to be Clark. Clark was educated at a local private academy and was admitted to the state university at Chapel Hill in 1822. He graduated in 1826 with an A.B. degree and earned a master's degree in 1832. In 1833 he joined the bar and moved back to Tarboro. (Courtesy Patrick Reddick Family Papers & Photos collection.)

During Clark's years at Chapel Hill, the university employed seven professors and two tutors, the tutors usually being recent graduates of the university and not much older than the students they taught. Three of the professors and one tutor were dedicated to language instruction, and two professors to science — one teaching chemistry, the other mathematics and natural philosophy. Of the remaining two professors, one taught logic and rhetoric, while the other taught national and constitutional law and served as university president. The second tutor taught math. The university served between one hundred and two hundred students a year, and the average graduating class in the 1820s numbered about thirty-five. Most of the students were age fourteen to eighteen.[45]

University life in the antebellum South differed in other ways from that of modern higher education. There were neither inter-collegiate athletics nor the wide variety of school and social activities that are available to today's university student. This lack of constructive after-school activity, combined with a rigorous curriculum, onerous rules, the isolation of university life, and a large number of relatively unsupervised, spoilt adolescent boys living in close quarters, encouraged misbehavior. Campus life was rowdy and student conduct often atrocious. Fighting, dueling, drunkenness, gambling, brutish pranks and riotous behavior were not uncommon. At the University of Virginia, in an extreme but telling example, a professor was shot and killed during a drunken student melée on the lawn. While nothing of this magnitude happened at Chapel Hill, students there were equally unruly. To combat student misbehavior, the University of North Carolina "forbade betting on horse races and cockfights, possessing liquor, guns, or dogs, public use of profanity and public intoxication," and required attendance to Sunday chapel services.[46]

Rules, however, were often broken or ignored. As the famed historian E. Merton Coulter once remarked, "The college student of the Old South was a happy creature; he had so many rules to disobey and did it so effectively." In universities across the South, professors and administrators alike complained about their students' conduct and refusal to obey the rules. But then, these young collegians were accustomed to issuing commands; obeying and submission to rules were for slaves and servants, not gentlemen. Many students were sons of wealthy planters, born to a life of privilege and ease, their estates, slaves, and property worth tens of thousands of dollars. Most professors, by contrast, lived on a salary of about seven hundred dollars per year. The college's president received an annual salary of $1,600 at a time when a planter could easily sell or purchase two slaves for the same amount.[47]

Professors and tutors lacked the social connections or pedigree of their charges, so they were often treated with contempt and defiance by the students (and their parents). In 1825 university trustees employed a superintendent of property to visit each student room once a week and "note the injuries [done to the room] and their perpetrators" who would then receive an appropriate fine. Any attempt to restrain these young scions, however, was usually an exercise in futility, and most punishments, if any, were light. Students could be expelled, but college trustees seldom dismissed these wealthy, truculent sons for fear of reprisal or the loss of student tuitions, which funded the college payroll.[48]

As future civic leaders and slave-masters-in-training, the students preferred to govern themselves, and formed clubs to do just that. The Dialectic and Philanthropic Societies were organized in 1795 to serve as social and academic releases for students apart from the prying eyes of their professors. Faculty members were forbidden to interfere with the societies' governance or attend their meetings. This practice of self-governance blossomed into an unofficial campus judicial system during the first seventy-five years of the university's existence.[49]

Clark joined the Dialectic Society upon entering the university and was active throughout his four years there. Clark's decision to join the "Di," however, was not taken without some pressure. Competition for student dues was fierce, as each society funded their own libraries and meeting halls, and members of both the Dialectic and Philanthropic harassed new students upon their arrival to campus, pressing them relentlessly to join. Apparently in order to stave off a particularly aggressive request, Clark gave a verbal promise to join the Philanthropic Society. However, this decision didn't sit well with him and word reached his father concerning his dilemma. His father wrote to him saying that he had heard some "difficulty had arisen about your entering one or the other of the Societies." He reminded his son:

> I placed you fully on your guard as to the polite treatment you would receive from the members of both Societies until you entered one. In order that you might follow my advise more effectually which you must remember was this — to become well acquainted with the standing and merits of the members of both and then join that Society, which in your opinion had the greatest number of respectable members that would remain at college the longest time with you. That in the name of Societies there was nothing to lead you one way or the other but that you were to judge from the members. Although you have not followed my advice, yet if you have made a choice and have given assurances in consequence thereof that you would join either society, adhere to your word; don't waver.[50]

However, Clark did waver. He withdrew his promise and joined the Dialectic. The club met each Thursday evening in South Hall to discuss current issues, recite poetry, or simply socialize. The club did monitor the conduct of its members, but how effective their "guarantees" were in combating student misbehavior is debatable. Rule violations and disrespect towards professors remained a problem throughout the antebellum period, and more often than not, the societies protected their members from reproach.

For example, a mathematics professor at the University of North Carolina decreed that students could no longer bring their math books to the recitation room. At the first meeting after this rule was announced, only half of the class obeyed. At another meeting, at least eleven shamelessly broke the rule and brought their textbooks to the recitation. After several weeks of disobedience, a faculty meeting was convened and the university president was asked to speak directly to the belligerents. He did so, but even after this lecture as many as a dozen students continued to flout the rule. A final meeting was convened and the students were called before the faculty and college president. They were told they would be dismissed should they continue to disobey. Most of the students complied, but three did not (one of these was the son of the state's governor): they were dismissed from the university.[51]

Other incidents at Chapel Hill during the antebellum period were more dramatic. After a particularly riotous night of drinking, dozens of students rampaged across the campus shattering the windows of the tutors' residence and throwing stones at members of the faculty: "The University bell was rung violently and long, the laboratory and recitation rooms were broken [into] and nearly destroyed [and] the stables of several Professors entered and the horses ridden." Punishment was light for most of the participants. Four upperclassmen were dismissed but the younger freshmen "were allowed to take the usual pledge and go free."[52] The student body, however, rebelled at the faculty's dismissal of the four upperclassmen. Students assembled in front of the South Building and began a "blasphemous revival of religion, calling up mourners, singing ribald songs, ringing the bell, and afterward painting the horses of a professor, cutting off [a horse's] mane and tail and placing him in Person Hall." Only two students were called out and dismissed. These two students, however, were readmitted after "taking the pledge of penitence and reformation." Two weeks later, students hijacked all of the campus blackboards, destroying several. After this infraction, the college promised criminal prosecutions for any student engaged in the destruction of college property.[53]

When several professors grew weary of the incessant talking in class and the drinking and card-playing, they "announced that the cords of discipline must be tightened." The students responded by forming "The Ugly Club." The members organized themselves in protest on the campus grounds and loudly denounced any attempt by the faculty to censure their behavior. Faculty members confronted the students but were "pelted with rocks." "Professor Mitchell" then "sallied forth with a sword cane and was driven back." There is no record of anyone being dismissed for this wild action.[54]

Heavy drinking was the favorite diversion, and rarely were students disciplined for this indulgence. Students and professors alike imbibed a variety of wines and spirituous liquors and in amounts that seem incredible today. Boozy fêtes honoring the memory of the American Revolution, and especially the memory of George Washington, were common. In one telling example, over thirty students hosted a party in honor of the nation's first president and invited all the professors "by special invitation" to attend. One student recalled that before the supper several of them began "drinking wine at 11 o'clock in the forenoon and continued drinking until one." Afterwards they took a nap to "sober up" in order to attend the evening party. Later, as expected, the party involved numerous toasts and everyone "drank pretty freely." Of the thirty in attendance, only "four or five" remained sober.[55]

It isn't known if Clark participated in such riotous behavior or whether he followed his father's advice to stay in his room and study. Letters from home suggest that young Henry stayed out of serious trouble, though he wasn't above cutting up from time to time. Given the wild, irreverent nature of campus life, it is safe to say that Clark, while perhaps not a leading participant, was at least an observer. He boarded on campus at both Old East and Old West dormitories and would have been an eyewitness to many scenes of revelry. Given the small community that was Chapel Hill at the time, the frequent occurrences of student misbehavior must have influenced Clark to some degree.

He was, in fact, caught skipping Sunday chapel. Attendance at Sunday morning chapel services was required of every student and while not as serious (or as exciting) an infraction as painting a professor's horse, it was reported to his father. "As I have understood, you have already been called on publickly for absence from prayer," his father admonished. "Inattention to one part of your duties necessarily leads to neglect of others, and so on, till you will become perfectly idle." He closed the letter by saying "see how soon news when it is bad spreads? You know when you were called on about your absence from prayers, and it is known here already. Let my bird, I pray you, bear me better news hereafter."[56]

Hoping to shame the boy into acting more responsibly in the future, he added, "I had hoped, however, that altho' young, and as thoughtless as ever, that on reaching the University, and becoming a member thereof, you would, for character sake, if for no other motive, become more thoughtful, more firm and less fickle; and more steady and manly and dignified in your conduct and deportment."[57]

1. Frontier Aristocrats

Clark's conduct was James West's constant concern. His father's letters are filled with worry, advice, and admonitions; he was well aware of the temptations and traps about campus lurking to ensnare a careless youth. A typical letter warned: "For want of one moment's thought, and by permitting my advice to be forgotten, you might, in the crowd of young men and boys who surround you, differing in disposition, in talents, in character, in their pleasures of amusement" follow their example and end up in trouble. He told his son to be a leader and to "answer for yourself, and I hope with candour and relieve my anxious mind."[58]

Clark, however, never wrote often enough to relieve his father's anxious mind. He was constantly scolded to write more often. "It is indeed surprising how soon we learn to do the things we ought not to do, and omit those we are in duty bound to do," his father said sternly. "When you left home I strictly required of you to write to me once in two weeks, and you faithfully promised to do so. But now six weeks have passed. You are verifying the old adage — out of sight, out of mind — not only of your parents, but of their advice and best counsels."[59] When "duty" proved an insufficient motivator, James West tried guilt: "Your grandmother is sick. She cryed because you did not write, therefore don't fail to write to her." Clark's reluctance to write letters, however, continued throughout his life.[60]

Like many fathers, then, James West worried about his son. While these letters reveal that he loved Henry, he was equally worried that something might happen to endanger the

Old West Building, University of North Carolina. Clark roomed in Old West when it first opened for students in 1823. As a state senator after the Civil War, Clark worked to keep the university open. Despite his efforts, it closed due to financial difficulties in 1870, but reopened five years later. North Carolina Collection, University of North Carolina Library at Chapel Hill.

family's reputation. Honor was to be respected and the family name kept from embarrassment. Failure was not an option. Clark's progress in school was closely monitored and his class standing was important to his father, as a measure of the Clarks' standing in the white male community. His father wrote, "What is your standing in the class, where does [your friend] Henry Hodge stand?" Another letter asked, "How does young Norfleet stand in your class, and a young man from Williamston by the name of Watts," while another letter reminded Henry to "Be of good courage, and maintain your standing."[61]

Clark's father was also free with practical advice, advice which the laconic future governor seems to have followed into adulthood. "Be not forward in your expression of opinion in any situation," James West wrote. "You have two ears and but one mouth. Hear twice as much therefore as you talk." And, "Weigh with any and every matter before you and keep a still tongue in relation to your companions, and tell no person not even your most intimate friend every thing you think." In a particularly witty mood, yet in all seriousness, he advised: "A horse may be led thro' college and be nothing the wiser for the trip."[62]

James West also encouraged his son to read good books. Being a university man himself, he was familiar with the texts and curriculum his son would experience. "When you finish [John] Gillie's 'History of Greece,'" he advised, "read Plutarch's 'Lives' attentively and minutely." This was a piece of advice that young Clark didn't mind heeding. Indeed, for young Henry history was a favorite, especially the ancient Greek and English variety. Mathematics, however, offered none of the excitement of Pericles or Marlborough. In fact, his father consistently nagged Henry to put down his history books and pick up his math work. In one letter, his father wrote sternly: "Listen to me — lay history aside for the present, and the moments you would have to spare to the reading of it, devote to the reviewing of your Collegiate studies, particularly Algebra and Arithmetic."[63]

Clark made it through his four years of university and while his academic record wasn't exactly stellar, it was good enough to earn him the designation of "honor man," allowing him the privilege to make an "Intermediate Oration" at graduation. Student orations and addresses by important people were the main features of antebellum graduations, but the number of speeches given by students had increased steadily over the years until the ceremony stretched into the better part of the day. No fewer than twenty speeches were given at Clark's 1826 graduation, and it was the last year that "honor orations" were heard at the final commencement. His oration, "On the English Character," was a 1,200-word speech that extolled the virtues of the English people and their history, arguing that "the character of a people is closely interwoven with the history of their country," and that we "discover the spirit and ruling passion of a people" in historical events. His address was well received, though his professor scribbled on the back of the document that "Mr. Clark is late in handing in his speech. I hope he will be particular in committing it to memory, remembering his embarrassment on a former occasion." Unfortunately, we don't know any details of this "embarrassment," though Clark's preternatural memory must have uncharacteristically lapsed during a recitation.[64]

Though Clark enjoyed history, family responsibilities and business matters dictated his career path. He was sent to New York City shortly after his graduation for reasons that are not entirely known, but most likely for additional study and an opportunity to see the larger world. He boarded and perhaps interned with a gentleman named A.H. Vanbokkiln, where, according to his father, he studied French. Living in New York was expensive, and there, as at Chapel Hill, Henry found it difficult to keep his money. He asked his father to replenish his purse but his father replied, "I regret the low state of your funds because I can't at present day say when I shall be able to replenish them as it depends on entering upon my time and means of collection. Husband therefore what you have."[65]

It is not known how long Clark remained in New York, but he returned to Chapel Hill and received a master's degree in 1832. He left Chapel Hill for Raleigh shortly thereafter and read law under his uncle, William H. Haywood, Jr. Haywood was a committed Democrat who greatly influenced the young Clark. From 1843 to 1846, Haywood served as a United States Senator from North Carolina and strongly supported President James K. Polk's expansionist policies. He resigned his Senate seat when the party lost control of the state legislature to the Whigs.

Politics would hold a lifelong interest for Clark, and contrary to what later historians have said about him, he did put his legal training to use. On February 15, 1833, he was admitted to the North Carolina bar to practice as counselor in Superior Court, though he never hung out his own shingle as a country lawyer. Rather, like many wealthy gentlemen, he used his legal training as an ornament to his station in life, and in a real and practical sense it served his business interests and acted as a springboard to a career in politics. For many years he served as a justice of the peace and chairman of the Edgecombe county courts, and his knowledge of the law would aid him in his career as a state senator and as North Carolina's governor. In his later years, he counseled friends and family members in estate planning, legal issues, and financial matters.[66]

The Clarks had indeed become members of the local and state elite. From their beginnings in the colonial shipping trade, the family's income and social prominence had steadily grown. Their business acumen, investments in slave property and the benefit of advantageous marriages had established them as members of the planter master class. Henry Toole Clark, with his university education and with political and social connections throughout the state, was ready for the next stage: elected office.

2

Coming Into His Own

As the 1830s began, Henry Toole Clark was moving rapidly toward his career as a planter and politician. Although classically educated, he showed a real and practical talent for accounts and figures and began proving himself a good steward of his family's affairs. He was considered handsome with black hair and dark eyes, and he stood at five feet, eight inches, the average height of the day. Known by many as a sincere and honest man, he also "possessed a wonderful intellect and knew the art of organizing men."[1] While still in his twenties, he was given more and more responsibilities by his father.

By the mid–1830s the Clarks had developed several successful businesses. They owned dozens of slaves and thousands of acres in North Carolina and Tennessee and had invested in bank and canal stocks. They managed trust funds and financial portfolios for family members. Their local ventures on their Edgecombe County properties included grain production and processing, raising livestock and a small amount of cotton, as well as wine and spirit distilling. But they wisely avoided the pitfall that ensnared many planters, that of committing all their resources to growing labor-intensive cash crops. They preferred to lease out small parcels of their land for others to farm, usually after harvesting the timber. And most importantly, they ran a slave-hire business. Slave-hire (as opposed to simple slave ownership) is a relatively little-known aspect of the southern economy. This rather grim practice was the first area of his family's affairs that Henry managed.

Slave ownership was a major source of income for white southerners. It granted cachet as well, conferring respect and social privileges, as it was an obvious sign of wealth and stability. For the Clarks, owning slaves was the key factor in raising them from the merchant to the planter class. Young Henry had grown up with slavery and had always known it. By 1790 his family had owned over twenty slaves and continued to invest in them. As a typical example, Henry's grandmother Hannah in 1797 bought "a negro wench named Easter" for two hundred dollars. Christopher Clark owned more than thirty slaves by the time he died in 1801, and he left several to his son in his will. Like him, James West Clark steadily increased his "inventory." By 1830 he had acquired another twenty-seven.[2]

Most of these slaves were female. In 1830, when federal census records first began noting the sex of slaves, James West owned seven males and twenty females. Ten were less than eleven years of age, and six were between the ages of twelve and thirty-five. The historian

2. Coming Into His Own

Walter Johnson has noted that besides being less expensive to buy, young female slaves were a good investment because they offered "the promise of reproduction." Whether the Clarks "bred" slaves isn't known, but according to the laws of the day, the slave's body and her offspring were the slave owner's chattels.[3]

The family came into possession of slaves over the years through direct purchases or gifts. The practice of giving slaves to friends or relatives was common among the slave-owning classes, for example: James West acquired a "mulatto girl named Ester about seventeen years of age" from John Byrne in New York in 1802. Ownership of slaves, whether bought or gifted, became an increasingly attractive and profitable venture, and over time southerners began to view slaves as a commodity. By 1818, Louisianan James Steer advised that "the best stock ... is negro Stock; negroes will yield a much larger income than any bank dividend."[4]

By 1840 the Clarks owned at least forty-seven slaves. Sixteen were kept in Tarboro, four males and twelve females; and at least thirty-one others were relocated to Alabama for hire purposes. Slaves were in great demand in that part of the country, and hiring them out became the most lucrative aspect of slave ownership for the Clarks.

Four main factors fueled the South's hunger for slave labor. The first was the invention and widespread use of the mechanical cotton gin, which made short staple cotton a viable cash crop for southern farmers. The short staple variety grew well in the inland areas of the southeastern states such as Georgia, Alabama, and Mississippi, but planters had generally avoided it because of the intensive labor needed to remove the numerous seeds imbedded in its fibers. When Eli Whitney patented his gin in 1794 to remove these seeds, the labor previously needed to process cotton could now be used for planting and harvesting. Cotton quickly became the region's dominant crop.

The second factor was the industrial revolution. The new steam-driven looms in British textile factories were able to produce a surplus of cheap cotton cloth. Transportation innovations like canals and railroads made it possible to move cotton quickly to market. What had been a rather exotic expensive fabric for most Europeans became widely available to the growing middle class. The American textile industry expanded rapidly in the 1820s, adding to the pressure to find more sources for raw cotton fiber. Finally, when Britain abolished slavery in its own colonies in 1833, southern farmers in the United States found they were overwhelmed by demand.

The third factor was the increasing availability of abundant fertile lands due to the Louisiana Purchase of 1803 and the acquisition of Florida in 1819. However, violent clashes over land rights between Americans and Indian groups presented a significant obstacle to white settlers. For decades numerous wars were waged by both sides, but during the 1830s virtually all of the remaining Indian tribes east of the Mississippi River were removed to Oklahoma. This relocation effectively ended native opposition to white settlement in the South. Whites poured into the region with abandon, hungry for slave labor to clear the woodlands, drain the swamps, till the fields and plant cotton.

The fourth development was the 1808 federal prohibition on the importation of African or other foreign slaves.[5] This drastic restriction on supply substantially increased the value of Upper South bondsmen. Many owners profited handsomely from the selling or hiring of slaves to areas where short staple cotton would flourish. Slave owners from the tobacco regions of the Upper South — Maryland, Virginia, North Carolina and Kentucky — supplied slaves to the cotton states.

By the 1830s, the demand in the Deep South for slave labor was very strong; in North Carolina, however, it was stagnant. Yeoman families were leaving worn-out farms, while younger sons of planters or those too poor to buy more land in the established eastern regions also sought opportunity in the less settled, more fertile agricultural areas of Alabama and points west. North Carolina's population declined severely during the period from 1800 to 1850, losing more people to out-migration than any other state in the Union. Once in the newer western regions, most could not afford to buy slaves outright but were able to lease enough slave labor on a temporary basis to meet their needs.[6]

Sumter County, Alabama, was a major cotton growing area and the state's most populous county by 1840. The majority of its inhabitants were slaves. This historical marker sits on the courthouse square where many of Clark's slaves were hired out for the year to other farmers or businessmen. (Photograph by the author.)

2. *Coming Into His Own*

Some of Clark's cousins had also moved away to Alabama. James West Clark and Theophilus Parker were brothers-in-law, and in the late 1820s or 1830s Parker's son Haywood had settled in Greene County, Alabama, buying land and establishing a plantation.[7] Haywood (the brother of Henry Clark's future wife, Mary) kept the Clarks informed about the new economic opportunities awaiting them in the region. Haywood told the Clarks of a boom area opening up within thirty miles of his plantation in what would become Sumter County, and suggested that they send some of their Tarboro slaves to Alabama to hire out. This new area was Choctaw Indian country; but, as the demand for land increased, whites began to covet the Sumter region. They eventually forced the Choctaws to sign the Treaty of Dancing Rabbit Creek in 1830, which ceded eleven million acres of prime cotton-growing land to the whites in exchange for fifteen million acres in Oklahoma territory. This gently rolling land in Alabama the whites now possessed was heavily forested with oak, hickory, and sweet gum trees, which could be cleared to make prime cotton fields. The region enjoyed a long growing season and its slow-moving streams and rivers supplied access to waterways on which farmers could ship their crops to Mobile and New Orleans, and eventually to New England and Europe.

It took three years to survey the area and remove the remaining Indians, and in 1833 the federal government announced that the lands would be sold from its offices in Tuscaloosa. During this brief interim period, Alabama organized Sumter County and laid out the town of Livingston in 1832. The land sold rapidly, the best of it by 1834, and whites inundated the region. Dirt roads and ferries brought in thousands of settlers, and by 1840 Sumter County was Alabama's most populous with nearly thirty thousand inhabitants. Of that number, nearly sixteen thousand, or fifty-three percent, were slaves. Livingston was a frontier boom town.[8]

This area was just one of many eagerly demanding more slaves. Historians estimate that as many as one million African Americans were forcibly relocated to the Deep South from 1800 to 1860. Known today as the "second middle passage," this journey mirrors the horrors faced by those Africans who were forced onto ships and made to endure horrific torments during their Atlantic crossing. Like their African ancestors, these slaves experienced an arduous and sometimes fatal journey across the unknown. Men and women were separated; individuals were chained in random pairs or burdened with iron fetters to prevent escape. Coffles of slaves were marched overland, shipped in mule driven carts, or packed aboard steamboats on a trip that could take weeks. These captive men and women endured exposure and malnutrition, and many thousands died.[9]

The Clarks forced many of their slaves to take this journey. In May 1835, thirty-one of the "Negroes of James W. Clark" were sent the eight hundred miles from their Tarboro plantation to the frontier of southwestern Alabama. The oldest slave, Tony, was fifty-seven. The youngest, Calvin, was one. At least half were men, better able to endure the long trip. Six, however, were under the age of ten. Averaging twenty miles a day, the journey would have taken about six weeks. The roads were in wretched condition and wound through remote swamps, thickets, and forests. Few towns along the way offered respite. Wild animals,

Negroes of James W Clark, 1 brought to
Sumter Co. Alabama May 1835

Names	Born	Names	Born
Tony	about 1778	Fabby	1793
Jepe	1780	Molly	1785
Ned	1798	Anna	Sept. 1800
Leml.	Sept 1806	Pallas	June 1816
Bill	April 1809	Matilda	Dec 1824
Lewis	Augt. 1811	Bednego	Jan 1827
Matthew	Sept. 1811	Nelly	15 Jany 1825
Frank	April 1817	Emily	March 1828
Fanny	June 1817	Hasty	Augt. 1828
Albert	Jany. 1818	Adeline	Sept 1832
Jerry	Sept. 1818	Teresa. Calvin & Augustus	
Daniel	April 1820	died on passage out	
Benjamin	Augt. 1821	Belongs to Maria J C	
Soloman	June 1823	Marina	July 1808
John	Nov. 1822	Virgil	Nov. 1829
Milly (child of Pallas)	Apr. 1837	Stella	Jan 1832
John (do)	1839	Bill	Jan 1836
Mary (child of Anna)	Nov. 1839	Frances	1839
		Infant (died)	1840

"Negroes of James W. Clark brought to Sumter Co. Alabama May 1835." Clark and his father, James, viewed slaves as financial investments as evidenced in this account ledger. The note that interrupts the list in the right-hand column reads: "Teresa, Calvin & Augustus died on passage out." Courtesy Special Collections Library, Duke University.

snakes, and the lash were feared, and often encountered. Food was coarse and bad. Sickness, disease, and death were likely companions and indeed, three slaves — little Calvin, Augustus, aged two, and Teresa, aged twenty-two — died on the passage out.[10]

There are no records to show who was in charge of this expedition, but it was likely Henry Clark himself. It is evident from his letters that later that same year he made annual trips to the region to manage the business, and this first trip would have been the most important of them all. The challenge was tremendous. He had to transport a major part of the family's assets, two thirds of their slaves, on a dangerous and uncertain journey fraught with potential for serious mishaps. James West was fifty-six years old and hesitant to undertake the long journey himself, while Henry, age twenty-seven, was vigorous and just reaching his prime. As Henry was proving himself capable, his father continued to give him more duties and trained him to take on the family's affairs. Setting up this new slave-hire business in a strange place would have been a responsibility that called for a family member's attention.

Livingston was the center of the cotton trade in west central Alabama and the seat of government for Sumter County. It was a rough-and-tumble community with little to recommend it, except for the prospect of earning great wealth by growing cotton on its rich lands, or providing services to those that did. As in other boom towns, men of fortune arrived early and set a bawdy tone. An "intense and eager pursuit of wealth" permeated the town as grogshops, billiard rooms and diversions of more a risqué nature arose. Public drunkenness was common. Fistfights and the public discharge of firearms occurred with frequency. It was reported that "there was a vast amount of dissipation of all descriptions, and nine tenths of the population participated in it with wonderful gusto." As in the California gold rush towns several years later, those who made the most money were the entrepreneurs who provided goods and services.[11]

Hiring out slave labor was the service the Clarks provided. For the first few years Henry tried to run the operation personally. Although needed in Tarboro, he traveled to Livingston after the autumn harvest. He had to be there every year for "Hiring Day," January 1, the start of the contract season, and also to collect rents from the previous year. He made the first winter trip in 1835, leaving Tarboro on December 17 and arriving on the 30th. All the slaves brought out the previous May had been hired out, some as field hands or skilled laborers, others in town as domestic servants or as help in local shops and businesses. These slaves generated $1,421 in cash and notes.

Clark also, however, needed to deal with problems. Two of his slaves, Bill and Lewis, were hired to "Mr. John Lake for $210." Bill and Lewis were field hands and highly valued as laborers. Almost immediately upon arriving at Lake's farm, the two slaves ran away into the woods. They remained hidden for several days, but not knowing where they were and with no one to assist them in their escape, they were recaptured. These runaways had cost Clark money. Lake demanded a reduction in the contract amount: fifty-six dollars for "lost time in the woods." Slaves who ran away were often thought of by whites as having the "habit" of doing so, a moral failing that served as "evidence of a vice of character." Many

Runaway Slaves. Two of Clark's slaves, "Bill and Lewis," ran away soon after arriving in Alabama. They hid in the swamps for several days but were recaptured. Angered at their temporary escape, the man who hired out the two slaves demanded fifty-six dollars from Clark for "lost time in the woods." (Courtesy of the North Carolina Office of Archives and History, Raleigh, North Carolina.)

doctors at the time treated this "habit" as a mental disorder. In the case of a runaway slave, the hirer of the slave might demand a deduction in the contract amount, or monetary compensation from the owner under state warranty laws that protected slave buyers and those who hired slaves from any "defects in the thing sold," but usually the hirer had to absorb the costs of lost time. Had Clark been in closer proximity, or had he hired an attorney to represent him in Alabama, he probably would not have reduced the contract amount.[12]

Other problems also arose over the years, and some expenses cut into the profits of the slave-hire business. Medical care — including child birthing, bleedings, cuppings, or extracting teeth — could average several hundred dollars a year for an owner of many slaves. One of Clark's slaves, Marina, bore four children in four years (1836 to 1840) at a cost to Clark of $108 (though the children did represent potential future profit). The slaves "Matthew, Albert, Tony and family" cost $153 in medical expenses during the same four year period. If a slave was not hired, the owner was responsible for clothing, and room and board. For example, Clark bought on average seven dollars worth of clothing each year per slave and over "$18 in boarding for Negroes" until they could be rented.[13]

Disagreements often arose over who was responsible for the slave. The death of a slave cost the owner future profits, but if the slave were hired out and died while under contract, the hirer was bound to honor the agreement for the full amount. For example, Clark's slave Solomon was a valuable, mature, and skilled worker. He did "smith work" and had been with Clark for a long time but "took sick and died" after a ten-day illness. His agent wrote from Alabama to say that "the [hirer] says that he is unwilling to pay the full year hire [but] there is no doubt he is bound for it." The hirer was duly taken to court and ordered to pay Clark the money owed.[14]

Nevertheless, the potential for substantial profit remained great. A healthy male slave could generate about two hundred dollars a year; a woman with children, about seventy dollars. Even children could earn money. As soon as someone was willing to hire them, slave owners leased them out, often at the rate of room-and-board expenses. The cheaper rate for children under twelve years of age was attractive to poor whites or those looking for help with small tasks, such as cleaning, sweeping, weeding, fetching water, scaring birds away from gardens, or any manner of similar tedious jobs. The affordability of child slaves gave less affluent whites access to slave labor and an empowering taste of mastery and social privilege. And of course, the children eventually grew up and the owner could command more money for their hire.

Clark made a longer, more extensive trip the second year. He left Tarboro by stagecoach on December 7, 1836, but fell ill on the way. By the time he arrived in Greensboro, Alabama, thirty-five miles away from Livingston, he was forced to stop. He lodged with "Dr. Rufus" (a North Carolina émigré from Raleigh) where he remained "quite sick." Writing to his family and extending Christmas wishes, Clark said that he was feeling better after a good rest and added his wish for "that good old Christmas custom of collecting the family around the same fireside." He noted that his cousin Croom "was very kind," inviting him to convalesce at his home, but that he declined the invitation, saying that he "preferred Dr. R[ufus] notwithstanding I should there [have] the privilege of being waited on by the beautiful Miss C." He recovered and made his way to Livingston where he arrived on December 28. There was no further mention of "Miss C."[15]

Clark remained in Livingston until January 27. According to his itinerary notes and ledger, he hired a boy and two horses for the start of his journey north to Tennessee. He wanted to visit Daniel Parker and look at his Dyer County lands and accounts. Antebellum travel in the South, however, was circuitous. To go north from Livingston, one had to catch a steamboat at Demopolis (about twenty-five miles to the east), travel south to Mobile and ride another steamboat to New Orleans. From there one steamed north up the Mississippi River.

Clark rode to Demopolis and, after boarding the steamboat, sent the servant and the horses back to Livingston. It was no doubt a relief: water travel was much more comfortable than riding a horse or traveling bad roads in a jolting stagecoach. The steamboat lazily journeyed the one hundred and forty miles south down the Tombigbee River to Mobile, where Clark disembarked and lodged for a couple of days. He purchased a new suit, an umbrella, a knife, a set of books, and an orange. That evening he attended the theater.

He left Mobile for a two-day steamboat journey to New Orleans, where he stayed for ten days enjoying the sights and sounds of the South's largest city, the nation's fourth largest. With a population of one hundred thousand people, New Orleans in the 1830s was vibrant, diverse, and exciting, and Clark found much to occupy his time there. He visited the slave markets, shopped for clothes and books, ate in restaurants and enjoyed the theater. He marveled at the city's technological advancements: natural gas lamps, a steam cotton press, and the railroads.

Clark left New Orleans in late February 1837 for the steamboat journey north to Memphis. This Tennessee city had been founded only seventeen years earlier in 1820, but it grew quickly thanks to the expanding cotton trade and its convenient location on the Mississippi River. Clark spent a few days there, again shopping and enjoying urban life. He bought "books, a cravat and a powder flask." He also rented a horse for fifteen days to make the seventy-five mile journey to Dyer County to visit Parker and survey the Clark family lands. After two weeks there engaged in business, he left for Nashville in early April.

Nashville was the state capital and while there, Clark purchased maps of Texas (the Texas Revolution had just ended), more books, a Bowie knife, and a pair of moccasins. He left Nashville on April 24 by stagecoach through Knoxville and eastward over the Appalachian Mountains to Raleigh, North Carolina. He arrived home in Tarboro by mid–May 1837. The journey took six months and covered over 2,200 miles at an expense of nearly eight hundred dollars.

These annual trips by horseback, stagecoach and steamboat continued until 1840, when he was able to travel by train. The Wilmington and Weldon railroad was completed that year and a spur line connected Tarboro to the depot at Rocky Mount. Clark left Tarboro by rail in early December for Goldsboro, where he met up with several friends who "constituted a large and pleasant party." The men dined together, enjoying "fruit, oysters and drinks," and then made their way toward Wilmington. Approximately thirty miles from its destination the train hit a cow, overturning the engine and cars. "No injuries were sustained," Clark wrote, though the party was detained for the night. He caught the train the next day to Charleston, South Carolina, and spent the evening enjoying the beauty of the city. He arrived in Greensboro, Alabama, without further delay on Christmas Eve. The train had reduced the journey from two weeks to one.[16]

The following day he and the Parkers went to St. Paul's, the local Episcopal church. Writing his sisters, he said that he found it "handsomely decorated with evergreen circles, wreaths and festoons of cedar, wild orange [and] holly." He "heard the best sermon" that he had "listened to this year, and you know I never compliment a sermon for form sake." After the service, the family "returned and ate Xmas dinner with Mr. P[arker]."[17]

Although he wrote that he enjoyed visiting family, he soon came to dread these yearly trips to Livingston, where he expected to find, as he told his sisters, "trouble and hard times." He was alluding to an inherent problem in the slave hire business: sharing slave mastery. In the South, slaves and mastery were both considered personal property, and sharing mastery often made slave hiring an acrimonious affair. Both owner and hirer felt

2. Coming Into His Own

St. James Episcopal Church, Livingston, Alabama, was established in 1836. Clark attended this church on his annual visits to the area from 1835 to 1842. (Photograph by the author.)

entitled to property rights in mastery over the same slaves: disagreements concerning contracts, and refusals to pay, were frequent. Given his great distance from Alabama, these disagreements were especially frustrating, as he could conduct his affairs only through letters and his annual visits each winter. They were but typical of the problems inherent in trying to run his business from afar. To try to stay abreast of things while in Tarboro, he subscribed to Sumter County newspapers and relied on his relatives in nearby Greene County to keep him informed.[18]

His cousin Haywood was his most reliable support. In one case involving non-payment, Haywood informed Clark that a certain "Capt. C. Jones" had had not paid his account, "but promises he will." "He says he has the money," Haywood continued, "and if he does not pay, I shall sue him and send the account over to Mr. Hair."[19]

James Hair and his son Sam proved to be the solution to Clark's problems. The Hairs were attorneys and slave agents, and in 1842 Clark employed them to represent him in Alabama. They proved to be trustworthy, reliable, and conscientious, managing all the

James Hair (1799–1863) was Clark's representative in Livingston, Alabama, after 1841. He was a reliable attorney and slave agent sending frequent updates to Clark concerning his slave property in Sumter County. Though considered a pious man who served in various leadership capacities in the Presbyterian Church, he was nevertheless a ruthless slave-driver who owned many slaves and died a wealthy man. (Photograph by the author.)

hiring-out and maintenance of the slaves. They sent Clark frequent updates and kept his accounts in order.

Hair (like Daniel Parker) had moved to the South looking for opportunity. Born in Pennsylvania in 1790, he married a North Carolina woman and moved to Sumter County in 1834. He opened a legal practice in Livingston and bought land "just east" of town which he farmed and where he boarded negroes. He quickly became a successful lawyer and businessman, acquiring sixty-six slaves and other property worth $140,000. He was a hardheaded businessman and a ruthless slave driver. Hair died a very wealthy man in 1863 at the age of seventy-two.[20]

Under Hair's management, Clark's profits increased steadily. In 1839, working alone, Clark held just over $5,100 in cash and notes for his hires. In 1840, he had about two thousand dollars on the account books. In fact, he lost over three thousand dollars in a five-year period from 1835 to 1840 due to bankruptcies, insolvencies, runaways, medical bills, and "compromises" with hirers. In 1844, two years after Hair was hired, twenty-one of his twenty-two slaves were hired for a total value of nearly nine thousand dollars. Most of his slaves were adult males, but Clark did possess four children under eight years of age. The youngest was three and the eldest sixty-three. Slaves were usually hired by year, but occasionally by the month or job.[21]

Drafting the slave hire contracts was an important part of the service that Hair provided. As a legal document, the contract bound the slave owner and hirer to certain agreements. These contracts usually required the hirer to provide each slave with medical care and "good and sufficient summer and winter clothes, hat, blanket and two pair of shoes." Most of Clark's slaves were hired as field hands to cotton farmers in the Sumter County area. They were brought to the courthouse square in Livingston in January and hired to the highest bidder at public auction. In most respects the man who hired the slave had dominion over him. The courts generally treated the hirer like the owner, except in cases where the contract may have been breached (non-payment, for example), or in cases of death or disfigurement.

Hair was especially efficient in getting Clark the money he was owed from delinquent hirers. For example, J. C. McGrew had hired several of Clark's slaves for the year but was unable to pay him the full amount. Hair tried several times to get the money. "His object is delay," Hair told Clark, "and the money will be made at the next term of our [Alabama] Circuit Court in November [1847] next." The case was settled in favor of Clark in the amount of $1,474.[22]

But not all slaves were bound to a year-long contract. Clark allowed certain slaves he deemed trustworthy to "self-hire." These slaves could find their own work and negotiate their own contracts, but the practice occupied shaky legal ground. Any breach in the "contract" was legally unenforceable, as slaves were considered property and could not enter into binding contracts that a court of law was bound to respect. Therefore owners needed to be very careful before allowing their slaves to hire themselves out, and the slave was given strict orders to turn over specific sums of money each week or month. For example, Clark allowed

Tony, Tab, and Bednego to "pay for themselves" in the amount of $150, and one slave in particular, Ned, self-hired for many years. Self-hiring predominated in cities and towns where the slave and their hirer could be monitored more closely by the slave-owner or his agent. Though the practice was problematic, it represented a financial boon for the slave owner and a labor solution for hirers looking for short-term, cheap workers.[23]

Hair also supervised the health of Clark's slaves, reporting for example in 1844 that twenty-two of his slaves were "in good health." "There has been," he said, "no difficulty with any of them this year except the deaths [of] Bobby" who died of "palsy" and "Nelly's child." He also told Clark about Virgil, a slave about twenty years old who had encountered a troublesome affliction. Virgil was served by "Doctor Trencheat" concerning a case of gonorrhea and Clark was charged ten dollars for "medical advice, and medicine." Virgil was sold two years later for eight hundred dollars.[24]

In contrast, healthy and skilled slaves, such as Ned, generated significant income for Clark. Born in 1798 in Tarboro, Ned was among the original group that had been forced to relocate to Alabama. He was a carpenter and was allowed to self-hire. Ned was often "busily employed" to "good men" about town. For him, Clark kept a separate ledger in which he meticulously noted his hours and location of work. Hair made sure he was hired to reputable people, and both Hair and Clark seem to have been particularly fond of him. As Ned aged and entered his sixties, his "hands and feet were swelled and [he was] unable to work." Clark allowed him to live in a "small house and cultivate a small piece of [Hair's] land." Ned's swelling eventually degenerated into a life-threatening form of dropsy, a disease from which "Doctor Smith [had] no expectation of his ever getting well." Ned remained in Alabama until his death shortly before the beginning of the Civil War.[25]

Not all people who hired slaves were reputable or trustworthy. In May 1849 Hair informed Clark of a "foul raid" involving his slave Yancy. The raid concerned a local slave patrol, runaway slaves, and a conspiracy to kidnap and sell those slaves "down river." Yancy's story offers an example of how slaves used what little power they had to exploit conflict between whites to alter their situation.

Yancy was born in June 1817, and like Ned, a member of the initial group of Clark slaves brought to Alabama. Given his age and high value of $650, Yancy might have been a skilled worker. He had been hired by a "Mrs. Curry" for the year and had been on her farm for approximately four months, but he grew dissatisfied with the arrangement. Mrs. Curry's neighbors had heard rumors that she was harboring three runaway Negroes and took it upon themselves to intervene. They launched a raid on her farm, but before word could reach Hair, Yancy ran into town and told him of the raid and Curry's conspiracy to kidnap slaves. He told Hair that the runaway slaves were secretly working for Curry and were to be "run to Texas" and sold after the autumn harvest.[26]

Hair visited Curry to verify this story. The raid had indeed occurred and Hair found that the "neighbors were much incensed [and they] threatened Yancy's life." Charges were made on both sides: Hair judged that "Mrs. Curry was as guilty as she could be," but Yancy was "accused [by the neighbors] of advising the runaways to run off" and of harboring and

Slave Hire Contract. This is a typical contract used by Clark when hiring out his slaves. Slave hiring was ubiquitous in the Old South and it gave less affluent whites access to social privilege and a taste of slave mastery. Though generally profitable, it came with some expense and Clark often sued hirers for non-payment or breach of contract. (Courtesy Special Collections Library, Duke University.)

feeding them in secrecy. To avoid any legal proceedings, Hair suggested that Mrs. Curry return Yancy and end the contract. She agreed, and Hair brought Yancy back to his plantation. As he reported to Clark, he "gave Yancy a good flogging" but "did not draw his blood or mark him and put him to work on my place." Hair told Clark that Curry's neighbors wanted Yancy taken out of the county, but since he had "flogged him and set him to work, all seems satisfied." There was no mention of what became of the three runaways, but in all probability they were returned to their owners to suffer Yancy's fate.[27]

Clark continued his relationship with Hair until at least 1858. His last letter was more that of a friend than a business associate. He had either sold most of his Alabama slaves or had them returned to him, but it is clear that slave ownership remained an important part of Clark's wealth. In 1860 he had thirty-three slaves at his Tarboro plantation, but he still seemed more interested in the business of trading slaves than employing them. Throughout the Civil War, despite threats of abolition, the price of slaves rose exorbitantly. Seeking to take advantage of the seller's market, Clark inquired of his friend, Confederate congressman Robert Rufus Bridgers, about high prices in the Richmond slave markets. "I have received your favor," Bridgers replied. "Negroes are selling higher here than ever known before. Likely Negroe men will readily sell for $1500 to $1600. Some sales as high as $1700.

I can not say how much higher Lewis [Clark's slave] would sell for being a carpenter, but as a field hand I think he would bring $1500 or there about. I do not know what to say of the woman & child, but all negroes sell well."[28]

All of these dealings with his slaves show a no-nonsense side to Clark's character that seems hard-hearted by today's standards. Slave-hire in particular could lead to brutal results. In spite of legal safeguards, people hiring slaves would seldom have had the kind of interest in the slave's well being, be it paternalistic or merely selfish, that owners would have felt. The nature of the practice, with its yearly termination and resetting of all contracts, would have created great anxiety and suffering among the slaves themselves. There would have been no continuity: slaves would have been hired to accomplish individual jobs, sometimes for far less than a year. Families were frequently splintered. People were sent to different farms, perhaps far away, perhaps never to be heard from again. It would have been devastating for them. Clark, as the records show, owned at least two families with children and often sent the parents to different plantations.

Yet he showed kindness to his slaves in some instances. His practice of allowing the few slaves he deemed trustworthy to "self-hire," to find their own work and to keep some of their own earnings, was considered generous. Owning slaves was not simply an aspect of his business, it was part of his heritage, and he believed the system to be the natural order that God had intended. It formed part of his deeply held beliefs which led him into his political career.

Planters of Clark's time and place served as political leaders. Clark had always been interested in politics, so embarking upon a political career was an obvious extension of his social standing and education. He had been exposed to statecraft at an early age and many of his family members had served their community in some political capacity. It was expected that Henry would follow in their footsteps. Yet there was always an ambivalence in his attitude toward politics. He thought it unseemly to be too interested or too ambitious, and some of his actions suggested that he preferred life as a working planter to that of a politician; as a relative recalled, it was his "unselfish interest in the history and affairs of the county which drew him into public life."[29] Though he may have felt this sense of *noblesse oblige*, Clark nevertheless made the choice to enter the fray and seek elected office.

Clark expressed strong political convictions as a young man. Like his father, he was a Democrat. In the early 1830s, however, he flirted briefly with the new Whig party — a party formed in opposition to President Andrew Jackson's alleged autocratic and dictatorial expansion of presidential power. Jackson was a popular leader in the South, but certain actions of his had alienated some supporters. He and John C. Calhoun had clashed over the Peggy Eaton affair, resulting in the resignation of several cabinet members and their staffs, including Clark's father. As Jackson pushed Calhoun away, the president began relying more on Martin Van Buren. This action angered many southerners who distrusted the New Yorker known as "the Little Magician." But two other events rankled Clark and finally turned him against Jackson.

The first was Jackson's threat to use force against South Carolina during the nullification crisis of 1832. When South Carolina defied the federal government's demand for the collection of tariff duties, Jackson called on Congress to increase his enforcement powers, resulting in the Force Bill of 1833. The bill empowered the president to use the military to enforce Congressional laws. The president's "willingness to coerce a state" resulted in a rift in the Democrat Party. Many Democrats "adopted the name Whig in 1833 to signify their resistance to [Jackson's] monarchial despotism."[30]

The second event was Jackson's removal of government deposits from the Bank of the United States in 1833. By executive fiat, Jackson ignored the will of Congress and "removed government funds from an institution where congressional law mandated they be placed." For states' rights southerners like Clark, the question was not the economic merits of the bank; it was "one of executive usurpation."[31] North Carolina's senator Willie P. Mangum broke with Jackson in an 1834 Senate floor speech, condemning the president for his arbitrary actions. Clark wrote Mangum an exuberant and revealing letter praising him for his bold stance. He said:

> I cannot omit this opportunity of adding a "well done" to your course as a North Carolina Senator. Disdaining the "shackles of party" at home and abroad you have acted as a high-minded independent Representative of a *Sovereign State*. However such a course may draw you the rancour of thos[e] who are thwarted, it must ultimately prevail and gain you the commendation of your people. The freedom of these remarks may subject me to the suspicion of flattery or pertness as my acquaintance with you is so slight. But Sir you are executing a public trust, and it certainly is becoming to express our satisfaction & opinions about public acts. I live in a strong Jackson county, the Politicians aware of the influence of Jacksonism nourish it for their *own support* & protection and endevour to spell-bound every subject by the magic of a name. But the future is more promising to freedom of opinion. For which we may feel indebted to the example *set us in high places*. I myself belong to the school of 'States-rights and State-remedies' — and the proclamation formed the epitaph of my Jacksonism — so I cant speak "By authority on the subject of 'the party.'" But if an alternative which can possibly be acceptable to No[rth] Carolina is presented, the influence of Jackson will certainly expire with his term, and the "malign influence" K[itchen]. C[abinet]. Regency *et id omne genus* will cease.[32]

Clark's flirtation with the Whig Party, however, ended by 1840. He came to believe that the Whigs would not protect slave property. He aligned himself firmly with the Democrats, as did much of Edgecombe County. Clark also began taking a more active role in the community. He joined the state militia as an adjutant in the Twenty-First Regiment and later rose to the rank of colonel. He served on the board of trustees of the Tarboro Male Academy, a local private school, and undertook increasing responsibilities within the Democratic Party.[33]

In his first independent political assignment, Clark attended a public dinner at Nolley's Crossroads on October 15, 1841. There he was selected to draft a Democratic platform proposal. He and four other men crafted a series of resolutions outlining the "sentiment of those present." Clark, on behalf of the committee, "reported the following preamble and resolutions, prefacing the same with appropriate remarks." The resolutions were decidedly proslavery and were unanimously adopted:

Resolved, That we view with much alarm and concern, the union of Whigism and abolitionism at the North; while our present President [John Tyler] stands pledged to vote any interference with our domestic institutions from the fanatic abolitionists, General [William Henry] Harrison is ominously silent on it — and the Whig party at the North have pursued such a course on this subject that no southern man should trust them with power. *Resolved*, That we feel grateful for the firm and manly stand assumed by northern democracy in favor of southern rights and the Constitution, and we feel indignant at the boastings of southern Whigs for the northern Whigs who are avowed abolitionists. *Resolved*, That the independent treasury bill, delivering us from the unholy alliance of corporations and the money power, is the plain interpretation of the Constitution and the true policy of the Government as marked out by our forefathers, and should be the uncompromising creed of the Democratic party.[34]

Earlier that same year, Clark had assisted with the local July Fourth celebration — a conspicuous civic duty. Edgecombe residents of the 1830s and '40s enjoyed elaborate ceremonies on the Fourth characterized by lots of eating, drinking, and a "Grand Exhibition of Fireworks." Celebrations often included a hot air balloon display. Residents gathered at "Mrs. Gregory's Hotel," the "finest in town," to watch the balloon and listen to dozens of speakers offer tributes to the county, state, and nation. At the end of the day's orations and festivities, a "profuse and sumptuous" dinner was prepared at Mrs. Gregory's and officiated by the local gentry. In 1842 Clark served as an assistant to the presiding officer, George Howard. As the local dignitaries gathered around the table, they raised their glasses in honor of the Fourth: no fewer than twenty-five rousing toasts were made by the dignitaries in honor of the Revolution, the founding fathers, and American liberty. Proclaiming that day the "political Sabbath" of the nation, the men entertained the guests in a feast of Jeffersonian rhetoric that included affirmations of white supremacy. Clark's friend William Dancy had begun the day with a "stirring, classical oratory" praising the freedom won for all white men. Dancy declared that the Magna Carta of 1215 "was reserved for the free Anglo-Saxons of America, to give birth to that great principle of popular liberty — the right of the people to govern — now regarded as the fundamental maxim of all free government."[35]

Following Dancy's example, the men made the celebratory toasts to the young nation's past, present, and future. When it came to Clark's turn, the planter stood amid the revelry with glass held high and reverently acknowledged: "The Constitution of the United States! Preserved from the constructions and misconstructions of the designing and ambitious, it will long guide us on to prosperity and happiness!"[36]

While such amicable bipartisan scenes might have been common at national fetes, the animosity between Democrats and Whigs had reached fever-pitch by the mid–1840s; Clark involved himself heavily in local Democratic Party affairs. His education, writing ability, and solid reputation won him an election as secretary for the local party in 1844, and later as an Edgecombe delegate to the state Democratic convention in 1845. This year proved to be an exciting one for Clark when his cousin, Henry Irwin Toole, found himself embroiled in a vitriolic congressional campaign.[37]

Toole had been a longtime Democratic leader in the Edgecombe community. An avowed "Democrat in principle," he was regarded by others as stubborn and inflexible.[38]

Toole was "an able and prominent man though never a successful one." He was a skilled public speaker," yet a "very deaf man who used a large ear trumpet."[39] His only real political experience came from his service as a presidential elector, but in 1845 he was asked by his friends to seek the nomination for an open congressional seat.[40] The Democratic Party, however, nominated Henry Selby Clark (no relation) of Beaufort County to run in the general election. Toole's supporters demanded "Justice to Toole!" But the nomination had been made. Toole's detractors called him and his faction "coons," likening them to a raccoon trapped in a tree with nowhere to go. The "coons" believed the convention had been "packed" to ensure Henry S. Clark's nomination, and as it turned out, relatives of both men had participated as delegates in the nominating process (including Henry Toole Clark). This situation resulted in the accusation that the nomination had been compromised. Toole believed he was the legitimate candidate, and he risked splitting the party over what he considered a matter of principle. He announced his candidacy as an Independent and inadvertently gained the support of the Whig Party. Democrats claimed unfairly that he had formed "an unholy alliance" with the Whigs and denounced him as a traitor. His former party accused him of "shaking hands with Federalism." His supporters, however, regarded him as a victim of factionalism.[41]

This acrimonious situation was more than the high-minded, quixotic Toole could bear. He wrote to his cousin, Henry Toole Clark, as the charges became increasingly personal and rancorous: "Please say whether you did not immediately inform me after the primary popular meeting in Edgecombe [that] you did not inform me that you had been appointed a delegate and whether I did not say instantly and earnestly that I regretted it because you are my cousin. I know you too well to suppose that consanguineal relations influenced your course."[42] Despite making appeals to his cousin and to the public, Toole offered to withdraw "as soon as a Whig candidate is presented" so that the people might have a choice.[43] True to his word, he withdrew when Richard Donnell of New Bern entered the race. Taking his leave in a letter to the Tarboro *Free Press*, he denounced those Democrats who had placed party over principle. "I make to you my strongest avowal," he proclaimed to the people, "that I have never at any time, or at any place, or to any person, compromised in the slightest manner my democratic principles. My only fault is that I have appealed from a packed caucus to the people. For years I have been the object of the political and personal vituperation of our adversaries. Strangely enough, I am now marked as the victim of the party that I have faithfully served, the target of democratic abuse."[44] His opponent, Henry S. Clark, won the election and Toole retired to his plantation. Toole's political misfortune was a significant lesson in party politics for his cousin: Clark never appealed to the public for sympathy.

Other events of 1845 included Clark's July Fourth oration. The town of Tarboro had asked him to give a eulogy on the death of former President Jackson, an odd choice given Clark's statement denouncing Jackson in an earlier letter to Whig Senator Willie Mangum. He accepted the invitation, however, "with reluctance, not from any want of disposition, but from a distrust in my ability to discharge the duty in a manner worthy of the great

Tarboro Town Common. Tarboro's town common is the second oldest in the United States and has always been a site for local celebrations. The memorial pictured here is the Colonel Louis D. Wilson Memorial. Wilson was a prominent state and local Democratic politician. He died of fever in Mexico during the Mexican War and his body was brought home to Tarboro by Clark. (Photograph by the author.)

occasion." The speech was well received, those present noting that he delivered a "beautiful and chaste Eulogium on the life, character and services" of the seventh president.[45]

By the mid–1840s, the key national issues were slavery, territorial expansion, and the war in Mexico. Though a colonel in the state militia, Clark did not serve in Mexico, but he faithfully supported the war. The 1845 annexation of Texas and the subsequent war with Mexico a year later was a divisive affair. Edgecombe Democrats overwhelmingly supported the war, but the county had provided few men to actually fight. Responding to criticism from the Whigs, two companies were formed in February 1847. The men were commanded by Edgecombe's state senator and speaker of that body, Col. Louis D. Wilson, and were sent to join the North Carolina Regiment in Mexico. The soldiers had departed for duty by March of 1847 but saw little combat action, battling instead with yellow fever and other deadly diseases.[46] They returned to Edgecombe County seventeen months later, much weakened by their travails. County leaders asked Clark to welcome the veterans home, and in a lengthy speech he congratulated them on their safe return. He reminded them of their country's call to arms and thanked them for their unswerving, if not unquestioning, response. "You did not hesitate when the appeal was made to North Carolina," Clark sermonized. "You never stopped to make the traitorous enquiry into the justice and constitutionality of the war, whether Mexico or your own country was in the wrong; but like true patriots you rushed to the side of your country, to fight her battles right or wrong.'"[47]

Though he did not fight in Mexico, he did travel there. Col. Wilson was one of the many soldiers who had died from "the malignant fever" in August 1847. His death at Vera Cruz, and the subsequent return home of this "ornament of his State" made headlines in many newspapers. The people of Edgecombe were "determined to bring his remains home" and asked Colonel Clark to collect the body. Accompanied by another militia officer and friend, William Norfleet, the men brought the body from Mexico to Wilmington, where they were greeted with great fanfare on February 6 "by the largest concourse of people that has assembled in Wilmington for many years past."[48] Bells tolled, flags flew at half-staff, and a great military procession of Wilmington's leaders escorted the group to the station, where the train departed for Tarboro.[49]

In 1848, Clark was again nominated by the Edgecombe Democrats to serve as a delegate to the state convention to be held in Raleigh. The local party approved a series of resolutions, which Clark helped to draft. The contents included support for President James K. Polk and the war in Mexico and thanked the president "for his able, energetic and faithful administration of the Government, according to the principles of Thomas Jefferson."[50] Clark's writing talents and his loyalty to the Democratic Party impressed state leaders. The president of the convention, Weldon N. Edwards, appointed him to a committee of thirteen to "prepare resolutions for the action of the Convention." The ensuing eighteen resolutions criticized the Whig Party's alleged financial mismanagement: "When the Whig party first obtained power in North Carolina our State was free of debt; that by their unwise, extravagant, or injudicious use of the public monies she became involved in debt; and that this same party shrunk from meeting the danger face to face." The resolutions also claimed that Congress had no authority to limit the expansion of slavery, declaring that "the Congress has no control, directly or indirectly, over the institution of Slavery; and that we are opposed to the Wilmot, or Winthrop, or Webster Provisio, in whatever shape it may be presented."[51]

Clark's prominent role in drafting the resolution prompted the state party to send him in June 1848 to the Democratic National Convention in Baltimore, along with twenty-two other delegates, including William Woods Holden. The North Carolina delegation voted overwhelmingly for James Buchanan and James McKay as the presidential and vice-presidential candidates respectively, though each lost the nomination to Michigan senator Lewis Cass and Kentucky's William Butler.[52]

For nearly a decade Clark had served the Democratic Party as a writer and delegate, having yet to seek political office. His hesitancy did not necessarily reflect a lack of ambition, but Clark was well aware that he lacked a key qualification needed to earn the respect and trust of his peers: a family of his own. Land ownership, slave mastery, and marriage confirmed to the community that an individual was ready to lead and to assume larger responsibilities. Clark's abilities were proven, but he had waited an unusual amount of time to marry. Elite men generally married in their twenties; Clark was forty-one and single. Marriage was an unspoken requirement for southern manhood, and bachelors of that day were looked upon with great suspicion. Families often worried about "reputation" should a son put marriage off for too long.[53]

There are several reasons for Clark's extended bachelorhood. First, he was preoccupied with his business dealings and with the care of his family. He had moved back to Tarboro probably in 1833 to help his father manage the family's fortunes. Both father and son were careful and responsible men. They were wealthy but not extravagant and it is likely Henry was needed at home. His father may have been ill; there is evidence that he was unable to manage without assistance. The Clarks owned several properties in Edgecombe County, including their plantations at Walnut Creek and Conetoe. Clark lived at the family's Tarboro house and for at least a decade, he lived in the shadow of his father until James West died at home on December 20, 1843, of "a lingering illness with much suffering." He was remembered for his "efforts to please, his gentleness, his smiles, sincerity, and generous care for others."[54] On his death, Henry came into the property, and thereafter had to single-handedly manage the family's affairs.

Another explanation for his delayed marriage is that the woman he loved was the wife of another man. Mary Weeks Parker Hargrave was Clark's first cousin and thirteen years his junior. She was the daughter of Theophilus Parker, Clark's uncle. The Parkers were a prominent and wealthy Edgecombe County family. Mary grew up across the street from the Clark's Tarboro home, so Clark knew her from childhood. His love for her went unrequited for many years. To his chagrin, she married, at the age of nineteen, and moved to Lexington, North Carolina, to live on the plantation of her husband, Franklin Hargrave. He died just four years later in 1845, leaving Mary to care for their little girl, Catherine. At his death some of the property was sold to settle debts. The "negro property," the most valuable part of the estate, was sold for a total of $12,940. After payment of all outstanding accounts, Mary was left with the house and a sum of $3,206.[55]

Another tragedy befell Mary when Catherine died in 1848 or early 1849. The death of her child was a great blow, but prompted her to renew her Christian commitment. She explained to Clark, "I have been made the child of God and promised to renounce the world and am bound to give my life to his desire." Clark and Mary began corresponding in earnest after Catherine's death and he proposed marriage in a letter of May 1849. But Mary expressed "unworthiness" and "unfitness" concerning his attention, and held back. However, she acknowledged, "I know you have always loved me and I have felt that you had a claim on my love more than ordinary — a kind of right to me." She asked Clark to wait a "little longer." "Think seriously and calmly of it," she said, "and write again." Several weeks later he did, and this time she accepted. They were married in Lexington on February 11, 1850, four days after Clark's forty-second birthday. The wedding ended his years of misery and heartache, and any suspicions about his single life.[56]

2. Coming Into His Own

Hilma, ca. 1860. Clark (pictured standing on the porch, center) named his plantation Hilma for his children — Haywood, Irwin, Laura, Maria, and Arabella. His horse, Little Sorrell, is being held by a slave, while his family, including his wife and mother, stand nearby. The decorative porch columns were copied from "The Grove," a local plantation home which today serves as the Blount-Bridgers Museum and hold several Clark family artifacts. (Courtesy Blount-Bridgers House Archives, Tarboro, North Carolina.)

The couple remained content for their twenty-four married years. Mary dutifully served in her role as "plantation mistress." She took care of the household, managed the domestic servants and supervised the children, while Henry farmed and busily managed his many business and civic obligations. The marriage produced six children between 1850 and 1862: Laura, Haywood, Henry Irwin, Maria Toole, Arabella, and Mary Parker. Five of the children lived to adulthood, most living well into the twentieth century. Laura, the first, was born ten months into the marriage; Arabella, the last, was born in 1862 when Clark was fifty-four years old. Little Mary Parker, however, died of unknown causes at the age of five in 1857 — a tragedy unrecorded in any surviving papers. Though he wrote few letters to his family, Clark's correspondence shows him as a dedicated family man who made sure each of his children received a proper education.[57]

Three slaves hoeing tobacco. Many of Clark's slaves were field hands hired out to pick cotton, hoe fields and harvest crops. A healthy male slave could earn Clark two hundred dollars or more each year. (Courtesy of the North Carolina Office of Archives and History, Raleigh, North Carolina.)

After his wedding Clark purchased a plantation of his own. In November 1850 he deeded his Tarboro home to his sisters and bought a farm from his friend, Robert Norfleet, located only blocks from the Town Common. The location was conspicuous and convenient, and he would later name it "Hilma" for his children (the first letters of their names). The spacious main house was built in the two-story frame style of the day and furnished with "home goods" Clark purchased on visits to New York City. The farm was three hundred and thirty acres, of which one hundred and seventy were unimproved. By comparison, ninety-two percent of Edgecombe County farms in 1860 were less than five hundred acres, and forty-six percent of all farms were between one hundred and five hundred acres. Clark's acreage was average for his area of the state, though it was large compared to farms in western North Carolina, most of which were smaller than one hundred acres.[58]

In 1850 the Clarks owned at least fifty slaves: twenty-one lived at Hilma (most of them children) and the others (mostly adult males) continued to be hired out in Alabama. Clark purchased two slaves in 1851—Nelson and Venus—for $2,200; but by the mid-1850s, he was curtailing his Alabama operations and instructed Hair to sell his chattels. In 1854 James Hair wrote that he had sold Bednego for nine hundred dollars and Marina and Pink for $1,250. He "could have sold John for $1,100 but he was not a blacksmith." Hair, with an eye for future sales, hired John "for $75 with an obligation to learn him the [blacksmith] trade." "There was no offer for Solomon," Hair said, so "he was hired for $200." After these transactions, Clark held in cash and notes nearly three thousand dollars, but Hair informed Clark that he had deposited $2,772 in the bank at Mobile, Alabama, "with instructions to buy exchange in New York," and apologized to Clark for "the small amount sent."[59]

Clark continued to hire his Alabama slaves for the next few years, but it appears that he ended his business relationship with James Hair by 1858. There is no clear indication why Clark sold these slaves, but he was doubtless concentrating on his Tarboro plantation, his growing family, and his political career. Ned remained in Alabama with Hair, and some of Clark's other Alabama slaves, including Lewis, were returned to him.

Ironically, back in Tarboro, Clark began hiring slaves from others. In 1853 he hired "Joe" for eighty-five dollars. Although Clark owned many slaves, before 1854 most of his twenty-one Tarboro slaves were under eighteen, and half were female. He did own one adult male, a "mulatto, age 39," who was very likely his personal valet, as well as two men in their thirties. He did not have enough mature male field hands to do the heavy (or skilled) agricultural labor needed in tobacco or cotton production, and much of his plantation income came from raising livestock and grain crops. However, his agricultural output increased as he increased his slave inventory at home. By 1860 thirty-three slaves were living at Hilma, eighteen males and fifteen females, but of these thirty-three, eleven were children under the age of twelve. Cotton was grown, but not in great abundance: Clark's 1859 crop produced twenty 400-pound bales, whereas other local planters with more cultivated land and more slaves could produce one hundred to two hundred bales a year.[60]

For Clark and Edgecombe County, the 1850s were prosperous years. Cotton production tripled and there was an increase in the export of naval stores such as tar and pitch. These were traditional commodities from North Carolina that had earned the state its nickname, the Tar Heel State. More than eighteen industries—including eight turpentine distilleries, a furniture factory, several timber and grist mills, and a large cotton mill—employed area laborers or hired slaves. The area boasted a newspaper, the *Tarboro Free Press*, which later changed its name to the *Southerner* in 1852, a change reflecting the nation's increasing sectional animosity.

There were forty-three public schools and four private academies. The county's population had grown from about fifteen thousand in 1840 to over seventeen thousand by 1850. The increase included nine thousand slaves and 270 free blacks. Slave owners numbered approximately 775 (4.5 percent of the county's total population), but most slave owners in the county possessed fewer than five slaves. The vast majority of slaves worked on small farms of two hundred acres or less and performed a variety of agricultural jobs.[61]

Farmers enjoyed these prosperous years, and Clark took special interest in his land and the agrarian life. His knowledge of new farming techniques was respected in the community. He actively participated in the revived Edgecombe County Agricultural Society, and like many "gentleman farmers," he employed the latest scientific agricultural discoveries. He subscribed to numerous journals. He experimented with "marl," a lime fertilizer, at a time when the use of commercial fertilizers was little known. Along with other Edgecombe farmers including John Dancy and John Bridgers, he encouraged progressive methods such as soil enrichment, composting and manuring, drainage improvements and more efficient use of labor. Guano, or bat dung, was used and promoted. Farmers in the area boasted of their "model farms" and of their new plows and improved implements.[62]

Clark often made wine and brandy. He kept a good supply of local wines and spirits and was very generous with his stores, especially during the election season. James Hair even solicited his knowledge of grapes. Hair asked his opinion in growing the famed Southern muscadine grape and requested that seedlings be sent for planting. "How are the Skuppernoge vines planted apart," Hair wondered, "how are they cultivated, [and] what quality of wine will they produce per acre?" Hair was confused by the grape itself, asking whether the scuppernong and muscadine grape were the same fruit. Clark obliged with vines and advice, and instructed Hair that the scuppernong, or "Big White Grape," was a variety of the muscadine.[63]

Shortly after his wedding, and anticipating prosperous times ahead, Clark was ready for a larger political stage. On March 12, 1850, he was named a delegate to represent Edgecombe County at a local "Southern Rights Meeting" that included several other nearby county delegations.[64] Many of Edgecombe's white citizens were furious over a series of debates raging in Congress over California, slavery, and the future of the Union. Edgecombe delegates passed nine resolutions outlining their pro-slavery stance. The preamble stated that local citizens "feel alarmed for the Safety of the Union, and have witnessed with deep regret the continued assaults and aggressions of the free soilers, abolitionists, and fanatics of the North, upon the property and institutions of the South." "The history of Northern action," said one resolution, "is one of unmitigated insult and aggression. Congress in our opinion, possesses no constitutional power to legislate on the subject of slavery."[65]

The Edgecombe delegates pressed hard for a state delegation to be sent to a larger convention in Nashville, Tennessee, in June. This convention, known as the Nashville Convention, had been proposed by Mississippi in an effort to present a united southern front against the 1850 Compromise. Clark was one of thirty-four delegates selected to travel to Raleigh and endorse North Carolina's participation in the Nashville Convention. This convention promised to lodge formal protests to Congress against the Compromise of 1850. As one ardent states' rights supporter argued, "I regard the admission of California as the great question which must decide the fate of the South. I hope to see every slave state represented in the proposed Nashville Convention."[66] William Holden, editor of the Raleigh *Standard*, echoed that sentiment, earnestly proclaiming: "The time has come for [the South] to UNITE AS ONE MAN."[67]

Holden had urged Democratic Party unity for some time and published hyperbolic editorials condemning the "abolitionist" Whigs for their willingness to support the Wilmot Proviso. He had written to Clark some months earlier to ask if the Edgecombe planter might "find time to give some numbers on the Slavery question." "Your esteemed favor," Holden said, "came duly to hand. I feel much gratified that my articles on the Slavery question meet your commendation and the approval of the Edgecombe Democracy."[68]

Unlike Holden, Charles Manly, the Whig governor of North Carolina at the time, did not support the Nashville meeting and hesitated to call a state convention. Thus, the General Assembly never convened to consider the proposal and North Carolina was not officially represented in Tennessee. Clark was disappointed, but by the time that nine states had met from June 3 to 11, 1850, Congress had passed the series of laws known as the Compromise of 1850 and the Southern rights movement lost momentum for a time.[69]

Now forty-two, Clark had served the Democrats faithfully for over a decade. When a vacancy opened for the Tenth District state senate seat, local party leaders asked him to consider running for the office of senator in the next general election.[70] Displaying the aloof character that befitted a plantation aristocrat, the future governor said that he would "consider the idea" if no one else wanted the job.[71] Clark left home for several weeks on business matters, and during his absence another man, William F. Dancy, placed his own name on the ballot. Dancy was a young Edgecombe County planter from an eminent, wealthy family. Like Clark, he was educated at Chapel Hill (Class of 1841), a lawyer, and a Jeffersonian Democrat. And also like Clark, he was not "inclined to mingle with the people generally, or to court their favor."[72]

Upon his return home, Clark learned of Dancy's announcement. Both men were active members of Calvary Episcopal Church and had served in some capacity together at virtually every civic event in the 1840s. This relationship put Clark in an uncomfortable situation. In a letter to the Tarboro *Free Press*, Clark praised his friend and wished him luck in the election. "Mr. Dancy's course toward me has been fair and honorable," he professed, "and it would be ungenerous in me now to array myself in opposition to him. He among others solicited me to be a candidate before my departure and it would be a want of good faith in me to oppose him on my return."[73]

The next week, feeling he had slighted a friend, Dancy replied in an equally magnanimous letter, and withdrew his name from the ballot. Disavowing rumors of treachery, Dancy was compelled by both public opinion and his own conscience to leave the race. "I had scarcely [announced my candidacy]," he declared, "before it was busily bruited about that Col. Clark had declared he would be a candidate upon his return and that I had come out to forestall him in his intentions, and to thwart the wishes of the people and especially his friends. Nothing has occurred which has given me more annoyance that this deliberate charge of treachery to a friend. This state of things shall exist no longer. I retire from the canvass." He went on to praise Clark for his "gentlemanly behavior" and to extend hopes for his success. Edgecombe County voters would later send him to the House of Commons, where he earned a reputation (like Clark) as a strict constitutionalist, and he voted regularly for sound money and against internal improvement projects.[74]

Between these two friends, both members of the local gentry, such polite behavior was not uncommon. For leading planters in their community, saving face was often more important than political gain. One's peers would have frowned upon any public show of ambition and for two old friends to contend publicly and acrimoniously for political office would have been bad form, considering the unwritten campaign rules of the day.[75]

Clark won the August general election, defeating William D. Petway, former sheriff of the county, by 326 votes to 200. Clark had been duly elected to his first political office. Democrats won large majorities in the 1850 General Assembly, and their gubernatorial candidate, David Reid, defeated the Whig incumbent Charles Manly by a wide margin—largest of all in Edgecombe County. Nationally, the Democrats gained majorities in both legislative houses and the national debate over slavery became increasingly rancorous.[76]

Edgecombe County voters would return Clark to the Senate for six consecutive legislative sessions. The local newspaper endorsed him, saying, "Col. Clark is one of the most attentive and faithful, as he is amongst the most useful members of the Senate."[77] His legislative record was one of consistency and quiet dependability, and he had a thorough understanding of the Senate's rules, procedures, and traditions. He occasionally introduced legislation and periodically proposed amendments, often items of a procedural nature. He is particularly noted for objecting to bills that increased government spending. He regularly voted with the Democrats for lower taxes and reduction of the public debt. In one motion, he moved to lower taxes on real property from twelve cents to ten cents on every hundred dollars of real property. His motion lost. He also opposed the ad valorem tax, a position he maintained throughout his political career.[78]

The 1854–1855 session was typical of Clark's legislative conduct. An amendment was proposed to an internal improvements bill to complete the North Carolina Railroad.[79] The attached amendment asked that fifteen thousand dollars of public monies "in the manner as other moneys are raised by provisions of this act be appropriated for the purpose of cleaning out and improving the navigation of [the] Tar river, between the town of Washington and the falls of said river; and that His Excellency, the Governor, is hereby empowered and required to appoint suitable commissioners to carry into effect the requirements of this section." Clark motioned to "disagree to said amendment." A voice vote was taken, but was too close to call. He then asked for a division of the house, demanding "the yeas and nays." The amendment failed by twenty-four to eighteen.[80]

It seems odd that Clark would obstruct a move to improve the Tar River, especially as the section targeted for improvement ran through his district and the improvement would have boosted commercial trade for his constituents. However, local projects were traditionally managed by the county justices of the peace, and the conservative senator distrusted the expansion of the governor's powers at the expense of local authority. He therefore rejected the amendment. Since colonial times, the North Carolina legislature had consistently constrained the powers of the state executive.[81] Clark simply distrusted any expansion of that power, even if such expansion might benefit his own district.

Clark was not, however, averse to all internal improvement projects. His voting record reveals that his association with anti-improvement Democrats was not always steadfast. During the 1852 session, Clark supported the construction of a forty-mile long plank road to run from Tarboro to Jamesville. He served on the Committee on Corporations and often recommended passage of improvement bills. He made a motion in 1852 to "encourage the investment of capital for mining and manufacturing purposes." The bill, however, was later tabled. Clark often voted against public projects in western areas, though he participated in the "logrolling" of bills to get favorable legislative bills passed. His increasing support for internal improvements reflects a trend among legislators of the 1850s as state funding for transportation projects found wide bipartisan agreement.[82]

Clark's record concerning internal improvements also reflects his strong states' rights, "home rule" perspective. While he supported certain state-funded projects that might benefit North Carolina, like banking legislation and public education, he was opposed to federal subsidies. As a young man, he had declared his support for "State rights and State remedies." Like many southern planters, he considered any increase in federal power to be the first step in federal legislation against slavery. Undoubtedly, much of his political action involved the protection of slave property from federal interference.[83]

Clark, however, exhibited a more progressive nature in his support for "free suffrage." Since the 1840s both Democrats and Whigs had fiercely debated the relative merits of extending voting rights to more taxpaying white men. Whigs opposed the idea, while Democrats endorsed it. In 1848, the Democratic gubernatorial candidate, David Reid, campaigned for a constitutional amendment to eliminate the fifty-acre property requirement for voters in state senate elections, or "free suffrage." For years white males who owned fewer than fifty acres of land could only vote for representatives to the House of Commons. By the 1840s, North Carolina remained one of the least democratic states in the nation and one of the few states to retain property qualifications for voters and certain officeholders.[84] These property qualifications eliminated more than half of the state's voters in the senatorial elections. An amendment abolishing the property requirement would undoubtedly have helped the Democrats, as the majority of Whig constituents met the landholding requirement. Reid, however, lost the 1848 election, and the amendment died in the Senate, though the issue remained broadly popular.[85] Reid ran again in 1850, still advocating free suffrage. This time he was elected governor.

When Clark entered the Senate in 1850, fewer than six hundred Edgecombe voters had elected him, as opposed to the more than 2,200 who had voted for their representative in the House of Commons. Clark supported extending suffrage to white taxpaying males and served on the Committee on the Amendment of the Constitution. Taking the floor to report the committee's recommendation, Clark recommended the "abolition of the freehold qualification." Every single Democratic senator voted for the amendment's passage, while only twenty-three percent of senate Whigs voted for the same bill.[86]

Democrats supported the amendment because the extension of suffrage to more white males did not threaten the interests of the Democratic landed classes. Since the amendment did not abolish the property requirements for holding office, the bill guaranteed that landowners would not lose power by retaining the redistricting rules that favored the status quo. Furthermore, the amendment "provided equality without changing power relationships in the state" and serves as an example of how the ruling, slaveholding class enlisted support from the white yeomanry. This liaison bolstered the continued political hegemony of the planters. Such political maneuvering was an object lesson in the "complex rules, bargains, and limits" that governed antebellum North Carolina society—a society where, as Paul Escott and Jeffery J. Crow observed, "structural and behavioral conditions had allowed functioning patterns of lower-class autonomy and upper-class control to operate simultaneously."[87]

Whigs and nonslaveholding westerners, however, desired representation according to a district's white population, a proposed system called the "white basis of representation." They hoped to replace the current system based on federal population, which included the numeration of three-fifths of slaves and served to increase the power of wealthy slaveholding districts, especially in eastern counties like Edgecombe. Redistricting based on the white population would favor the Whig Party and reduce the power of the eastern planters. It was on this issue that Whigs supported an open, popular convention. The Democrats, including Clark, opposed the "white basis" and defeated the proposed convention bill.[88]

Passage of the free suffrage amendment required a two-thirds majority vote of the legislature. For a time the Whigs were able to suppress the amendment. But support for the bill grew among North Carolinians, and opposition became increasingly difficult. Whig representatives in the House of Commons now began supporting the bill, but the traditionally conservative Whig senators, the group most affected by the amendment, consistently blocked its adoption. Not until 1857 did the amendment pass from the General Assembly to the people, and on August 6, North Carolinians voted overwhelmingly to abolish the property requirement. Voters in Edgecombe County passed the measure by a vote of 749 to 240.[89]

But Clark did not always vote along party lines. While he supported the extension of suffrage, he did not support the proposal to make judicial offices elective. Nevertheless, the Democratic Party recommended its passage.[90] Often a defender of the status quo rather than a blind supporter of Democratic legislation, Clark was usually consistent in his conservative views, as his opinion on slavery's protection and extension attests.

Clark's view of slavery was consistent with that of most white men of his day. He believed that slavery was a necessary and just institution, essential to the South's social and economic way of life. Conservative white southerners like Clark considered slavery the foundation of republican virtue, necessary to maintain the social order and an engine of human, moral, and material progress. He also thought that free blacks threatened to undermine the white male republic. He no doubt shared the opinion held by the editor of his local newspaper, who proclaimed, "The free negro population entails more crimes and nuisances upon us than all other classes together." Clark believed that any blacks freed from slavery should be colonized outside the United States. He felt so strongly on this point that he introduced a Senate resolution to fund the colonization of free blacks to Africa.[91]

Although he was a Democrat, Clark's dependability, honesty, and knowledge of the Senate's rules and procedures commanded bipartisan respect. He never spoke with the "thrilling eloquence of the orator," but was esteemed for his intelligence and unassuming manners, and senators elected him speaker in 1858 by a wide majority.[92] Upon taking the speaker's chair, Clark thanked his colleagues with a short, gracious speech:

> The flattering vote which has just elevated me to this high and honorable position I must regard as an evidence of your partiality, and not my merit. It shall be my steady purpose to administer these laws faithfully and impartially — to ensure the most general satisfaction by being plain and direct in their interpretation, and *rigid* in their enforcement. The obedience of the citizens to your legislation demands of you in return a full and ample protection of their interests and rights. We live in times of great political embarrassment, when not only our rights but the very principles of our Government are imperiled; and while in our own borders we are endeavoring to reconcile apparently conflicting interests, we are equally bound to protect our rights to a fair and equal participation in all the benefits of this great confederacy of States. We have inherited from our ancestors the most inestimable blessings of liberty, and a system of government the parallel of which is not found in the history of the world, and we are bound by every consideration of duty and patriotism to preserve these blessings and this government, sound, unimpaired, and without blemish to our posterity.[93]

Two years later, in 1860, Edgecombe voters re-elected Clark (facing no opposition) to the Senate. Democrats won slim majorities and returned Governor John W. Ellis to the executive chair. The Senate retained Clark as speaker. He again thanked his colleagues and reminded them, as a newspaper account reported,

> of their duty to press and carry out those interests [of their constituents] with zeal and the most jealous vigilance. But experience had taught us that party strife is the bane of legislation, and that the surest way to ensure wisdom and success in our councils is by calm consideration and mutual forbearance, and that due respect for all differences which must prevail in consultative bodies. This was essential, not only to the harmony of the body, but to the dispatch of business. No rules were required for the deportment of an association of gentlemen, but for the regulation and dispatch of business it would be necessary to prescribe proper rules. The rigid and faithful enforcement of the rules was the best guarantee he could offer for the approbation and support of the Senate.[94]

By 1860, escalating sectional tensions threatened to boil over and tear the nation apart. Clark's call for calm consideration was apt, given the high level of emotion running throughout the state and indeed the country. In North Carolina, Democrats had survived a strong challenge from a resurgent Whig Party during the August elections, a campaign which had divided the state over issues of secession and ad valorem taxation.[95] Nationally, charges of corruption in President James Buchanan's administration hurt the Democrats, but it was slavery and its expansion to the territories that remained the most divisive and discussed political topic among all Americans.

Democrats split over the question of slavery. At the party's convention in Baltimore, disgruntled Lower South delegates, including all but three North Carolinians, broke with the party after the convention failed to seat the secessionist delegation from Charleston, South Carolina. Northern members and a few moderate southern Democrats nominated Stephen A. Douglas on his "popular sovereignty" platform. Southern Democrats reconvened in a separate convention and nominated John C. Breckinridge on a platform demanding federal protection of slavery in the territories. Meanwhile, the Republican Party opposed any expansion of slavery to the territories and nominated Abraham Lincoln.[96]

Fearing any threat, real or perceived, to the institution of slavery, secessionist fire-eaters pledged to leave the Union if the "Black Republican" was elected president. Such extreme rhetoric alarmed cooler heads. A large group of former Whigs and American (or Know-Nothing) Party members joined together to encourage support for the old Union, and advocated continued compromise between the nation's sections. This new coalition called itself the Constitutional Union Party and nominated John Bell of Tennessee.

Clark voted for the Breckinridge ticket, as did Edgecombe County in the November general election.[97] John Hill, a former principal clerk of the Senate, wrote to Clark shortly before the election, expressing "the earnest hope that Breckinridge and Lane may carry this State November next."[98] Though Breckinridge won North Carolina, he lost the election to Lincoln, who did not appear on the ballot in nine southern states. Lincoln had won the election without the votes of the South, and fire-eaters were convinced that their slave property would be unprotected. By February 1861 seven southern states had left the Union and formed the Confederate States of America.

Though a secessionist, Clark advocated a "watch and wait" policy for the crisis. Like many North Carolinians, he took a cautious approach and believed Lincoln's election an inadequate excuse for leaving the Union.[99] Though he did not deny the South's constitutional right to secede, the future governor bowed to the reality that most Tar Heels did not favor an immediate dissolution of the Union. As a result, he publicly supported a statewide convention to settle the question.

On the evening of February 13, 1861, two weeks before the first convention was scheduled to convene on the 28th, the North Carolina General Assembly officially received Samuel Hall, a "commissioner" from the state of Georgia. Hall was sent to encourage support for secession among Tar Heel legislators. He addressed the group "in behalf of Georgia and Southern Rights," and his speech was "characterised with great beauty, eloquence, and ability."[100] At its conclusion, Clark rose and said to the gathered joint body:

> Senators and Gentlemen of the House of Commons, in times of ordinary embarrassment we are prone to turn to those for counsel who are in similar difficulties. But now when we are in the midst of dangers, threatening our dearest rights and even the very existence of our govern-

ment, we must welcome with great satisfaction, the mission of our sister State of Georgia, whose common interests with us indicate too plainly a common fate. These times call forth the undivided heart and best abilities of every patriot of the land, and no exertion should be left untried, on an occasion fraught with such deep and lasting consequence to us and our posterity. After giving this momentous question our best and most anxious deliberations, we have referred it to the sovereign people in convention assembled. Their judgment and decision will form and guide our faith and the rule of our conduct; and to that tribunal alone can we look for any authorised response to the friendly counsels and suggestions of our fellow suffering sister State. But without reference to the amount of sympathy or the extent of our co-operation with her in her present struggle, we at least will assure her that no hostile foot shall ever march from or through our borders to assail her or hers! (Cheers)[101]

The impromptu speech reveals the Edgecombe senator's commitment to Southern rights within a framework of vigilant caution. A month later, in March 1861, Clark left Raleigh for Richmond "to become acquainted with some of the members" of the Virginia Convention, which met from February until June. He held a letter of introduction from Thomas L. Clingman, U.S. Senator from North Carolina and later a Confederate general, who described Clark as "a thorough Southern Rights man in all things."[102] Though never a radical fire-eater in the mold of the extremist William Lowndes Yancey, Clark undoubtedly believed in the constitutional right of a state to secede.[103] His views on "Southern rights" did not waver: secession was an article of political faith. The conventional and cautious Clark, however, met the current crisis with his customary cool, methodical manner. Only after the firing on Fort Sumter in April 1861 did he publicly support North Carolina's decision to leave the Union.

3

"We rely upon his honesty"

As the war began in 1861, Henry Toole Clark had been Speaker of the Senate for over two years and had served his district for a decade. He had proven himself a good leader, quiet but firm, with a thorough knowledge of the Senate's rules and traditions. He was well liked and respected by his colleagues, both Democrat and Whig, who had reelected him to the speakership by a clear majority.

Those very qualities which made him a successful senator, however, proved harmful to him as governor. His strong political beliefs were accepted and applauded by other men of his class, owners of property and slaves, but they proved too rigid when he needed to adapt to change or reach a consensus among men of many different convictions. He worked well from behind the scenes, relying on his friendships with his colleagues to accomplish the Senate's business; but when the public came to demand answers from him, when he needed to rally public opinion as a war leader, he disdained to speak out. He was good with his peers, but he lacked the common touch.

His new office was to make unprecedented demands upon him: quite unexpectedly, Clark found himself occupying center stage and facing the glare and scrutiny of the public eye. Besides having to execute the routine administrative work required of a governor, he had suddenly become responsible for putting the state on a war footing. Thousands of raw recruits were already arriving in Raleigh for muster into the new southern army. The law required the state to equip, arm, clothe, and organize them as quickly as possible before turning them over to the Confederate government. He had to lead that effort while making new government appointments and issuing military commissions. And almost immediately he had to establish a Confederate prison to deal with Union prisoners-of-war taken in Virginia and shipped unexpectedly to Raleigh.

At the same time, Clark's very status as governor was being threatened. As soon as he took office, some former Whigs in the General Assembly challenged the legality of his succession. They raised the question of whether the powers of the governor should belong to "His Accidency," as some people called him, until the next general election, or whether the General Assembly should elect a new governor as soon as possible.[1] Could Clark continue to serve as speaker, or even continue to represent Edgecombe County? The state faced a constitutional crisis.

3. "We rely upon his honesty"

View from the Speaker's chair, Senate Chamber, North Carolina State Capitol. Clark was first elected to the state Senate in 1850 and served as speaker of that body from 1858 until July 1861, when the governor's duties were conferred upon him. (Courtesy of the North Carolina Office of Archives and History, Raleigh, North Carolina.)

The state's original constitution of 1776 had been extensively altered in 1835 by several sweeping amendments. These changes modified North Carolina's government to reflect the growing popularity of "Jacksonian Democracy"—a political movement that emphasized the common white man. Other states in the Union at the time were updating their constitutions and North Carolinians, especially in the state's Piedmont section, were dissatisfied with the extensive property requirements needed to vote or hold state office. They were also dissatisfied that the governor was elected by the General Assembly rather than directly by voters. These concerns culminated in the Convention of 1835.

The constitutional amendments drafted by Convention were ratified by popular vote. Membership of the House of Commons was fixed at one hundred and twenty and the Senate at fifty. House membership was based on population and each county received at least one seat. Senate membership, however, continued to favor the wealthy areas of the eastern

Senate Chamber. As Speaker of the Senate, Clark used the office, located on the left of this room, to conduct business and meet with colleagues. In 1866, Clark's final senate term, the former governor served on the joint committee that drafted an official recommendation to reject the Fourteenth Amendment. (Photograph by the author.)

half of the state — senators would be elected from districts drawn according to the amount of taxes that counties paid to the state. Other amendments called for biennial sessions of the General Assembly, rather than the traditional annual meetings, disenfranchised free Negro men, and relaxed somewhat the property and religious requirements ("Christian" was substituted for "Protestant") for holding office.[2]

The legislative branch of government retained its dominance. The convention still reflected a deep-seated suspicion of granting power to the executive. Under the old constitution, North Carolina's governor was probably the weakest in the Union. He was not elected by the people, but was chosen by the legislature for a one-year term and was eligible for only three terms in six years. The Amendments of 1835 introduced direct popular election of the governor and extended his term to two years. Both changes strengthened the office, although the governor was still denied veto power.

None of the amendments, however, addressed succession to the governorship. The amended constitution failed to alter the old custom of conferring the duties of the governor onto the speaker of the senate in an emergency situation. A problem with this method was that a successor to the governorship would not have the support of a popular mandate. A senator was elevated to the speakership by the senators themselves, not the voting public, and without a lieutenant governor who had won a state-wide election, there would be doubts about the legitimacy of a senate speaker as the state's chief executive.[3] Governor Ellis's death and Clark's succession to the state's highest office exposed these weaknesses.

Although Clark was the first man in North Carolina's history to become governor on the death of an acting chief executive, the situation in which he now found himself was not without some historical precedent. Two previous senate speakers, Alexander Martin and Warren Winslow, had assumed the duties of governor when the acting governor had either left the state or resigned his office to accept election to the U.S. Senate (state legislatures elected senators until 1914). But these previous occasions on which the speaker acted as governor had been temporary and short-lived.

Senate Speaker Alexander Martin had twice assumed the duties of governor. In 1781 Governor Thomas Burke was captured by Loyalists under the command of David Fanning, taken to Charlestown, South Carolina, and jailed. Martin acted as chief executive until Burke was freed and returned to North Carolina two months later. The second time, in 1805, Governor James Turner was elected to the United States Senate. Governors were not yet popularly elected, so Martin simply assumed executive powers until the General Assembly could elect a new executive.[4]

Winslow's elevation to the office, in contrast, was governed by the 1835 amended constitution which provided for a popularly elected executive. When Willie Mangum resigned his U.S. Senate seat in March 1854, the General Assembly needed to fill the vacancy, but the next biennial session, by law, could not meet again until after the August general election, when a new governor would also be elected. When the next General Assembly convened in November, it selected David S. Reid, the lame duck governor, to fill Mangum's senate seat. However, Thomas Bragg, the new governor-elect, could not take Reid's place until the scheduled inauguration ceremony in January. Reid therefore turned over his duties to Winslow, the current speaker of the senate, until Bragg took the oath of office. Winslow qualified as governor on December 6, becoming the first governor not elected by popular vote under the new constitution. He served for a total of twenty-five days.[5]

When Governor Ellis departed from North Carolina for Virginia on June 27, 1861, seeking a cure for his tuberculosis, his powers were transferred to Clark, as the state's constitution mandated: "On [the governor's] death, inability, or absence from the State, the speaker of the senate, for the time being ... shall exercise the powers of government, after such death, or during such absence or inability of the governor, or until a new nomination is made by the general assembly."[6] It was expected that Ellis would return and that his executive powers would be restored. When he died twelve days later, however, the questions concerning Clark's status began. Should the General Assembly elect a governor to fill what a few members thought was a vacancy in the office, or should Clark serve only as "acting"

North Carolina State Capitol, 1861. Constructed between 1833 and 1840, the state Capitol is one of America's finest examples of Greek Revival architecture. The General Assembly met in this building until 1961. During the Civil War, Governor Clark conducted official business from the executive office located on the ground floor, three windows from the left. (Courtesy of the North Carolina Office of Archives and History, Raleigh, North Carolina.)

executive "for the time being," until the next general election? The legislature would not meet again until the special session in August to take up the matter. In the meantime, Clark exercised the duties of governor.

Josiah Turner, the caustic senator from Orange County and former Whig, was the first to bring the question of Clark's status to the floor. He made a motion to form a joint select committee to "investigate and report whether or no it be the Constitutional duty of this General Assembly to elect a Governor for the State of North Carolina, to fill the vacancy caused by the death of his Excellency, John W. Ellis."[7] Continuing as speaker and acting governor during both extra sessions, Clark himself saw the situation as straightforward.[8] He believed that the powers of the governor devolved to him until the end of his elected term as senator from Edgecombe County. He rose from the speaker's chair in the senate and reminded the other senators that two previous speakers had served as acting governor. He spoke briefly but effectively: "A difference of opinion may exist in the minds of some about what the Constitutional powers are, devolving to duties of the Executive of the State. So our Constitution says the powers of the Governor shall be held and exercised by the Speaker 'after the death' or 'during the absence' of the Governor. The Speaker does not become the Governor. He still holds his original office, which enables him to exercise the duties of the other." After his speech, Clark "called Mr. [James P.] Speight to the chair and withdrew from the Senate chamber" just before the vote was taken on Turner's motion.[9]

Clark prevailed. The majority of legislators agreed with him, and the motion to consider a new election was tabled by a vote of twenty-four to sixteen. It was a vote of confidence which confirmed him as Ellis's successor. The Raleigh *Standard* reported that "this action of the Senate settles the question; and Gov. Clark is, therefore, acting Governor."[10] His tenure, however, was not officially defined until the state ratified a constitutional amendment in May 1862 clarifying his situation. "An Ordinance Concerning the Election of Governor" stated that the speaker of the senate "shall exercise the powers of Governor [until] the election of his successor in the next succeeding Senate." The amendment also declared that Clark would hold the office of governor until the "second Monday in September [1862]," at which time a new executive would be sworn into office.[11] During the interim period, Clark occasionally signed official correspondence as "Henry T. Clark, Governor Ex-Officio," but after this clarification he simply signed "Governor."

Most North Carolinians wasted little effort in debating the matter and had accepted Clark as their governor when Ellis died. The newspapers had lamented Ellis's death but reassured readers that a capable successor would take his place. Assessing the character of the state's new chief executive, the Raleigh *Standard* commented, "We have known Mr. Clark for many years. He has been a good deal in public life, has been observant of men and things, and brings to his aid a knowledge of our public men, the character of our people, and the demands of the present crisis. He has a cool judgment, a modest estimate of his own abilities, an honest heart, and a purpose to do his duty to his entire State and the South. We rely upon his honesty, his prudence, his cool judgment, his patriotism, his readiness to counsel with the wise, and more than all, upon his will and ability to do *right.*"[12] The *State Journal* concurred: "[Clark possesses] large experience, honesty above suspicion, capacity beyond doubt, and fidelity whom all can trust."[13] His high reputation earned him a nomination from the General Assembly to serve as a Confederate States senator, but he withdrew his name from consideration in August 1861.[14]

As governor, Clark needed to devote his full attention to the problems at hand. His first order of business was the preparation of his predecessor's state funeral. He ordered all military posts to fire guns on the half hour from sunrise to sunset and display colors at half-staff. State militia officers were to wear "usual military mourning for thirty days." All regimental standards were shrouded and virtually every business and public building in Raleigh was draped in somber black bunting.[15]

North Carolina state troops received Ellis's body on Tuesday evening July 9 at the train station in Petersburg, Virginia, and escorted it to Raleigh, where it arrived the next morning under armed guard. A great cadre of mourners, "the largest ever witnessed in a Southern city," including the now-governor Clark, greeted the train upon arrival. The funeral procession escorted the body past the Capitol and to the Executive Mansion, where it lay in state for twenty-four hours until transported to Davidson County for burial.[16]

Clark was sympathetic to Ellis's family and he handled the difficult situation with grace and dignity. Upon assuming the duties of the state's highest office, he immediately contacted Ellis's grieving wife through her family and offered her the use of the Executive Mansion: "I will thank you to convey to Mrs. Ellis," said Clark, "in the kindest terms, my deep sympathy with the great affliction which has fallen upon her in the death of Governor Ellis and how gratifying it would be to me to offer a word or an act which would alleviate her distress. I desire to tender to her the continued use of the Executive Mansion. It would gratify me, if it would prove agreeable to her to do so. Assuring her that it would not in the least interfere with any personal arrangements, I shall have made for my own residence in Raleigh." Though he made plans for his "own residence" he moved into the Executive Mansion once Mrs. Ellis left Raleigh.[17]

Clark immersed himself in his work, seldom making public appearances and seeing few friends. Kenneth Rayner, a former Whig congressman from Bertie County and a good friend of his from Tarboro school days, paid a visit to Clark shortly after he became governor, but found him busily occupied. Writing to a friend, Rayner said, "I called this morning to see Gov. Clark, but found company with him, and therefore had little opportunity of conversing with him. I know very little of how he is getting along, having seen but little of him since he became Governor."[18]

The new governor had much to sort out. One of the more vexing problems he faced was deciding what to do with a group of forty Union prisoners

Henry T. Clark, ca. 1850. This original oil painting of Clark hangs in the home of the Governor's great-grandson, Dr. Henry T. Clark, Jr., and his wife Blanche, of Chapel Hill. The portrait was probably completed shortly after Clark's marriage to his cousin, Mary Weeks Parker. (Photograph by the author.)

"taken in the various skirmishes" in Virginia and unexpectedly shipped south to Raleigh.[19] Confederate army regulations stated that prisoners of war were to be disarmed and sent to the rear of the lines. The Confederate Congress had enacted rules in May 1861 clarifying that captives were to be transferred to the secretary of war, but because there were no proper prisons constructed at this early date in the conflict, Secretary of War Leroy P. Walker transferred the prisoners to North Carolina.[20]

The prisoners were placed under the guard of "a company of Irishmen commanded by a good officer the first lieutenant being a brother to Lincoln's wife."[21] The "good officer" was Confederate Lieutenant David Todd, brother-in-law to the American president — the irony of which was not lost on North Carolinians, as newspapers and letters attest. The whole affair electrified Raleigh citizens who were "curious to see a real live Yankee Lincolnite soldier," some observers noting that the Union soldiers resembled "foreigners."[22]

Arriving in Raleigh on July 17, Todd received orders to "turn over the prisoners to the State authorities, take a receipt for them, and return to [Richmond]."[23] There were, however, no instructions as to what the "state authorities" were to do with the prisoners upon receiving them, nor had anyone been given an advance warning of their imminent arrival. Contacted by Lt. Todd only upon his arrival in Raleigh, Clark decided to lock up the prisoners at a local church for the night until they could be moved to the state fairgrounds the next day.[24] The fairgrounds at the time had been transformed into a "camp of instruction," a Confederate base to muster troops. It was by no means a military prison.[25]

The situation was awkward. Nevertheless, Clark wrote to Lt. Todd to relieve him of his charges, saying, "Your arrival here with the prisoners was unexpected, and having received no notice of their intended transfer to this State, no preparation has been made. Under these circumstances I deem it advisable to receive them here, and relieve you of the further charge of them."[26] He thus relieved not only Todd, but also the Confederate War Department, of the responsibility of the prisoners' care and incarceration. The next morning Todd escorted them to the camp and turned them over to the commanding officer, Maj. Henry King Burgwyn.

Clark held the prisoners at the fairgrounds until more suitable confines could be arranged. He sent agents throughout the state in search of a good location to build a prison. He considered sites in Wilkesboro and Greensboro but decided that there were "no buildings of capacity suitable." A site in Alamance County came under consideration and was "in every way a proper place" but the "Proprietors objected" to its sale.[27]

Finally, one agent, Col. William Johnston, told the governor about a fine building located in Salisbury that could easily be converted into a prison. Clark quickly wrote Secretary of War Walker informing him of the find. "I have the honor," he told him, "to enclose you the Report of Col. Johnston." But reminding the secretary of the difficult situation he had put him in, Clark said: "I must respectfully ask that no more prisoners be sent here unless I am notified in advance that preparation can be made. The prisoners brought here by Lt. Todd are most inconveniently situated here. Having no suitable place for them and being unapprised of their coming till they were present."[28]

The building Johnston discovered was an old cotton-processing factory located on sixteen acres of land and adjacent to both the town and a rail line, which would facilitate the transport of prisoners and supplies. The lot and buildings were "shaded by a beautiful grove of oaks and well supplied with good water" and would maintain upwards of two thousand inmates.[29] Being sympathetic to the Southern cause, the owners offered the property at an agreeable rate, asking only fifteen thousand dollars in Confederate bonds. Clark estimated an additional two thousand dollars for repairs and fittings, such as iron bars for the windows, and calculated the property would sell after the war for between thirty to fifty thousand dollars.[30] The governor immediately contacted Richmond for approval to close the deal.

Secretary Walker responded three days later, authorizing the governor "to have the purchase consummated at an early day, and to make arrangements for the necessary repairs and additions, so that the Building may be ready for early occupation." As an apology for the difficult situation in which he had placed Clark, the secretary added, "In conformity with your request, you will be duly notified in future of the intention of the Department to forward prisoners to your Capitol, should that be again necessary, in order that you may have time to make arrangements for their reception."[31]

Before the prison could become fully operational, however, guards had to be hired. The task of raising a guard detail fell to Clark, but it wasn't clear if Confederate troops or state militia units would be assigned to the duty. In any case, he dreaded the project because he expected few men would volunteer for such an onerous, low-paid job. Guards received ten dollars a month, a dollar less than a Confederate private, and guarding prisoners wasn't nearly as exciting as a possible cavalry assignment.[32] Fighting Yankees, as opposed to guarding them, had much more romantic appeal at this early date.

Worrying that he might have to impress the labor or draft unwilling individuals into the militia, Clark wrote to Walker asking for assistance. "I shall meet with great difficultly in providing a suitable guard," he said, "as volunteers for the war entertain the greatest repugnance to such a confinement themselves, and it will be very difficult to enlist persons for the specific duty, and if other arrangements could be made, it would relieve me of an unpleasant and very difficult duty."[33] He received an unhelpful reply: "It is hoped that the difficulty of which you speak in procuring volunteers to act as guards for the building may soon cease to exist," said the secretary. "Should it continue however, you are requested to notify this Department as some arrangements must be made for this necessary service."[34]

The governor did eventually succeed in raising a guard force. He recruited students from nearby Trinity College (now Duke University) and placed them under the command of their college president, Braxton Craven, who was named prison commandant. There was some confusion, however, concerning the actual chain of command. Craven wrote Judah Benjamin, the new Confederate war secretary, asking, "I am commander of this post by appointment of the Governor of this State. Am I to report to you in reference to the prisoners and other matters connected with the post? Am I to be recognized by you as commander of the post? The Governor of the State does not know your intentions on this

3. "We rely upon his honesty"

Salisbury Prison. Clark organized the establishment of the first true Confederate prison. The empty cotton factory was located near a major rail line and good water. It opened on 9 December 1861 to one hundred and twenty prisoners. (Courtesy of the North Carolina Office of Archives and History, Raleigh, North Carolina.)

subject." Craven's predicament lasted only a few weeks. Col. George C. Gibbs arrived from Richmond to take command of the facility and Craven returned to the more comfortable confines of his college. On December 9, 1861, the Salisbury prison opened its gates to one hundred and twenty prisoners of war.[35]

Salisbury was one of the first true prisons in the Confederacy: earlier ones had been simply unused buildings or tobacco warehouses.[36] The Confederate government established policy on the administration of prisons, and the state governors executed and enforced that policy.[37] Once the Confederate government authorized a transfer of funds, the day-to-day operations fell almost entirely to the state, as Clark unhappily acknowledged. "The resources of our State," he declared, "are being largely called on for our troops and the support of a large army of prisoners is an exhausting and very profitless undertaking."[38]

Another of Clark's early duties included making appointments to the state Military Board, and his appointments brought him into conflict with an influential newspaper man, his old acquaintance William Holden, editor of the Raleigh *Standard*. The General Assembly had established the Military Board on May 10, 1861, while Ellis was governor, to "advise [him] on appointments of officers, or such other matters respecting naval and military

79

affairs." The board consisted of three members, one of whom "at least shall be skilled in military affairs." The Board was a temporary measure designed to ease the transition of the state's armed services into the larger Confederate military organization and assist the governor with his numerous military responsibilities. The legislature had scheduled it for dissolution on August 20, 1861.[39]

The board was never popular with the public, who viewed it as a conduit of questionable patronage advising the governor to issue commissions or plush appointments to well-connected political friends. Its membership did little to alter this image. Upon assuming office, Clark appointed to the Board former Democratic governor Thomas Bragg and Democratic Party leader Daniel M. Barringer as "aides-de-camp." Barringer was a friend and classmate of Clark's from Chapel Hill. The Board's chairman, Warren Winslow, was another former governor and a secessionist Democrat, furthering the perception among observers that the leadership in Raleigh was little more than an exclusive country club of slave-owning secessionists, which indeed was generally the case.[40]

Holden blasted Clark for his three appointments, writing that the Board was a wasteful and unnecessary expenditure of public funds. He thought the salaries paid to the Board's members would be better spent on the military itself, and that its very existence smacked of "favoritism and partyism." "The Governor appointed two civilians and one military man to comprise this Board," Holden fumed, "neither of who[m] possessed peculiar qualifications for the position. It is to be regretted the Legislature did not take matters into its own hands. Dismiss the 'parlor colonels.' Let him dismiss the Military Board."[41] Holden's criticism proved to be the first of many attacks on the governor (and later, in a similar vein, on Vance).

Despite criticism, the Military Board did facilitate several burdensome tasks, and what some regarded as its drawback—its membership—added in fact to its success. One of its missions was to vet the hundreds of candidates who had requested appointments and military commissions from the governor, and the board's former politicians knew many of the applicants personally, and probably knew better than anyone else their strengths and weaknesses. The Democratic newspaper, the *State Journal*, came to the Governor's defense, responding, "The people see that nothing is too gross for Mr Holden," and called him a "civil dictator."[42] In one case, however, Clark responded uncharacteristically to these charges of political favoritism: when Haywood Guion, a Lincolnton native and president of the Wilmington, Charlotte, and Rutherfordton Railroad, resigned from the Military Board, Clark replaced him with Charles Manly, the former Whig governor.[43]

Nevertheless, his other appointments continued to provoke criticism. The majority of his appointments to top government jobs and military positions were men with viewpoints and backgrounds similar to his own. As Gordon McKinney has noted, "[his] appointment policies created a highly partisan atmosphere. [Clark] apparently distrusted anyone who had been a Whig or who had not been a proponent of secession before the firing on Fort Sumter."[44] But while the governor did appoint a majority of Democrats to many various positions, his nomination of Manly to the Military Board shows that he was not entirely oblivious to the charge of "partyism," nor was he suspicious of all former Whigs, many of whom were his friends.

Despite early criticism from Holden, the new governor enjoyed the public's support in his first few weeks, helped no doubt by news of the first Confederate victory at Manassas. This Union defeat near Bull Run Creek, Virginia, on July 21, 1861, greatly excited southerners, reinforcing Confederate delusions of a quick war while hardening Northern resolve. President Jefferson Davis received praise from all over the South.

Clark offered his congratulations as well, but he also used the opportunity to address a serious issue — and one that rankled North Carolinians: Richmond's apparently deliberate refusal to promote North Carolinians to high Confederate commands or government positions. Tar Heels were often bypassed for advancement while men of other states, Virginians in particular, received the lion's share of appointments and recognition.[45] Advocating for his state, Clark wrote to Davis, reminding him that, "The active participation of three North Carolina Regiments in that great triumph [at First Manassas] appeals to our State pride to claim to share in its trophies and hence I will respectfully submit to your consideration that No[rth] Carolina with 14 Regiments in the field and many others now ready as soon as equipped to join them, has some claim to have her Regiments commanded by her own sons. I need not speak to you of its influence on the soldiers, or on our State pride in a contest where <u>equal</u> states are struggling shoulder to shoulder in a common cause. No[rth] Carolina yields to no State in her loyalty to the common cause, and her sincere and ardent support of the administration."[46]

Clark was addressing more than an insult to state pride; he was reaffirming North Carolina's commitment to the Confederacy, and he went on record early to assure Davis that North Carolina was loyal to the cause. But because Tar Heels had been reluctant to secede, and only did so after Lincoln's call for troops following Fort Sumter, President Davis and members of his administration, as well as a number of Confederate generals, viewed North Carolina as less than fully committed to the cause of Southern independence. Such suspicions persisted from the beginning until the end of the war.[47]

A more pressing issue demanding his attention was the very defense of the state itself. North Carolina was ill prepared for war. Long regarded as the "Ireland of America," it was predominately agricultural, exceedingly rural, and lacking heavy industry. As historian John G. Barrett has written, out of a population of nearly one million people, there were fewer than 15,000 employed in any sort of industrial manufacture.[48] Its long coastline was virtually undefended and open to attack. What few coastal batteries and forts existed were outdated and in need of serious repair. These defenses could be easily outgunned. In the spring of 1861, the state's defense rested on a poorly trained and even more poorly equipped militia. What passed for an organized defense system was little more than local groups of men with fowling pieces who often passed the time socializing rather than training for military action.

As commander-in-chief, the governor was responsible for placing the state on a proper war footing. Its citizens expected him to take whatever steps were necessary to defend them, including the mobilization of volunteers. At the same time, he was also expected to send troops to the Confederacy.

Raising troops was not a difficult task at first. North Carolina was filled with men eager to come to her defense, but to raise an army when none previously existed, the Confederate government had adopted the method long employed by the Union itself; the president would issue calls for volunteers, and the state governors would raise and equip troops. Recruits were organized into regiments, equipped with uniforms and supplies, and tendered to the national government. Though North Carolina did not officially secede and join the Confederacy until May 20, 1861, the state, for all practical purposes, had been supporting the southern war effort for at least a month with men and materials.

During the 1860–61 secession crisis, North Carolinians were divided about whether to join the lower Southern states or stay in the Union. Most favored the latter course. A statewide vote was held on February 28, 1861, to decide if North Carolina should hold a convention to answer the secession question. The Unionists prevailed by a clear majority. Union sentiments changed, however, after April 12 when Fort Sumter was fired upon and President Lincoln called for troops to "put down the rebellion." Governor Ellis told the president, "You can get no troops from North Carolina."[49]

On April 17, Virginia, North Carolina's neighbor to the north, left the Union. Two days later Lincoln declared a naval blockade of the seceded states. North Carolinians felt threatened. Responding to the escalating military crisis, Gov. Ellis began putting the state on a war footing. Militia units were ordered to occupy coastal fortifications and the Federal arsenal at Fayetteville was seized. The governor called the General Assembly into special session for May 1 and recommended that it establish a convention of delegates to meet in Raleigh and address the crisis. As historian Drew Gilpin Faust suggests, it was also hoped by secessionists that such a convention would serve "to create the need for widespread political consensus on secession."[50]

Ellis's recommendation was approved and, on May 20, one hundred and twenty convention delegates unanimously passed an ordinance to quit the Union and join the Confederacy. It must be noted, however, that this secession ordinance was never put to a popular vote. The decision to secede was made by delegates convened into a special convention dominated by secessionist planters and those otherwise tied to the slave economy. Clark did not serve as one of the delegates, but was certainly a member of that elite group. As enthusiasm for the war faded, the lack of broad public support for the war effort would greatly undermine Clark's efforts as governor.

The other principal business of the General Assembly's special session was to provide troops to meet the request it knew would be forthcoming from President Davis. On May 8 it voted to authorize the governor to raise ten thousand state troops for the Confederacy for a three-year enlistment period, and he was given authority to raise an additional twenty thousand twelve-month volunteers. Over the next few weeks, volunteers thronged to recruiting centers to offer their services to the Southern cause. They were formed into regiments, equipped, and mustered into service.[51]

The Convention of May 20, in turn, voted to transfer all those troops that would soon be raised to the authority of the Confederate government. The act would "muster out, disband or dismiss from the service of the State" all volunteer companies and regiments. Unfortunately, the Convention did not provide a substitute bill to regulate the raising and equipping of troops for service within the state, and North Carolina was left without a militia to defend itself.[52]

When he became governor, Clark saw the need to correct this oversight and he raised the issue in his "state of the state" address, which was read aloud to the House of Commons on August 16. (As was the custom, it was read by the House Speaker, rather than the governor.[53]) The governor called on the legislature to correct this "injurious" state of affairs. The constitution authorized him to provide for the state's defense and he needed men to repopulate the ranks of the militia. He suggested that the state call directly upon those counties that had furnished few men. He believed it "fair and equitable, that in each county a just proportion should be observed between those who remain to take care of the homes, and make provisions for the absent soldiers, and those who go forth to risk their all for the country."[54] The *State Journal* described the address as "Business-like. No display is made. It is a plain, straightforward, commonsense document."[55] It was also effective. The General Assembly authorized him in September "to credit the respective counties, as to place them as near as practicable on an equal footing." The law also gave the governor the authority to raise men by draft—an authority he would exercise in the coming months.[56]

Eager volunteers requested from the governor the authority to raise companies of troops; but, while Clark did not initially have trouble finding men, he did have trouble providing the volunteers with equipment. Supplying uniforms and weapons to the many thousands of soldiers in the field was a great challenge, exacerbated by the state's lack of industry and its meager transportation system.

Getting uniforms was especially problematic. The high demand for cloth was putting pressure on existing supplies of cotton and wool, making them scarce commodities. By the end of 1861 a yard of good cloth cost no less than twelve dollars. Forty regiments, or approximately forty thousand men, needed to be clothed as the first winter of the war approached. It was the sort of challenge Clark could handle well. He had once been an adjutant in the state militia and knew that logistic efficiency was needed. He reorganized the state's various war departments in September 1861, placing them under the skilled command of James G. Martin. They ordered all cloth manufactured in the state's forty-eight mills be sent to Raleigh to be made into uniforms. Women supplemented that output with their spinning efforts from home. To help obtain the blankets, quilts and socks that were sorely needed, Clark issued a circular to the state's sheriffs asking them "as agents of the State, to solicit a contribution," to collect donations of woolen goods and handmade items to supply the troops, and explaining that "The scarcity of material for sale in this State, and the uncertainty of procuring supplies from abroad, force us to rely on our domestic resources. Transportation of all goods will be at the expense of the State."[57]

Arming the troops proved as challenging as clothing them. Confederates had seized over 150,000 stands of arms from U.S. arsenals across the South, but that amount wasn't nearly enough. Most of the rifles confiscated from the Fayetteville, North Carolina, arsenal were ancient flintlocks, and as late as the autumn of 1861 a number of Tar Heel soldiers went to the front armed with pikes! This want of weapons obviously limited the state's ability to put effective fighting men in the field, leading a member of the Adjutant General's staff to comment that at least ten thousand men were held back that winter because there were no proper rifles for them.[58]

Like other state and Confederate leaders, Clark turned to Europe to make up the shortage. He authorized John Lewis Peyton as an agent to purchase arms for North Carolina. Peyton was born in Staunton, Virginia, in 1824. As a "Virginian gentleman of ancient family, large possessions, and connections of first-rate respectability," he received a classical education and trained as a lawyer. One of his connections was William A. Graham, a former North Carolina governor and U.S. senator. Like Graham, Peyton was a former Whig and had opposed secession, but when his state left the Union he "placed his services at the disposal of the Confederate Government." Peyton was "called away from his Virginia home to the city of Raleigh during that first wild outburst" when seven southern states formed the Confederacy. He remained for several months detained there by a "domestic bereavement."[59] Graham recommended him to the governor, suggesting that he would make a good agent for the state in Europe. Clark met him during his stay and provided him with official credentials, instructions and credit.

Peyton departed Charleston, South Carolina, for Great Britain as a "Confederate State agent" on a "secret service" in late October 1861. His vessel, the *Nashville*, was a "fast boat," two hundred and sixteen feet long with "very heavy" armament. It successfully ran the blockade, only stopping at Bermuda to take on coal and other stores. The ship was detained for about six days there and Peyton spent his time dining with the colony's English governor, enjoying the mild weather and the "hospitality of the island's gentry." However, the final leg of his journey was much less pleasant, though full of adventure. The ship left Bermuda "with a light fair breeze, and under the happiest auspices" but steamed headlong into a tropical storm. The ship and passengers alike "suffered much from tempest" but they suffered even more when they discovered that seawater had entered the hold, spoiling their food and drinking water. Their concerns increased when they saw a Union warship giving chase. That ship failed to overtake them, but they soon encountered another vessel, a "Yankee packet ship" named the *Harvey Birch*. In the action that followed, they were able to capture and sink it, and when Peyton finally landed at Southampton, England, he described his journey of twenty-six days as "very disagreeable."[60]

He set off for London immediately but met with disappointment. Other agents from both Union and Confederate states had gotten there before him. "I regret to have to inform you," he wrote the governor, "that I have not been able to get anything here upon credit. At the period of my arrival, there were no arms to be had here." Later that winter, however, he was more successful, placing an order for arms which he paid for with funds from the state and had them shipped to North Carolina.[61]

3. "We rely upon his honesty"

CSS *Nashville* burning the *Harvey Birch*. Clark commissioned John L. Peyton a state agent to buy arms and supplies in Europe. Peyton left Charleston, South Carolina, aboard the *CSS Nashville*, which ran the blockade in November 1861. The *Nashville* encountered the *Harvey Birch*, an American packet ship, in waters near Southampton, England, and sank the vessel. Peyton described his journey as "very disagreeable."

It isn't known how much more Peyton contributed directly to North Carolina's war effort other than this one shipment, but he remained in Britain as a "Confederate State Agent" for the duration of the war. He served as a diplomat, meeting with government officials and working to obtain official recognition of the Confederacy. He charmed many Britons and was even appointed a Fellow of the Royal Geographic Society. After the war, "driven by stress of politics into temporary asylum," Peyton relocated to the Channel Islands. He remained there, "beguiling his own leisure," traveling the continent, and writing books before finally returning to Virginia in 1876.[62]

The arms he succeeded in purchasing were English Enfield rifles. The first installment of two thousand arrived in Wilmington in April 1862. It was sent via steamer, and the weapons, "stamped with N.C. on the rifle stocks," shared space with supplies purchased by the Confederate government, reflecting the "cooperative federalism" shared between state governors and Richmond authorities during the war's first year.[63] Writing the Confederate Secretary of War, George Randolph, about the forthcoming delivery destined for both North Carolina and the Confederacy, Governor Clark reported, "I am notified of the shipment from England on board of the *Southwick* of a lot of Enfield Rifles for the State of North Carolina bought by her agent [John Peyton]; and I understood the Steamer was also loaded with arms and munitions for the Confederate Government. Will you be pleased to forward me the earliest information you may receive of the fate of the *Southwick*?"[64]

Besides rifles, soldiers also needed swords, bayonets and scabbards. Other essential equipment included cartridge boxes, waistbelts, and bridle reins and saddle skirts for cavalry mounts. When Peyton could not find them overseas, Clark sent agents to other Confederate states and authorized manufacturers at home to supply them to the state's troops. For the first year of the war, at least until more southern industry could be brought into production, state governors contracted with small, privately owned weapons manufacturing enterprises. These enterprises were often a single weapons maker or family working out of a home or small shop. Each required a contract, and here Clark's business experience was a definite asset. He vetted many requests for this lucrative state business, including some from war profiteers who were not always respectable.[65]

One example that illustrates this process, and Clark's determination to get quality arms, concerns the Wilmington, North Carolina, firm of Froelich and Estvan. In November 1861, its owners, Louis Froelich and Bela Estvan — émigrés from Bavaria and Hungary, respectively — lobbied the state to obtain a weapons contract. Fortunately for them, they were acquainted with Clark's brother-in-law, William George Thomas, a Wilmington physician, who wrote the men a sterling recommendation. Estvan personally delivered the letter to Clark in Raleigh and the governor awarded the company a contract to provide edged weapons to state troops. North Carolina received from them "1,474 saber bayonets and 312 cavalry sabers between December 20, 1861 and February 15, 1862."[66]

A good number of Froelich and Estvan's weapons, however, were found by inspectors to be substandard, and Clark threatened to revoke the contract. It was soon discovered that Froelich's now-estranged business partner, Estvan, was "a thief, a low blackguard, and improvident vagabond." Froelich pleaded with Clark to let him keep the contract. To convince him that he was an honest businessman, the arms maker dissolved his partnership with Estvan and settled his company's debt, convincing Clark to retain the contract. Froelich soon began producing quality weapons, and from March to September 1862, "he sold to North Carolina 855 saber bayonets, 565 cavalry sabers, 129 foot officer swords and belts, 318 artillery short swords, and 216 lances."[67]

The scramble for arms was ongoing, often leading to confusion and mistrust. On one occasion Clark accidentally appropriated a shipment of Confederate arms intended for Virginia. When a supply of rifles en route from Charleston to Richmond stopped at the Goldsboro, North Carolina, depot, he believed the shipment to be long-awaited supplies from the Confederate government, and ordered the weapons dispersed to North Carolina troops.[68] When the arms failed to arrive in Virginia, President Davis, Secretary of War Randolph, and even General Robert E. Lee telegraphed the governor, criticizing him for the apparent theft. He claimed a misunderstanding had occurred rather than an intentional disregard for the law, and wrote President Davis explaining the situation in a characteristically assertive tone:

> The telegraphic dispatches recently received from yourself, Genl Lee and the Secretary of War induce me to believe there is some misapprehension prevailing. Under your direction and in compliance with your requisition I have established here a Camp of Instruction and made a call upon the State for her quota of five Regiments which has been handsomely responded to by the tender of more than a hundred companies — besides filling up ten War Regiments with new enlistments. When I saw a lot of arms stopped accidentally at our Depot, I supposed they were intended for our Regiments. I am fully aware of the scarcity of arms and would have quietly acquiesced in the loss of these arms, had not their removal to a post where they were not then needed led me to regard it as a mistake on part of the [Confederate War] Department. North Carolina will report her quota [of men] ready as soon as they are furnished with the indispensable requisite of arms. [North Carolina's] own arms have been exhausted by furnishing all of her own Regiments with arms and thirteen thousand stand to other troops in the Confederacy, and I know of no reason why she should be slighted now.[69]

Davis acknowledged the support he received from Clark, thanking him for his efforts to arm Confederate troops, replying, "I did not know before the receipt of your letter, that your State had done so much for the Confederacy in the way of arms."[70] Under Clark's leadership, the state spent over five hundred thousand dollars on arms and ammunition from October 1861 to September 1862.[71]

To make up for its initial shortage of weapons, the Confederate War Department had asked state governors to purchase private weapons from its citizens. When this practice failed to produce sufficient numbers of guns, some authorities turned to impressment. Though the practice was not authorized by the Confederate Congress until March 1863, it was sometimes sanctioned by orders of military commanders. Clark cooperated willingly with the War Department's efforts to find guns, but when Confederate officers attempted to seize arms from state citizens without payment, he protested vehemently.

In April 1862 President Davis ordered William S. Ashe, a former rice planter from the Cape Fear region and by then a colonel in the Confederate Quartermasters Department, to "collect guns from the citizens for the soldiers until the blockade runners could provide the needed rifles."[72] Colonel Ashe enthusiastically executed the order and rounded up all the weapons he could find, seizing guns when citizens refused to surrender them. His aggressive tactics infuriated Clark, who consistently defended the individual's right to keep and bear arms, believing an armed citizenry to be the foundation of the nation's defense.[73] He addressed the House of Commons: "A militia system, with arms in the hands of the people, should be sustained as one of the main institutions and props of a free country. They are the volunteer national guards of a republic, a substitute for the standing army of despotism."[74]

These illegal impressments continued, however, becoming so common that Clark issued a proclamation on April 12, 1862, informing citizens of their legal rights and declaring that "Any attempt [by agents] to seize the arms of our citizens is directly at variance with the Constitution, and in opposition to the declared policy of the Government." Still, he reminded them, "as an act of the highest patriotism and duty, that you should discover to the proper State authorities all public arms, muskets or rifles within your knowledge, and of selling to the State all the arms, the property of individuals, [that] can be spared."[75]

Ashe was enraged with Clark's response. He had seized the weapons because he thought the governor had no money to buy any arms. Clark shot back:

> I could not have said so, for at that time and for six months previous, I had been buying and paying for them, and in some instances advancing money for them; and in making known to the President [Davis] as you say you did, that "I had no means to purchase the arms," you greatly mislead him and did a great injustice to both me and to the State, which has been so liberal in procuring arms and so generous in supplying other States,[76] and the Confederacy itself with them. My objection was not to your purchasing any arms that could not be spared, but to impressing whether they could be spared or not. To disarm a country is the first step towards its subjugation! The spirit of a freeman is gone when he is not allowed to keep his arms! You say it is "useless to discuss the Constitutional rights of impressment." I say 'tis equally useless to discuss it on any other consideration, for 'tis a question of might not right — the power alone confers the right. "No one refused to sell" because the threat was made and a sale was preferred to a seizure, others have concealed and some have refused. These are the representations made to me; and I want it understood in North Carolina that private arms — one for each man — cannot and shall not be seized. My card was so worded as to produce or invite no collision or controversy with the Confederate Government, or its agents, and regretted the necessity for it, but the exercise of such a power must be stopped at once, and complaints and appeals from various quarters called for my interference.[77]

Although Clark was committed to Confederate war aims, it was not to be at the expense of what he perceived as individual liberties, or of a state's right to protect its citizens from an overreaching federal authority. Generally, however, he supported Confederate requests for more men and arms, and worked diligently within the law to arm and equip North Carolina's troops.

Clark received little reciprocal support from the Confederate government. Under its commutation policy, the Confederate government was supposed to repay each state the cost of provisioning its soldiers. It often failed to do so, and North Carolina, with its large areas of widespread poverty, was especially hard pressed to make up the difference. It was Clark's fastidious stewardship, his attention to detail, and his wise appointment of Adj. Gen. James G. Martin that allowed the state to supply its soldiers. Though North Carolina troops were often crudely clad and equipped below regulation standards, they had what they needed to fight and remain in the field. As one soldier later said, "the troops of North Carolina were clothed the first winter of the war, if not exactly according to military regulations, at least in such a manner as to prevent much suffering."[78]

Furthermore, North Carolina became the only state to supply clothing for its troops

3. "We rely upon his honesty"

for the whole of the war. It spent over $4.5 million in clothing its soldiers over the course of the conflict.[79]

As war governor, Clark was initially a success. He was accustomed to conducting business, and his skill with figures, contracts, and accounts enabled him to accomplish a great deal. He established the Confederate prison at Salisbury and he mobilized thousands of soldiers for the Confederate cause. Almost every one of North Carolina's seventy-two Confederate regiments was organized under his leadership. But as the war expanded and more men were called to the front, the governor began to face greater challenges, which he was ill-equipped to handle. Too many troops had been transferred out of the state leaving North Carolina open to attack. Hardships on the home-front increased but Clark remained indifferent to public opinion. He dutifully attended to administrative tasks, but failed to realize that to wage war successfully, he needed to set larger goals and engage with the public.

4

"North Carolina has been neglected"

The most immediate and pressing problem Clark faced as governor was the defense of coastal North Carolina. From the 1790s coastal forts and batteries had been the nation's primary means of strategic defense, and after the War of 1812 many new forts were built and existing ones strengthened; but, on the eve of the Civil War, most of these forts had aged badly. Clark recognized their importance to the overall war effort and knew that repairs were needed. He realized that engineers, gunpowder, and cannon were essential; he urged the General Assembly to fund the construction of batteries and the purchase of ordnance, pointing out that "the great length of coast that requires guarding has also drawn largely on our funds, but not larger than its immense importance deserves; and whatever amount of men and money its needs must be furnished." The legislature had appropriated $5 million for war expenditures in early May 1861 and spent all of it by the end of the month. But more was needed, and Clark requested an additional $6.5 million. Though dismayed at the war's rapidly mounting costs, legislators approved his request.[1]

Much of the money went to the purchase of rifles, ammunition, cloth, and other supplies for the soldiers; but it also funded the construction and repairs of the state's coastal fortifications. The old forts at Wilmington and Beaufort, though stout, were nearing obsolescence. The newest forts, Macon and Caswell, were built in the 1820s and constructed of brick, which would crumble if exposed to sustained fire from the new powerful artillery being developed in the 1860s. North Carolina provided the manpower (including slave labor) to refurbish or rebuild shoreline fortifications, but Clark had to rely on Confederate officers to plan and supervise their construction.

The Confederate government, however, was slow to provide trained officers and skilled engineers. Their frequent delays in providing assistance troubled him from the beginning. In August 1861 he informed the North Carolina legislature, "An officer of the Confederate States has also been sent to inspect our coast defenses and batteries, preparatory to assuming control of them, but as yet it has not been accomplished. I have lately addressed a communication to the President on the subject."[2] The Confederate War Department was consistently slow in responding to North Carolina's defense needs and only halfheartedly supported Clark in his efforts to defend the state.[3]

The War Department's slow response forced Clark to rely on local resources, and he looked to the state's Military Board for assistance. The Military Board was divided into two departments, North and South, to supervise coastal defenses. Its officers immediately began strengthening the state's existing garrisons, including Forts Macon, Caswell and Johnston, and earnestly began erecting new forts and batteries. Guns, laborers, ammunition — and fresh water, especially — were needed at coastal locations. And the Outer Banks were an unforgiving place. Everything but the sand needed to be shipped in from the mainland. Its barren shores were a remote wasteland of mosquito swarms and biting flies. In winter, bracing nor'easters and high tides made water travel difficult and uncertain. Despite these obstacles, numerous forts and batteries were constructed at the mouth of the Cape Fear River and at the inlets of Ocracoke, Hatteras, Oregon. One of the new forts at Hatteras, Fort Clark, was named in honor of the governor.

It was not only for guarding the coast that Clark wanted these forts. Like Ellis before him, he saw clearly the potential value of the barrier islands as a base for offensive operations. In early 1861 the state had purchased a fleet of old merchant ships and converted them into scrappy gunboats, known as the "mosquito fleet." Letters of marque authorized their captains to capture enemy vessels. Like the pirates of the eighteenth century, these roving bands of privateers used the North Carolina Outer Banks as a base. They would dash out from the inlets, capture a prize, and dart back behind the dangerous shoals, their shallow-draft vessels easily evading the heavier Union warships. They organized an elaborate system of signals to coordinate attacks on merchantmen while the Union blockaders patrolled other areas. Storms, gales, and rough water also kept blockaders far out to sea, increasing the difficulty of federal surveillance.[4]

These raiders were highly successful. The very first commissioned steamer, the *Winslow*, a speedy two-gun "public armed vessel," bagged sixteen enemy merchant ships in only six weeks of operating out of Hatteras Inlet.[5] In one typical adventure, the *Winslow*, armed with one mounted swivel gun and a crew of forty men, captured the *Transit*, a schooner transporting "Government stores" from Key West to New York. The *Transit*'s master later complained to Union authorities that the mosquito fleet was seizing vessels and outfitting them for privateering service. He reported that sailors from these captured vessels were taken "to a masked [Confederate] battery which was being constructed on Hatteras Inlet, and that some of his own crew joined the pirates." The master also reported that "a large number of privateers [from] the Gulf, and even as far as New York" were using Hatteras as a base of operations.[6]

Like all captured ships in this area of the Atlantic, the *Transit* was sold at auction in New Bern under authority of the Confederate Admiralty court. It fetched $3,053, of which nearly $1,400 was paid to the state of North Carolina, and "a similar amount was distributed to the officers and men of the *Winslow*." The *Transit* was a relatively small catch; other prizes could fetch upwards of twenty thousand dollars. The prize business was lucrative — and romantic — and it attracted additional privateers from all over the South, many of whom no doubt believed themselves modern-day swashbuckling versions of Blackbeard the Pirate.[7]

The location of Hatteras at the midpoint of the eastern seaboard made it ideal for these attacks. The increasing frequency of this "piracy" and the growing boldness of the ships' crews concerned the New York Board of Underwriters and other insurance syndicates, which demanded that the Union navy intervene. As the Wilmington *Journal* reported, "One dismal universal howl has gone up from Yankee-land for giving shelter to a nest of pirates who slide out and in 'confiscating' the property of the Lincolnites in the coolest manner imaginable."[8]

The Union navy also recognized the tactical value of coastal North Carolina, control of which would provide a springboard for larger operations, facilitating a Federal push into lower Virginia and possibly the Union capture of the Confederate naval yards at Norfolk. On August 26, 1861, Maj. Gen. Benjamin Butler of the Union army and Cmdr. Silas Stringham of the Union navy led a combined amphibious expedition from Hampton Roads, Virginia, with nine hundred men and seven warships, intent on capturing Hatteras Inlet. The determined force arrived off the wind-swept cape two days later. The warships soon began firing on Forts Hatteras and Clark and three hundred and twenty Yankee troops made their way ashore. The small forts lacked sufficient powder, ammunition, and long-range cannon, and never seriously threatened the gunboats, which had simply sailed to a safe point beyond the reach of the ancient Confederate smoothbores. Fort Clark was abandoned as its garrison fled to the larger Fort Hatteras for protection.

The Federal landing party, however, did not find conditions as favorable as their navy counterparts. The soldiers' wooden crafts foundered in the heavy breakers and were dashed on the beach, while the iron-hulled ones "filled with water and sank." Their powder and rations were spoiled by sand and salt water. The August heat on the Outer Banks furthered their troubles. The troops encamped inside Fort Clark to await the morning, but their grave situation deteriorated further as night fell. A heavy thunderstorm kicked up the surf and sent the warships out to sea. The weary Union troops were now bereft of support, bone-tired from the day's exertions, and racked by thirst. To their further dismay, Confederate vessels were able to land some reinforcements.[9]

Rebel leaders called a council of war and discussed the possibility of recapturing Fort Clark, but when a larger contingent of reinforcements from New Bern did not arrive, the order to advance was never given. They had "failed to appreciate the importance of an attack" and lost their opportunity to win the battle. Had the Union landing party been taken, it's likely that Stringham and Butler would have been forced to return to Hampton Roads, but the storm abated and, as the morning broke, the warships resumed their bombardment of Fort Hatteras. At about noon on August 29, Col. William F. Martin surrendered the Confederate garrison of six hundred and seventy men. Not a single Federal was killed and only one had been seriously wounded.[10]

The capture of Hatteras was the first Union victory of the war. Within two weeks all Confederate military property from Oregon Inlet to Portsmouth Island, a stretch of more than one hundred miles, was either abandoned or destroyed. Forts Ocracoke and Oregon were given up without a fight. Reports of the Confederate disaster boosted Northern morale, and given the purchase of the Outer Banks at such an extraordinarily low cost in blood and treasure, the Hatteras campaign remained one of the most material Union triumphs of the war. Union Admiral David D. Porter considered it "one of the most important events" of the four-year sectional conflict.[11]

North Carolinians were stunned. They questioned why the small landing party wasn't attacked and why the forts had been given up so easily. North Carolina's Outer Banks defenses had utterly collapsed with hardly a shot fired. Such an ignominious defeat eclipsed any enthusiasm that had been gained by southern arms at Manassas a month earlier.

Newspapers from across the country and in Europe reported the glum mood among southerners. A foreign correspondent in Richmond observed that the Hatteras affair had "thrown a dark shadow across the South." The inlet's capture denied Confederate marauders the use of the Outer Banks as a base and strengthened the Federal blockade, and without reinforcements from Richmond, the Pamlico Sound region and the interior were open to attack. As the Wilmington *Journal* stated before the inlet's fall, "Privateers are the militia of the seas. They are the protection that a nation that does not keep a standing navy has against one that does." The smaller, weaker Confederate navy had lost a key advantage in the naval war. The *Times* of London prophetically observed: "The South may resist long, and will certainly do so with energy, [but] her troubles will come by water."[12]

Clark reacted quickly. He sent delegates to Richmond to beg for the return of some of North Carolina's veteran regiments — state troops that, by law, had been transferred out of Clark's command and to the Confederacy. The governor also emphasized the state's defenseless condition to Confederate Secretary of War Leroy P. Walker. "The loss of Fort Hatteras," Clark said, "exposes so many points of attack and invasion, some of them of great importance from their connection with the railroads and public works, that I must ask for the immediate assistance of four regiments."[13] Several weeks passed without a response. Clark wrote again, requesting at least a shipment of powder, saying, "If soldiers can not be spared [from Virginia], I may at least hope that the requisitions for arms and powder and other munitions may be speedily and favorably attended to. I desire to impress upon the Confederate Government the great and pressing importance of defending the coast of North Carolina."[14] His requests had little effect, though Maj. Gen. Benjamin Huger in Norfolk did send a disgruntled detachment from the Third Georgia Regiment to Roanoke Island.[15]

This episode suggested to Clark that he would get little support from Confederate authorities. He decided to act independently to improve the state's defenses, and he focused first on the loss of the state's small navy. Its initial "mosquito fleet" had been largely destroyed and many of its sailors transferred to the Confederate navy. Therefore Clark requested and received money from the General Assembly in September to purchase "five steam propeller boats." He had each vessel fitted with "suitable rifle guns" for protecting the state's inland waters of "Albemarle, Pamlico, and Currituck Sounds and the waters connected therewith." Legislators also approved $150,000 and the authority to establish a battalion of marine artillery staffed by as many as one hundred and sixty-eight men.[16]

It wasn't much, but it was start. And he continued to hound the Confederate War Department. Undeterred by Walker's cold shoulder, Clark bypassed him and wrote directly to the Confederate president, suggesting that the Confederate command structure in North Carolina be divided and made more efficient. He told Davis: "Sir, the possession of Hatteras affords the enemy a position or nucleus to form expeditions, almost without observation, to radiate to different points, even in opposite directions.... Let me therefore respectfully ask of you to divide our coast defense (now two divisions) into three or more." He requested the appointment of Maj. Gen. D. H. Hill to oversee the Cape Fear region, and then added sardonically: "An examination of the map will satisfy you of the propriety of this suggestion" (and this to a West Point graduate, decorated veteran of the Mexican War and former war secretary of the United States). Confederate authorities, however, disagreed with the governor and appointed Brig. Gen. Joseph Anderson, and, of course, they never properly responded with enough men, guns, or engineers.[17]

Clark was not meek. As governor he was responsible for defending the state, and he confronted Confederate authorities when he thought it appropriate and prudent. But his confrontations and requests for more men went largely unseen by the people on the Outer Banks, and the loss of Hatteras unleashed disaffection there and in the state's other isolated coastal communities.

The day after the island fell, August 30, 1861, Hatteras citizens approached Col. Rush Hawkins, the flamboyant commander of the Ninth New York Zouaves, and told him that they had never "taken up arms against the Government." The next day they held a meeting, swore their allegiance to the U.S. Constitution, and cooperated with Union forces. Following this meeting, civilians Marble Nash Taylor and Charles Henry Foster rallied support for a provisional government on the island loyal to the United States. Taylor was the island's Methodist minister and had reportedly given aid to the Federal landing parties during the battle. Foster was a native of Maine who had only recently relocated to Hatteras. The men held a meeting at a Hatteras church on October 12 to select delegates for a "constitutional convention," an action that was neither endorsed nor discouraged by U.S. military authorities. No more than a few dozen islanders cast ballots in the election which selected Taylor as "governor" and Foster as "congressman." For several months Taylor issued "executive proclamations" and Foster went to Washington seeking Congressional recognition of their government, but nothing much came of their scheme. It did, however, attract the attention of the press and Clark closely followed its development in the papers. He called the whole affair a "regular bogus government" of "radical statesmanship," but with Taylor and Foster behind Union lines there was little Clark could actually do about it.[18]

The fishermen who inhabited this remote region had little or no financial stake in the war and little love for the Confederate cause. If the war meant anything to them, it meant disruption of their livelihood. Describing the lack of patriotic ardor among the bankers, Confederate diarist Catherine Ann Devereux Edmondston complained that the people "in that region are mere nomads owing allegiance to Neptune & Boreas only selling their services to the highest bidder."[19] As Flag Officer Louis M. Goldsborough, now commanding the North Atlantic Blockading Squadron, observed, "Five of the enemy's soldiers came to us yesterday from Middletown, Hyde County, N.C., in a small schooner, loaded with wood, which they had taken, without authority, to effect their escape. They tell us that at least two-thirds of the population of both Hyde and Beaufort Counties are in favor of the Union, but that the poor are held in entire subjugation by the rich."[20] Governor Clark was also aware of the increasing disaffection among coastal residents. He wrote the secretary of war informing him that "seven or eight islanders had come over into Hyde County, bringing proclamations with them, and offering inducements to the citizens to take the [United States] oath of allegiance." "These persons," he said, "were immediately arrested" and "held as prisoners."[21]

Clark aggressively prosecuted traitors to the southern cause and showed little compunction in turning dissenters over to Confederate authorities, but given the inchoate relationship between Richmond and the states, certain legal procedures were not clearly defined or understood—especially in cases involving alleged treason and the possible suspension of habeas corpus. Habeas corpus is a petition filed by a prisoner demanding to be brought before a judge, allowing the judge to determine whether the state has the lawful authority to hold that person in custody. Its suspension was not authorized by the Confederate Congress until February 1862, thus Clark found himself in this instance without legal guidance in the matter regarding the islanders. He didn't think he could charge the prisoners with treason against North Carolina for "offering inducements," but what about treason against the Confederate States? Who had jurisdiction? He decided to hold the prisoners without charge, in effect suspending habeas corpus. With the prisoners under guard, he wrote Secretary Benjamin for clarification and instructions: "In our State there is no law of treason which will reach these men, and as they are now held by the officers of the Confederate Army, I should like to know what disposition to make of them." "I wish especially," he continued, "your opinion as to the legal course to be taken against these prisoners. I herewith inclose a copy of our [North Carolina] law of treason against the State, as defined by the recent Convention."[22] On receiving this information Benjamin replied promptly, explaining that "the mode of procedure against such persons will be through the Confederate courts ... they will be indicted for treason by the District Attorney of the Confederate States in North Carolina." Clark complied and had the men turned over for indictment.[23]

Union advances in the coastal region dealt a blow not only to the Confederate war effort in eastern North Carolina but also to Clark's political career. Criticism of his administration increased. The people of Washington in Beaufort County held a public meeting on September 10, 1861, to address the crisis near their borders and "decried the state's poor efforts" at defending the Coastal Plain. Clark's apparent aloofness only acerbated the situation. Confederate officer John W. Graham wrote his father, William A. Graham, former governor and prominent politician, saying that Clark "seems to be still in a stupor" after the fall of Hatteras. David Schenck, a Lincolnton judge, opined that "his incapacity is so enormous that it is becoming the subject of everyday remark."[24] The Wilmington *Journal* blamed both the governor and his advisors. "Thank God the Military Board is gone," exclaimed its editor. "Let Governor Clark do something to redeem the state from the disgrace inflicted upon her by the disaster [of Hatteras]. Brave men have fallen into the hands of the relentless [Benjamin] Butler while men lean back in their chairs at Raleigh and poo-poo at any demand for adequate protection."[25]

But Clark was demanding adequate protection and not all North Carolinians blamed him for the fall of the coastal defenses. A few military men, such as Confederate Col. William J. Clarke (no relation), believed the governor had done all he could do to protect the region. He wrote to his wife, the journalist-poet Mary Bayard Devereux Clarke, "I don't think Gov. Clark is to blame about the coast defences & I hope you will always defend him." Indeed, Clark had sent what few men he had at his disposal to counteract Union advances and shore up Confederate loyalty in the region. In one instance, for example, Maj. Edward D. Hall and his Seventh Regiment of state troops were ordered to Hyde County in September 1861. But such efforts by the governor were only marginally effective and did little to alter his public image.[26]

Clark thought that President Davis was failing to fulfill his promise to defend North Carolina. In June 1861 the state Convention had sent Thomas Ruffin and William A. Graham to Richmond as commissioners to confer with Davis on his plans to defend North Carolina after the transfer of its state troops. The president told the commissioners not to worry, saying, "The Confederate government will defend every part of all the States." Secretary of War Walker reinforced the president's commitment, announcing that "it is unnecessary for a State to keep up a separate force for its own defense" and that "proper measures would be duly provided by the common government."[27]

"Proper measures" never materialized. Clark continually emphasized his state's defenseless condition to Richmond officials, but his pleas for assistance fell on deaf ears. He angrily wrote the War Department in September that "besides the arms sent to Virginia in the hands of our volunteers, we have sent to Virginia 13,500 stands of arms, and we are now out of arms, and our soil is invaded and you refuse our request to send us back some of our own armed regiments to defend us. We have disarmed ourselves to arm you."[28] And, writing again the next month, he complained that "We see just over our lines in Virginia, near Suffolk, two or three Regiments, well-armed, and well-drilled, who are not allowed to come to the defense of their homes. This is not a criticism of the military position, but rather a suggestion of anxiety to have their services when we are so seriously threatened."[29] As one diarist noted, "No[rth] Ca[rolina] has been neglected, her troops sent to other points, while she is left to the tender mercies of the enemy."[30]

In the face of these military setbacks, Clark encouraged resolve and asked citizens to pray. In a November 1861 proclamation he declared Thursday, December 5, 1861, a "day of thanksgiving" to "give thanks to the Almighty God." Jefferson Davis had made a similar proclamation in October, but Clark's was less ornate and more reserved than the president's. With Union forces on the Outer Banks, Clark reminded North Carolinians that "instead of peace" God has "afflicted us with the calamities of war." Whereas Davis's proclamation centered on requests to the "Sovereign Disposer" to humble the enemy "to confusion and shame," Clark asked for forgiveness from the Heavenly Father for past sins. He recommended that the "usual avocations be suspended" so that citizens could go to their houses of worship to render thanks for the "manifold blessings we enjoy."[31]

Although prayers and heavenly supplications were used by both Confederate and Union leaders, Clark understood the need for guns and bullets. He urged President Davis to consider authorizing the recapture of Hatteras Inlet before Union troops could solidify their foothold on the Outer Banks. Writing Davis in December 1861, Clark said, "My favorite idea of defending the towns, rivers, and sounds on our coast was to recapture Hatteras. I don't think there has been a day since its capture that 3,000 men could not have retaken or destroyed it."[32] But his advice went unheeded, and in the end, the Confederate War Department deemed the defense of North Carolina secondary to the needs of Virginia. The Confederacy's decision not to defend coastal North Carolina to any appreciable degree led to further Federal encroachment in eastern North Carolina and gave the Union army a base from which to threaten vital railways, ports, and even the Confederate capital itself.

Clark's suggestion about recapturing Hatteras was valid. The Confederate victory at Manassas in July 1861 ended major fighting in Virginia for the year, and the threat to Richmond wasn't nearly as grave as President Davis thought it was. There would not be another major engagement on that front until March 1862 — nearly nine months — when Union army Maj. Gen. George B. McClellan began his advance on the Confederate capital, inaugurating his Peninsular Campaign. It was a mistake by the Confederate high command not to authorize a rapid assault to recapture Hatteras during this lull, which would have likely altered McClellan's plans and the war in North Carolina.

The action for the moment was in coastal North Carolina and Union forces were secretly planning an offensive to capture Roanoke Island. McClellan's demand for secrecy concerning this mission kept his officers guessing, but Clark correctly surmised the Union's objective. Roanoke Island was strategically situated between the Albemarle and Pamlico Sounds, a vital link in the system of waterways connecting the state's river network, and its loss would leave much of eastern North Carolina open to attack and occupation. More importantly, its ownership ensured control of direct links to Norfolk, the Confederacy's largest naval base. Recognizing the need to hold such a strategic point, Clark wrote to Davis in December:

> I will invite your special attention to Roanoke Island. It was understood that [its fortification] was to have been done immediately after the fall of Hatteras, but yet it is so imperfectly done as to amount to no protection. A little promptness may even now effect much; for the possession of Albemarle Sound would entail one of the heaviest calamities of the war, not only to North Carolina, but would cut off Norfolk, and ensure its capture or starvation. The direction of a superior engineer officer at Roanoke Island for a few weeks might now render the most material service of the war. Having failed to impress these views [to undertake offensive action] on the various commanders, I must now urge the fortification of Roanoke Island to defend one-half of the exposed territory; and it is necessary for the superintendence of a separate command, as the other positions on Pamlico require.[33]

The island's importance should have been obvious, yet Richmond regarded Clark's suggestions as "damned meddling." Jefferson Davis believed Union forces were only making

Battle of Roanoke Island. Roanoke Island occupied a strategic location in the Pamlico and Albemarle Sounds. After the fall of Hatteras Inlet in August 1861, Clark immediately recognized the importance of holding the island. Despite his urgent pleas to the Confederate government for more men and arms, the island fell to Union forces on 8 February 1862. (Courtesy of the North Carolina Office of Archives and History, Raleigh, North Carolina.)

"demonstrations" in North Carolina, that any movement against the island was a ruse. Confederate Maj. Gen. Benjamin Huger, commander of the Department of Norfolk and the nearest concentration of significant troops and supplies, kept control of over fifteen thousand idle soldiers to guard that city, refusing to reinforce Roanoke Island's small garrison of fewer than two thousand soldiers. In fact, the Confederate Third Georgia Regiment, which had been sent to Roanoke Island after the fall of Hatteras, was withdrawn by Huger in January 1862 just when its services were needed on the island the most. Clark immediately stepped in and sent the Thirty-First North Carolina (militia) Regiment to replace it — a poor exchange. Though undoubtedly brave, the few soldiers left to defend the island were all "greener than Spring grass." Despite Clark's urgent and prescient pleas to Richmond for help, the island and its outnumbered force fell to Union troops on February 8, 1862.[34]

"A little promptness" might have indeed affected much, but President Davis and his generals remained unwilling to comply with Clark's eminently reasonable advice and requests for troops. North Carolinians now openly doubted the Confederate government's commitment to their state. Davis's neglect fueled speculation that there was an "anti–North

Carolina cabal" in his administration, and while there was some truth to the charge (given the state's Unionist history), the main reason for the neglect of its coastal defenses was that Confederate authorities believed a withdrawal of soldiers would "weaken and demoralize the army in Virginia."[35] Clark realized he'd have to act on his own initiative to achieve any results.

Clark needed soldiers, and Confederate colonel William J. Clarke of the Twenty-Fourth North Carolina informed the governor of the military's desperate straits. "I need men," the colonel proclaimed. "Militia will answer my purpose. I do not, as many do, undervalue the militia. With them we could line the banks of the rivers and kill every man who exposed himself."[36] To fill the ranks, Clark executed those war powers granted to him by the state convention and called up the militia in late February and early March 1862, more than a month before the Confederacy adopted the Conscription Act.[37]

By calling up the militia, Clark hoped to raise enough troops to repel Union forces from North Carolina's coast. But the militia proved too little too late, and despite his aggressive measures, public opinion turned decidedly against the governor. Since the fall of Roanoke Island, the Federals had steadily tightened their grip in the east. In March 1862 Union troops under General Ambrose Burnside's command captured New Bern, a key river port town and commercial center for eastern North Carolina. Its loss rendered Fort Macon, the state's salt works in Morehead City, and the important port town of Beaufort, each of which were now behind Union lines, "practically valueless" to the Confederate war effort. By the end of April, all ports in North Carolina, except Wilmington, would be closed to southern trade. The public was again outraged at how easily it all had fallen into enemy hands.[38]

New Bern's capture finally convinced Confederate authorities to pay attention to North Carolina. More than twenty-four thousand troops were rushed in from Virginia to prevent a Federal push into the interior, a move which would have threatened Raleigh and, perhaps more importantly, the vital Wilmington-Weldon railroad which supplied Lee's armies in Virginia. To strengthen the state's defenses further, the Confederate War department appointed more senior and experienced officers to the North Carolina command, including Theophilus Holmes, North Carolina's ranking Confederate general. Richmond's quick response prompted Burnside to turn his attention away from the rail depot at Goldsboro and toward Beaufort. He took Fort Macon in late April 1862 and ended any realistic hopes that Union forces would ever be dislodged from North Carolina's shores.[39]

Clark was heartened at Richmond's quick response to New Bern's fall, but he wondered why those soldiers had not been sent sooner (there was no good reason why they hadn't). His wondering turned to consternation when Confederate authorities withdrew the troops almost as quickly as they had arrived. General Lee was preparing his Antietam campaign and had ordered them back to Virginia during the summer of 1862. Without the protection of those troops in his state, Clark worried that Federal forces from New Bern might move on Wilmington or take Goldsboro at any moment. Moreover, the western road to Raleigh was virtually undefended. Clark begged Lee to send an expedition to retake New

Bern and drive the enemy from its positions. The whole region, the governor complained, was "swarming with Yankees, Negroes and Traitors." Lee, who saw little to be gained in North Carolina, refused to send any aid. He told Clark that the force required to retake New Bern "would lead to a subdivision of our forces [in Virginia] from which we could anticipate nothing but disaster." Though the Confederacy would attempt to retake the town in 1863 and 1864, the area was occupied for the remainder of the war.[40]

Clark worried about the effect of the strengthening Union blockade on commerce and North Carolina's ability to obtain supplies, and he took these concerns to the General Assembly. A firm believer in self-reliance, he maintained that southern dependence upon northern industry had weakened the state's ability to supply its own needs. "It is mortifying to our State pride to think that we have hitherto been so dependent on the Northern States," he insisted. He told legislators that North Carolina should strive not only for political independence, but economic and industrial self-sufficiency, and he encouraged the state to fund the production of war material. Self-reliance, Clark declared, "would render the blockade ineffective. We have the means and material for supplying all [of our] wants within our own borders. The continuance of this war and the blockade for two or three years may inflict much personal suffering, but it will surely accomplish our national and commercial independence. Once check and turn off the great flood of northern trade, and southern labor, southern trade, and southern capital will roll their strength together to establish southern prosperity and independence."[41]

When that policy proved ineffective, he decided that the state should purchase a blockade runner. He and Adj. Gen. James Martin became increasingly concerned about the shrinking cargo space the state was forced to share with the Confederate government. They believed that a state-owned steamer used to transport supplies from England might be the most effective solution. Clark's suggestion was not made earlier, however, because of his concern that it might conflict with Confederate efforts to obtain British recognition. A state entering into competition with the Confederacy for supplies would have been seen as undermining those efforts. Clark believed that the South should present a united front to the world. Though the blockade runner was "suggested and taken up by [Clark's] administration," it was left to his successor, Zebulon B. Vance, to actuate the purchase. The iron-hulled sidewheel steamer, the *Advance*, was the most successful blockade runner of the war, and its success was a credit to Vance's administration.[42]

Clark's hesitancy to purchase the ship lends credence to historian Michael Albert Powell's assertion that state governors initially "provided troops, arms, and equipment to both the Confederacy and each other with minimal conflict over constitutional lines of authority." However, the lengthening war increased hardships, giving rise to internal dissention and increasingly vocal peace movements. These developments threatened the "cooperative federalism" that state governors sought to cultivate early within the Confederacy. Proliferating demands upon a shrinking pool of southern resources by mid–1862 resulted in the emergence of a "negotiated federalism" between the states and Confederate authorities. Governor Vance's purchase of the *Advance* is representative of this transition toward compromise and away from unequivocal obedience to Richmond, and it helps to explain Clark's reluctance publicly to jeopardize Confederate solidarity by doing the same.[43]

Despite the failure to purchase a state blockade runner, Clark did actively monitor shipping that passed through state ports, especially Wilmington, the state's largest, most important port. He attempted to prevent foreign vessels from leaving Wilmington loaded with cargoes that ship owners intended to sell to northern states. This monitoring of trade effectively bolstered the Confederacy's "cotton diplomacy" policy, which restricted trade in an effort to enlist foreign assistance in lifting the blockade.[44] He revealed his sentiments to Confederate Secretary of State Robert M. Hunter, explaining, "I approved of the policy of controlling the exports of cotton and naval stores as based on the doctrine of self-preservation."[45]

Clark's enforcement of a tight export policy, however, brought him into conflict with Great Britain, and into the midst of an international diplomatic incident.[46] In August 1861, overly excited members of the Wilmington "Committee of Safety," a quasi-legal body of citizens led by the mayor of the city, passed an ordinance forbidding vessels entering town "in ballast" to leave the port with cargo. The Safety Committee had gathered "for the purpose of taking into consideration measures essential for their own security," and was comprised of zealous Confederates (some so zealous that they called for New Hanover County to secede from North Carolina). One of the first ships detained under the new law was a British vessel, the *Carrie Sanford*, recently arrived from Havana, Cuba. Inflaming matters more, ardent citizens believed the schooner to be a Yankee ship carrying on illicit trade under a false flag. The Safety Committee agreed to release the ship only if it could be proven that the vessel was indeed British.[47]

Captain Daggett of the *Carrie Sanford* contacted the British vice-consul in Wilmington, Donald McRae, and appealed for assistance. McRae wrote to his superior, Robert Bunch, chief consul for the North and South Carolina Department in Charleston.[48] Bunch, furious at the detaining of a British ship by a "self-constituted body" of unruly Wilmingtonians, decided first to confer with Governor Clark rather than Confederate authorities in Richmond. He immediately wrote the governor, asking "that the intended wrong to a British vessel will be promptly and efficaciously addressed by Your Excellency."[49] More than a month passed and Clark did not respond. The British consul then directed a letter to Confederate Secretary of State Robert M. Hunter. The Confederate government attempted to turn the letter into an incident that would force British recognition. Bunch's correspondence apparently failed to acknowledge the official nature of the Confederate State Department. He had addressed Hunter as "Mister," rather than "Confederate Secretary of State" and did not write "Confederate State Department" anywhere on the letter. Hunter thus ignored the correspondence because, as it was claimed, Bunch had not "properly addressed Mr. Hunter's official character." Hunter did finally reply, after leaving the British consul to fume for a while over this legality. He suggested the British consul rewrite his letters by addressing them to a *de jure* Confederate government. Bunch claimed that he could not do so, or admit to any intent of making a mistake, because the letters were addressed to a *de facto* government.[50]

While this diplomatic wrangling continued, Clark finally replied to Bunch after more than a month. The reason for the delay, Clark explained, was that he had discovered "an illicit trade was carrying on between [North Carolina's] ports and the United States under the protection of the British flag." Clark apologized for his late reply, but pressed for official British recognition of the Confederacy as a legitimate nation. His letter was reasoned, clear, and showed restraint. It also revealed his support for Confederate authority and his desire to act in concert with Richmond regarding the matter. He explained:

> Information has been laid before me that, and that Mr. Vice-Consul McRae either failed to sustain the good faith of his government, or was himself implicated [in illicit trading]. The investigation of this has occupied my time, but for want of intercourse with parties in the United States, I have made no satisfactory conclusions. I trust this will account for my delay. You allude to the 'disagreeable necessity' of making a remonstrance to the authorities in Richmond. That is the proper tribunal, and I see nothing disagreeable in resorting to it. It certainly would be agreeable to me that you should pursue that course. The 'claim for damages' which you notify me will probably be made against us, I would suggest that they would be more suitably be brought against the United States, with whom you have a <u>treaty</u> to trade with Wilmington, but who you allow to block you out the Port, and despite the terms of the treaty refuse you to load in or sail in or out of Wilmington. You will not make a treaty with us and consequently trade becomes a matter of policy — and it surely is not our policy to allow vessels to come in ballast and load out with that which alone sustains our trade or renders it desirable. Free trade is our cherished policy but there must be reciprocity. We would be glad to establish some relations of trade with you and we would faithfully carry out all such and would always listen and respect which you as Consular Agent would bring before us.[51]

Though British recognition never materialized, the *Carrie Sanford* was eventually released. The ship ran the blockade a second time into Wilmington the following November.[52]

Clark faced many challenges during his thirteen-month tenure, and none was greater, or had more telling political consequences, than coastal defense. The Union invasion and subsequent capture of the Outer Banks ensured Federal control over the state's inland waterways, leading to the eventual fall of Roanoke Island, New Bern, and Fort Macon. These losses irreparably damaged Clark's ability to lead effectively the people of North Carolina, though the greater part of the blame lies with the Davis administration and several Confederate generals, including Benjamin Huger. They did not support Clark with enough men or materiel.

North Carolina lacked sufficient troops because the Confederate military strategy was to consolidate men on as few fronts as possible. North Carolina was deemed a secondary theater of operations and the best soldiers were siphoned to the Virginia front. Clark bristled at this strategy, though he obeyed it. Before the loss of Hatteras in August 1861, six regiments and at least seven forts defended the length of the state's four hundred mile long coastline. By September, most of those forts, and their heavy cannon, were lost. Only "seven regiments, one battalion, and one light battery" were available to defend the state. Yet the Confederate government absolved itself of any fault and allowed Clark to suffer the full force of the public's dissatisfaction.[53]

4. "North Carolina has been neglected"

Clark made no attempt to defend himself publicly, nor did he lash out at Richmond's ineptitude regarding these Confederate disasters. North Carolina's coastal defenses had swiftly collapsed, not through Clark's negligence, but due to the shortage of heavy artillery, ordnance, engineers, and soldiers: all of which the Richmond authorities should have provided. (If it was a mistake by Richmond to neglect North Carolina, then that mistake was made also by the North, which could have knocked the state out of the war quite early, saving perhaps thousands of lives.) Unfortunately for Clark, most of the troops available to him were untrained recruits and inexperienced officers. They were, he lamented, "taken from the ordinary occupations of civil life, with no military instruction or education except what they have acquired amidst the labors of camp life, and I hear serious complaint of the inefficiency of all the gun batteries from the want of instructors or suitable drill masters."[54]

The governor was not without energy or intelligence, and given the limited resources available to him it's difficult to see how he could have done more. He continued to work within his power to defend North Carolina while simultaneously enforcing Confederate policies that drew men and supplies away from his state. His sensible requests for soldiers, however modest the number, to reverse Confederate defeats on the coast were denied by those authorities who deemed Virginia a more important political and tactical front.

Despite setbacks, Clark showed initiative. He authorized the replacement of the "mosquito fleet" and called up the state militia, however small their numbers. But unfortunately for Clark's political career, he kept his difficulties with Richmond confidential, and citizens therefore perceived him as a weak and incapable leader. His aloofness and his refusal publicly to explain himself or to criticize Richmond speaks to his loyalty, but also to his rigidness and political naiveté. His desire that the South maintain a united public front and his strict enforcement of Confederate law would eventually bring his career as governor to an ignominious end.

5

"With no man to protect us"

The Civil War affected every aspect of North Carolinians' daily lives. Ever-diminishing supplies of food and essential commodities such as salt, medicine, leather, and cloth, as well as the drain of manpower from home, combined to increase civilian discontent. Hoarding and speculation by some merchants and the impressment of supplies by armies in the field exacerbated an already difficult situation. Women and those men not called away to the battlefront faced increasingly grim prospects. For Clark, finding a solution to homefront hardships proved as challenging as the military situation he confronted.

Clark was not unsympathetic to the plight of his state's people, but as the war dragged into its second year, his policy of fighting the enemy "to the last man and the last dollar" required sacrifices that many were becoming unable or unwilling to make. Unlike his successor, Zebulon B. Vance, he did not mobilize public opinion or support. Instead, with stubborn determination, he continued to prosecute the war effort and to enforce unpopular Confederate policies. Furthermore, he relied on existing laws and customs to guide him, rather than adapting the traditional role of governor to meet wartime demands. He never stretched his authority, as Vance did by following through on the purchase of a state-owned blockade runner. Nor did Clark's naïve belief that the state possessed the "means and material for supplying all wants within our borders" take into account the state's lack of specie, its feeble rail transportation, and its anemic industrial infrastructure.[1]

Clark did, however, work diligently within the existing legal framework to alleviate certain shortages, especially those having a direct effect on the war effort. His handling of the salt shortage, for example, was a great success. Any shortage of salt was considered a serious crisis. Its availability meant life or death. Indeed, salt was one of the most important commodities of the day, being necessary for the preservation of food and essential to the everyday health and diet of humans and their livestock. Its consumption was enormous and without it armies could not be fed. Salt-cured pork was the staple protein source for most southerners (it took approximately ten pounds of salt to preserve 100 pounds of pork) and each month the typical Confederate soldier received, in addition to flour and meal, ten pounds of bacon and a pound and a half of salt.[2]

Before the war most of the state's commercial salt had been brought overland to the central and western areas of the state from Saltville, Virginia. The eastern regions were often supplied by salt works scattered along the coast. As the war progressed, most of those supplies were disrupted, and Clark knew the state had to assume a direct role in salt's manufacture and distribution. Salt works were established in Currituck County but were lost when Roanoke Island fell to Union troops in February 1862. The state operated a saltworks near Morehead City but abandoned it when Gen. Ambrose E. Burnside captured New Bern. Thereafter most of the in-state salt operations were confined to the Wilmington area where Confederate troops could offer protection.[3]

Clark took innovative steps to meet the growing demand for salt. He recruited scientific help from the state's geologist, Professor Ebenezer Emmons of the University of North Carolina, who investigated underground salt brine deposits in Chatham County and encouraged the governor to set up boring operations for the substance.[4] The state incorporated the Chatham Salt Mining and Manufacturing Company in January 1862 and Clark asked John M. Worth, the state's salt commissioner, to procure a boring machine to assist the company in extracting the brine, writing: "Let me therefore urge you to use the authority and means in your hands to bore in that region and do so immediately. I want to leave no expedient untried for the supply of salt and I will render you every assistance in my power."[5] Worth was given wide latitude by state authorities to obtain this most vital of substances.

The governor especially encouraged salt's manufacture from seawater, salt marshes, and artesian wells, and he sent out agents to locate the materials needed in the production process. In July 1862 Clark sent two agents to Saltville, Virginia, telling them, "I desire to lose no time in carrying out the manufacturing and supplying of salt." His agents, N. W. Woodfin and George W. Mordecai, negotiated a contract with Stuart Buchanan and Company for a supply of cast iron salt pans and enough brine to produce 300,000 bushels a year at a charge of seventy-five cents per bushel.[6] The state constructed furnaces and kilns to boil the brine into a usable commodity. Using special war powers that allowed the governor to bypass the General Assembly's budgeting process and draw directly on the treasury to fund certain essentials, Clark was quickly able to advance thirty-five thousand dollars for the purchase of the equipment and supplies.[7]

No matter how it was done, getting salt was difficult, dirty work. Whether it was mining rock salt or chopping wood and keeping fires lit to boil brine and extract the mineral, the process was laborious and dangerous, and finding enough labor to pack and ship it presented a further problem. Hired slaves had done much of the hard, tedious work, but the war forced much of the available slave labor into constructing military defenses. Clark looked to other sources. Many conscientious objectors such as Quakers or disaffected citizens were put to work manufacturing salt, but their numbers were not enough. Commissioner Worth requested permission to impress labor, often from the state's small free-black community, and Clark approved. In one instance in June 1862, for example, he gave Worth the "authority to impress one hundred and fifty free negroes."[8]

Keen on ensuring its success, Clark urged salt production to continue, even into the last days of his tenure. The governor wrote Worth in late August 1862: "Put everything to work and make salt and you will receive the thanks and commendations of the people. So let me urge you to spare no labor, money, or pain in making salt."[9] Clark's resourceful salt policies were immensely valuable to the state. Governor Vance reported to the General Assembly on November 17, 1862, that, due to Clark's efforts, North Carolina was producing over 1,200 bushels of salt a day.[10] Although sporadic shortages continued, especially in the remote mountainous areas, Clark's work provided a solid foundation for Vance to supply salt to the troops and the state's citizens for the remainder of the war.

Gunpowder was another scarce commodity and its manufacture offers a good example of Confederate-state relations in prosecuting the war effort. In September 1861, the North Carolina General Assembly passed an act to "Encourage the Manufacture of Gunpowder," and Clark advanced ten thousand dollars to George Waterhouse and Michael Bowes, presidents of a Raleigh construction firm, to erect a powder mill.[11] The mill was located on House Creek in Wake County and by the summer of 1862 was producing two thousand pounds of powder a day. A fatal explosion in June, however, destroyed the original mill and killed four laborers. Working quickly, Clark had the state purchase a paper mill and advanced twelve thousand dollars to convert it to powder production. The mill proved a success: by the winter of 1862 the factory had doubled its production to four thousand pounds of gunpowder per week.[12]

Most of the powder, however, was sold to the Confederate government. By December 1862 the state had "turned over to the Confederate government over half a million dollars' worth of powder." Though the powder was sold to the Confederate Ordnance Bureau, the governor pressed his concern for his state's defense. "I suppose," he wrote to Josiah Gorgas, chief of the Ordnance Bureau, "it is part of your duty and wishes to supply powder to the N[orth] Carolina batteries and will readily sanction my course in giving them the preference under present circumstances." Clark also made considerable efforts to locate sources of saltpeter and niter, sending agents throughout the state to locate these gunpowder ingredients. He informed Gorgas, "I am very solicitous about the supply of Salt Peter and designed sending agents in any and all directions that will not conflict [with] your purchases. Send me transportation tickets for [my agents]. I shall send out these agents, but will instruct them not to enter into competition with the Confederate States if they can discover it."[13]

Clark was less successful in combating North Carolinians' disaffection with the war, and dealing with anti-war activity became a wearisome task for him (and likewise for Vance). The state had been divided about secession and Southern independence, and attachments to the Old Union remained strong for some Tar Heels. Although most white North Carolinians overwhelmingly supported the Confederacy after the firing on Fort Sumter, a sizeable peace community quickly developed in certain parts of the state. Clark's willingness to suppress dissent with force, and his determined, dogmatic approach toward prosecuting the Confederate war effort likely fueled their anti-war sentiments.

Immediately upon taking office, Governor Clark had been informed of a particularly vocal group of about one hundred and fifty dissenters in the Quaker Belt, a large region located near Greensboro which was home to significant numbers of Quaker settlements. In a letter to Clark, High Point resident and Confederate sympathizer James H. Moore confirmed the presence of this group who were "opposed to the Southern Confederacy and openly advocate the Union." These were men of "considerable property (not slave owners)," Moore wrote, who mustered under the United States flag and vowed to "kill any man or set of men that should attempt to prevent it."[14]

This Unionist group was led by a John Helton (sometimes referred to as Hilton), a sixty-six year old farmer and father of four who lived near Thomasville. Confirming Moore's observation about property ownership among the protestors, Helton owned no slaves, but did own his farm and was worth about $1,500.[15] Helton had reportedly declared that he would "never submit to the Southern Confederacy" and that there were "certain secessionists in the neighborhood that would 'feel the rope' in a short time." The alarmed Moore told Governor Clark that, "[I think] it best to inform [you] of the condition of affairs, and … take the necessary legal steps to investigate and suppress the movement."[16] Clark quickly replied: "This thing must be promptly put down or it may give trouble." The governor "requested the immediate action of the Civil Authorities of Davidson [County]," and told Moore that he had demanded "the arrest of the offenders," who, failing their good behavior, "ought to be committed to jail."[17] A few days after receiving Clark's letter, Helton was arrested for "making many threats of violence."[18]

Citizens in the central Piedmont especially disapproved of the governor's call for militia, and some citizens held public meetings protesting it and demanding an end to the war.[19] The cantankerous Helton, now freed from jail, continued his anti-war demonstrations in a series of meetings in Davidson County. According to historian William T. Auman, these "peace meetings" became the "forerunners of the meetings that inaugurated the larger peace movement in the state during the summer of 1863."[20]

The governor issued a proclamation on March 4, 1862, denouncing the Davidson County protestors as traitors. He authorized the militia to "procure such proofs as may be legally used to establish the guilt of the parties." He further directed the sheriff "to prepare for the arrest of any of the parties implicated and to notify [me] that if necessary for this purpose, a sufficient force will be at [your] disposal."[21] Two days later on March 6, Clark ordered three hundred state troops into Davidson County to aid in "keeping the peace" and authorized Col. Spier Whitaker to "capture all the arms in the infected district," telling him to "send down whatever information you may collect" and emphasizing that "if necessary we may increase our force." Helton escaped to Union lines and reportedly joined the Federal army.[22]

Disaffection in eastern counties still under Confederate control also presented difficulties for Clark. Unionists in Washington County staged a campaign to elect "Lincoln men" to officer positions in the local militia (officers below the rank of colonel were elected by their men). The General Assembly had enacted a militia law in August 1861 requiring elected officers to register with their local commanders, who were attached to the state adjutant general's office in Raleigh. This provision allowed these local commanders to dismiss undesirable candidates from leadership positions. In October 1861, that law was challenged by a Henry Ambrose, who declared his candidacy for a captain's position. Ambrose was a

Unionist and an independent white subsistence farmer with little to fear from the secessionist planters who controlled Washington County. He openly declared to an assembled audience that "I am a Lincoln man and I do not care who knows it." Furthermore, he told the crowd that North Carolina had never legally separated from the Union and that anyone who had voted for William Pettigrew (a leading Washington County planter and secessionist Democrat elected to the state's secession convention) was a "damned fool," as were supporters of Confederate President Jefferson Davis, all of whom he thought should be hanged. His strong words found support in the audience and when the elections were held a few days later, Unionists had won several officers' positions.[23]

When Pettigrew heard of Ambrose's remarks and the success of the Unionist campaign to pack the militia, he petitioned Governor Clark to intervene. On October 28, Pettigrew personally delivered to Clark his "memorial and various other papers and certificates having reference to the disloyalty existing in the County of Washington." In the meantime, Gen. Daniel (D. H.) Hill, Confederate commander of the northeastern military district in North Carolina, had also been informed of the situation. He ordered a squad of twenty-one cavalrymen to arrest the Unionist ringleaders. This action seemed to quell Unionist enthusiasm in the ranks, but Pettigrew was not convinced of its total success. He begged the governor to send more troops to Washington County to ensure that the militia remained in Confederate hands. Clark agreed. He dispatched three companies to support Hill and subdue any lingering Unionist activity in the area.[24]

The presence of armed troops, however, did little to assuage the discontent that only grew among the people as Federal troops tightened their grip on eastern North Carolina. Alarm and anxiety increased when slaves and those white men who no longer wanted to serve in southern armies fled to Union lines. For example, five state militia soldiers deserted in January 1862, telling Federal commanders that Union feeling was growing in the eastern counties of North Carolina. In February 1862, months before Lincoln's Emancipation Proclamation, nineteen slaves escaped to Hatteras from Hyde County. Such events frustrated Clark and emboldened Unionists, who began recruiting men openly in Beaufort County to serve in the First North Carolina Union Volunteer Regiment. By May 1862, the *New Bern Progress* reported that the regiment was "rapidly filling up." Confederates retaliated on May 9 when one hundred raiders attempted to capture the Unionist ringleaders in Washington. Two men were killed in a savage confrontation between the raiders and soldiers from the Twenty-Fourth Massachusetts Volunteer Infantry, outraging local citizens who felt that state and Confederate authorities had abandoned them to the violence that increasingly surrounded them.[25]

North Carolinians in the western counties also became increasingly critical of the Confederacy as the war continued. As one Polk County man warned the governor in March 1862: "Your proclamation calling for volunteers will not receive a cordial response in those counties along the blue-ridge [mountains]. There are some among my acquaintances who say that they never will go into the army unless compelled to do so. And that the war is on account of slavery and the rich may fight it out."[26] More than a few western Tar Heels thought the war was over slavery and refused to join the Confederate cause. "We have many Union men under guise among us," said a Baptist clergyman from Polk County. "[My people] have no negroes to defend and will not take up arms for the South."[27]

Clark believed that much of the Confederate disaffection in the western region was encouraged by Unionists in east Tennessee who were crossing into North Carolina looking for supplies and recruits. To thwart what he called "East Tennessee treason," Clark established a Confederate "camp of instruction" in Ashe County; and when that failed to stop the border crossings, he asked the Confederate War Department for help. In November 1861 he informed Secretary of War Judah Benjamin that "For the last few days I have received numerous communications from the North Carolina counties bordering on East Tennessee asking assistance. That portion of North Carolina is now very weak and exposed from the large and undue portion of volunteers furnished from this section." The Confederacy sent no assistance, however, other than occasional help from its troops stationed in East Tennessee, so Clark ordered a regiment of state troops to Madison County in November 1861 to "look after the Lincolnites." They were led by Robert B. Vance, brother to the future governor."[28]

But these efforts were not enough. The western region became a haven for deserters and bushwhackers who often raided farms "taking money, powder, threatening death, and on occasion beating Southern men." In early 1862 a large band of Unionist bushwhackers from eastern Tennessee crossed into Madison County. They used the Laurel Valley area as a base to launch raids and escape arrest from Confederate and local authorities. Confederate troops had previously attacked these men "at the head of the Laurel" but their efforts were unsuccessful. The governor therefore ordered a detachment of state militia to do what Confederate troops had failed to accomplish. These state troops, many of them local men, knew the terrain and blocked several key mountain passes, quickly capturing about forty of the ringleaders. Those captured were forced into the Confederate army, but most of them deserted at the first opportunity and returned home to continue their lawless activities.[29]

One of Clark's few supporters in the western region was the eccentric "white chief of the Cherokees," William Holland Thomas. Thomas was a white man from Jackson County near the Great Smoky Mountains who befriended the Cherokees at a young age. He learned their language and publicly promoted their interests (and his) in the state government. He had served with Clark in the state senate as a Democrat for twelve years from 1848 to 1860, and voted for secession at the May 1861 state convention. When the war broke out, Thomas promoted the idea of a "Highland Brigade or Legion" made up of North Carolina Cherokees and whites to defend the mountain passes. He wrote to Clark in October 1861 for permission to enlist Indians. In spite of opposition from the state legislature, which refused to recognize Cherokee citizenship, Clark supported him. By the summer of 1862 eight companies of Indians and local whites fiercely loyal to Thomas had been raised. In August Thomas received ten thousand dollars to pay bonuses to recruits and enlarge his command. He was named colonel and his "Highlanders" were officially recognized by Confederate authorities in September 1862, just weeks after Clark had left office. These soldiers spent much of the war in western North Carolina frustrating Union forces and helping prevent east Tennessee bushwhackers from crossing the border.[30]

The need for additional troops became more apparent as the war expanded and Unionist activity increased. By early 1862 Clark had few men left to call upon. Militia companies were being called up, sworn in as state troops, and transferred to regular Confederate army units. Many of the men who volunteered for militia service had done so to stay close to home where they could more easily defend their families and their property. While these men may have thought they could escape the distant, deadly battlefields of Virginia, they soon discovered they were not exempt from being transferred out of the state. By law, it was Clark's responsibility to enforce this transfer of troops, but his enforcement of the law was not popular with the militia. A militia officer told his brother of the rank and file's discontent with the governor's severity:

> I have never seen so much disaffection among men at the manner in which they have been treated. They do not do that much but abuse Gov Clark and the County Court of Edgecombe. About ½ of our company has been sworn in as state troops. I understand there is great dissatisfaction in Edgecombe at this thing as well as in the Companies. They are now talking of getting up a petition to send to Gov Clark remonstrating against the thing. And if they do every man in each company will sign it. I think our County has not been treated right and must confess I do not feel satisfied as having to stay here. I am in hopes that Gov Clark will take some steps to have this company sent home as nearly all the men have families.[31]

Clark, however, was not about to send any soldier home. Men were needed, and of the many problems that the governor faced, few were as difficult or exasperating as the enforcement of the Confederate Conscription Act.

To acquire the large numbers of men needed to maintain the war effort and protect against the loss of thousands of the twelve-month enlistees, the Confederate Congress enacted the Conscription Act in April 1862.[32] The law called into service all white men between the ages of eighteen and thirty-five. Legislation in September 1862 would extend the upper age limit to forty-five, and ultimately the range became seventeen to fifty by February 1864. Though Confederate records are incomplete, by the end of the war, nearly 100,000 men were drafted for military service. In North Carolina alone, over twenty-one thousand were conscripted.[33]

The draft touched virtually every white family in the South and proved to be the most hated of all Confederate policies. Conscription was a radical departure from the volunteer method of raising an army, and made a difficult adjustment for the independent-minded southern soldier. As one North Carolina soldier writing home said, "I am doing pretty well only for one thing and that is Congress is about to pass a bill to keep all of the men in the field that have not enlisted for the war and bring out all the men between the ages of 18 and 35. But I hope they will not do it for I want to come home. But if they do press us I dont know what will be the consequences for the men seem to think it is not justice and that is what I think."[34]

Hearing that they were to be pressed into service for the duration of the war, some soldiers walked away from the army, if only for a few weeks. More than twenty-three thousand North Carolinians deserted during the war (more than were conscripted), and estimates claim that straggling and desertion in all the Confederate states deprived the Army of Northern Virginia of one-third of its effective fighting force during the September 1862 Antietam campaign.[35] To counteract the effects of this loss of manpower, Secretary of War George W. Randolph wrote Clark for help in capturing deserters. "Our Armies," Randolph explained, "are so much weakened by desertion and by the absence of officers and men without leave that we are unable to reap the fruits of our victories. I must therefore beg your Excellency's aid in bringing back to our colours all deserters."[36]

Clark initially believed that stern enforcement of the law would be effective in controlling disaffection and desertion. In a report to the Council of State in March 1862 the governor explained, "The [militia] draft which has been ordered in conjunction with the recent disasters on our coast has developed a spirit of disloyalty in a few sections of some of our middle counties. I have taken prompt measures and with much success putting these manifestations down."[37] He found, however, that as quickly as he could put them down, others popped up. By mid-summer he was exasperated. He informed Davis that he had heard of "much complaint and disaffection" among the soldiers about conscription. He said that their "complaints had increased almost to mutiny" and reported that numerous conscripts had deserted and "left in disgust for their homes."[38] His efforts to apprehend deserters proved especially difficult in parts of the state where disaffection ran high, as in the Quaker Belt counties. To entice them back into the army, Clark offered them a reprieve, proclaiming, "All such persons as are absent from the army without leave, if they will report themselves to me [or to other authorized agents] and return to their duty on or before the 15th day of August [1862], they shall be received and restored without any punishment." Those who refused the governor's pardon, however, "will be captured and punished as the law provides."[39]

Though conscription placed Clark in a difficult political position, he nevertheless enforced the law and deemed it necessary for the war's successful prosecution. Whatever doubts he may have had about Confederate supremacy, however strong might be his fundamental belief in states' rights, he was willing temporarily to set aside this belief and support the national war effort. Declaring his intention to support the draft shortly after the Confederate Congress passed the Conscription Act, he wrote, "I desire to carry out the Conscription Act fairly and to the fullest extent of the wants of the country."[40] He informed President Davis in April 1862 that "I propose to turn [twelve thousand men] over to you for service in the State, as designed by the law. My design was to furnish the full quota required for the Confederate States, and also to furnish any additional quota that might hereafter be required."[41] Declaring his support more emphatically to President Davis a few months later, the governor described how, "feeling a deep interest and even anxiety in the speedy and faithful execution of the conscript law, I cannot allow myself to be represented as opposed or even neutral toward it."[42]

The Confederate Conscription Act took recruiting out of the governor's hands, ending the volunteer system and making Confederate military service compulsory with few exceptions.[43] Clark had no control over the conscripts or their destination; this limited his ability to defend the state. As he stated often, "The passage of the Conscript Act takes all further control and management of the military out of my hands."[44] The Confederacy shipped the conscripts north to Virginia or to the western theater, leaving North Carolina depleted of manpower. State militia commanders begged the governor in vain for more troops. Clark told one officer in Kinston, "I would gladly comply with your request [for men] but I have none. Neither have I any control over the conscripts to say where they shall go. I can only recommend you to keep a bold and threatening front, and keep Burnside [in New Bern] restless."[45]

Though the law was despised by many at home and in the field, conscription filled Confederate ranks. Some men enlisted before the law went into effect, volunteering rather than waiting to be drafted. Some of the twelve-month enlistees rejoined, if only to get the thirty-day furlough. Others, however, signed on voluntarily with the more adventurous, mounted units called "Rangers." Authorized by the Confederate Government in April 1862 under the Partisan Ranger Law, these bands of irregulars harassed Union troops and their supply lines. The Confederacy offered monetary rewards for all war materiel captured and turned over to the government. Critics of the law claimed that the rangers disrupted regular army enlistments and that their guerilla actions exceeded the intent of the law.[46]

Clark was such a critic. He thoroughly disliked ranger units, believing that their existence was a drain on the treasury (the state had to furnish the horses) and, more importantly, that they interfered with his prosecution of the Conscription Act. Writing Secretary of War George W. Randolph, Clark said tersely (if not rudely), "I called your attention to the great number of partisan-ranger companies getting up in every section of our State [and] their inefficiency unless well officered. I greatly regret that it cannot be made manifest to you what little service they are and what a great and serious damage they are doing to the conscript act and through it to the whole country. Disband them and return them to the conscripts. If that cannot be done it would be of some service to the country and save a deal of expense if they were dismounted."[47]

The dragnet of conscription also rounded up non-citizens. Confederate agents would scour the country and press men into service, but many of those pressed were quick to appeal to civil authorities. Agents drafted Robert Gadd, "a subject of her Britannic majesty's" who was "called upon to do military duty for the Confederate States." Gadd was living in Cabarrus County near Charlotte, but had remained a British citizen. Claiming immunity, he appealed his conscription to Confederate, state, and British authorities. Investigating Gadd's appeal, Clark wrote Robert Bunch, the British consul in Charleston, South Carolina, telling him, "I will further state to you that other persons claiming to be British subjects have appealed directly to me. In all such cases I have ordered an immediate enquiry to ascertain the facts and where they really are British subjects, their rights shall be respected." An investigation revealed that Gadd was a British citizen and Clark released him from military duty.[48]

For draft-eligible men, however, avoiding military service was difficult. Substitution and exemption were the only two ways to legally escape conscription, and both practices generated confusion and discontent (as it did, in fact, in the Union). As historian Albert Moore observed, these laws were "not generally understood or accepted."[49]

Substitution, the method whereby a conscript hired someone to take his place, proved unpopular with the poor who could not afford a replacement. The perception quickly arose that it was "a rich man's war and a poor man's fight." The law was also abused. To complete the process of hiring a substitute legally, the conscript and his substitute visited the nearest camp of instruction. If the substitute was not liable to the draft and deemed fit, the conscript received a discharge from the camp commandant.[50] Some substitutes sold themselves only to desert the army and sell themselves again. Clark received frequent inquiries from citizens expressing frustration, which he did little to assuage. Replying to a typical inquiry from a Bladen County man, the governor said that substitution was "a law of the Confederacy and the State authorities have no control over it, consequently appeals to me are useless — all the information I have is what has been published by Richmond authorities."[51]

Exemption from the draft was rare and limited to a few occupations deemed essential, including government officials, postal workers, ferrymen and rail pilots, and hospital and factory superintendents.[52] Average North Carolinians, a large proportion of whom already lived on the margins of existence, felt more acutely the hardships caused by the war and the drain of manpower from their communities. Virtually every aspect of daily life was disrupted and basic public services were curtailed for want of qualified personnel. But hardship was not a cause for exemption. No matter how dire the situation, citizens had little recourse except to petition civil authorities, the very men intent on filling the army's ranks.

In an attempt to stem the loss of manpower, some communities formed petitions to keep skilled laborers or professionals at home. For example, more than fifty people in a Chatham County community signed a petition to have Joshua C. Causey discharged from the service, as he was "the only public blacksmith in our District." The petitioners entreated the governor to exempt Causey, claiming "there will be no one that can shoe our horses or keep our tools in order," and without proper tools, the community would "therefore be unable to make bread to feed our families" or "support our gallant soldiers in the field."[53]

Citizens in Asheville petitioned Clark to exempt medical doctors, pleading, "the undersigned citizens of the County of Buncombe take the liberty of representing to your Excellency that the Conscript Act will deprive the County of Physicians sufficient to supply the wants of the people."[54] Though the Confederate Congress eventually exempted blacksmiths, physicians, and some others from military service in October 1862, Clark enforced the conscript law to the letter during his tenure. His decision not to plead with the War Department on behalf of those requesting an exemption undoubtedly undermined public support for his administration.[55]

Clark also received petitions from women burdened by the drain of men taken from home. Women suffered greatly when husbands and sons were called away to the front, leaving many wives vulnerable and often overwhelmed with the added responsibilities of maintaining a home or farm with little support or protection. A letter to Clark from a High Point woman is a typical expression of the difficult circumstances that women and their families endured: "I am a poor woman with one daughter," she wrote. "My present husband is afflicted so that he cannot make a support of me. I have five sons [that] have all volunteered and have been in service ever since the War commenced. Their has been no provision made for my support. If you can contribute any thing to me I will ever be grateful to you." In July 1862, more than a dozen "Ladies of Halifax County" petitioned the governor to exempt "J. C. Randolph" from military service, asking that he "may be left at home for our protection. We all reside within a mile and a half from his farm with no man to protect us." But Clark could do little to aid the destitute families of soldiers because the state legislature did not pass a state law providing for poor relief until December 1862, about three months after he left office.[56]

Basic commodities that were in limited supply before 1861 became even scarcer as the war continued. Inflation, speculation, and high prices made a difficult situation worse. Parts of North Carolina had suffered also from various debilitating livestock diseases and crop blights, which limited the availability of grain, meat, and leather. As the Wilmington *Journal* reported in the summer of 1861, "The supply of meat demands grave attention. Hogs have been terribly thinned out by disease. The scarcity of food for several past winters has greatly diminished the number of cattle."[57] With the approval of the legislature, Clark issued a proclamation in November 1861 prohibiting "the exportation beyond the limits of the State of all Bacon, Pork, Beef, Leather, men's shoes, Woolen Goods, Jeans, Linseys, and Blankets, etc., etc., except through the orders of the proper Officers of the Confederate Government or of the State Government."[58]

Getting enough cloth for the state's troops remained a priority, and because cloth was in such high demand, Clark issued a proclamation in March 1862 prohibiting the "exportation beyond the limits of the State of all cotton and woolen goods."[59] The governor also asked the state's women to help: "Let the Ladies and their friends prepare for such underclothes as [the Confederate soldiers] need and, for their coats and pants. Let their Captains make a requisition on Richmond and if Richmond can't furnish right off, bring the requisition to Raleigh and we will."[60]

Clark sought other states' assistance in enforcing his proclamations against exportation of goods. Gov. Francis W. Pickens of South Carolina agreed. "We desire to act in concert," said Pickens. "I would be glad if you would inform me if the exportation of any provisions of any kind has been prohibited from North Carolina. The strength and support of one state is the strength of every other state in this great revolution. We should stand together, as far as our mutual supplies are concerned, as one in the same."[61]

Despite such efforts by southern governors, shortages continued. The Union navy tightened the blockade, further limiting goods and commodities. Inflation continued to rise and prices reached record levels. Clark came to believe the solution lay in price controls. Writing Weldon N. Edwards, the governor urged the state convention (the acting legislative body when the General Assembly was not in session) to authorize him to set maximum prices on goods. "There must be some corrective for an evil which is now drawing the very life-blood of the community, feeding on the distresses of the people and growing, and increasing with their distresses," he told Edwards.

Clark claimed his earlier embargo on trade and woolen goods was but a "partial remedy" and an "imperfect corrective." He desired stronger means to control speculation by suggesting "a regulation of prices on some of the prime necessities of life, by establishing a maximum price, which shall not be exceeded." The governor suggested that the states work together to set and enforce price caps. He insisted that "if a joint action can be had with those States, of which there seems no doubt, it must prove highly beneficial." In April 1862, the state convention granted him the power to regulate prices of essential commodities such as food and clothing by "fixing the highest price at which any of the said articles may be bartered or sold." The governor was given the additional power to "draw upon the Public Treasury" to enforce the act.[62]

Clark's concern for the population's suffering led him to an uncharacteristic leniency in one regard; he came to believe that citizens caught trading with the enemy for such essential items as medicine and salt should be treated with compassion. The blockade and faltering Confederate fortunes in eastern North Carolina prevented essential items from reaching the general public. Areas in eastern North Carolina controlled by the Union army had access to at least some of these supplies, and citizens near these localities often risked capture and arrest from both Confederate and Federal forces if found trading with the wrong side. For example, a William Atkinson was arrested and jailed by Confederate soldiers for allegedly trading with Union forces near Plymouth. Atkinson appealed to Governor Clark, assuring him that he had only crossed enemy lines to purchase salt. Clark was sympathetic but stern, telling Atkinson's Confederate captor, "If his offence is only the trafficking of salt or passing the lines for that purpose, he should be discharged with a proper caution as to [its] impropriety."[63]

Horses, carriages, and wagons were also in high demand, and army officers on both sides had little compunction in impressing these necessities. Citizens near the Virginia border or near Union lines in disputed regions of eastern North Carolina were particularly vulnerable to the depredations of marauding army units scavenging these provisions.[64] Edenton planter Richard Paxton, whose slaves and property had been previously pressed into Confederate service, informed Clark of his latest dispossession. Confederate raiders had confiscated Paxton's horses and other necessities from his plantations in March 1862. Paxton wrote the governor and demanded protection from raiders, or at least compensation for his losses. "Yesterday," he complained, "I was visited by a company of dragoons from Smithfield, Virginia, who have come to impress horses in Eastern Carolina, a district almost depopulated in consequence of prior impressments made for the State and Confederacy. These dragoons took my two carriage horses. As a compensation they furnished me with a script payable at Suffolk [Virginia], to which I have no means of getting."[65]

Paxton worried also that the close proximity of Federal troops and the disrupted status of eastern North Carolina's plantation economy might lead to slave unrest in the region. "Is it designed," he asked, "that we shall abandon our farms, omit cultivation, and permit the negroes to run wild to commit depredations for the want of employment? Are we to be reduced in this manner?"[66]

Confederate loyalty often wavered when the struggle for independence interfered with the strict maintenance of the racial order. Paxton had addressed the fear of every slaveholder, if not that of every white Southerner — blacks, slave and free, operating independently and outside of white supervision. African-American chattel slavery and its inherent racial caste system was the bedrock of the South's social and economic way of life. As Governor Ellis said on the eve of war in November 1860, "Our whole social fabric is based upon and sustained by slave labor. There is scarcely an occupation of our people, whether mechanical, manufacturing, mercantile, or professional, that does not mainly depend upon it for support." Any suggestion of wild Negroes free to commit depredations upon the country incited alarm among the state's white population.[67]

As a large slaveholder himself, Clark harbored such fears. Most overseers had been drafted or had volunteered for military service, leaving communities without enough white men to continue regular slave patrols to prevent slaves' escape, or even to prevent slave insurrections. Clark had sought strong, overarching powers as governor to keep the slave system intact in the midst of wartime disruptions. He urged the state to create a slave patrol system to maintain "law and order" on the plantations, but it was never implemented, and communities where slaves were in or near the majority especially remained fearful of uprisings. For example, one overwhelmed Northampton County overseer, Thomas Goode Tucker, begged the governor for a detachment of troops to put down a local slave disturbance. Clark replied:

> Yours of the 11th [March 1862] is received asking for a detachment of soldiers to aid in seizing and bringing off Mr. Capehart's negroes who are represented as in a state of quasi-insurrection. I fear it is too generally the case with the large plantation of slaves in that portion of the country. I have no force now that I can detail for that service, and the Convention declined to legislate on that subject, or in aid of the planters. South Carolina has an armed police to remove the negroes into the up country and provide for their support. But the North Carolina Convention refused to give me any power or means to move in this matter. It is a most important matter, and should be considered. It is nothing more nor less than an institution of the greatest wealth and prosperity to the Southern Confederacy — not merely in danger of being, but of being converted into an engine of destruction to us.[68]

Clark maintained that any incident or indication of possible slave unrest should be summarily dealt with. He suggested to Tucker that he request soldiers from the commanding officer of a nearby cavalry unit and urged him to reestablish his authority at once, coldly advising him, "At the first instance of opposition, [a slave] should be shot." "Some act of this sort will resuscitate your authority," Clark said, "and I think the men, particularly the slave holders, unless in the service, should remain on their farms, and keep order not only among the negroes but among the disaffected."[69]

By mid–1862, the political and military situation had worsened. Clark's rigid compliance with Confederate policy, coupled with the Union victories in the east, jeopardized his political career. Though he had attained a degree of administrative success, he was losing the support of both the planter and yeoman classes. His administration became increasingly unpopular, yet the governor did little to mold or alter public opinion. The August elections loomed ahead but he made no effort to win his party's nomination or the public's confidence. He continued to work diligently but invisibly, often spending long hours addressing the business at hand.

The people, however, sought more forceful, reassuring and visible leadership. They rarely saw Clark and he never made public speeches as governor. In an April 1862 letter to the Raleigh *Standard*, a disgruntled citizen who called himself "Gaston" suggested an early election to replace Clark, saying, "If the war lasts, greater wisdom and a greater reach and quickness of intellect if possible will be required in the Gubernatorial chair."[70] Other North Carolinians criticized the governor for not defying the Confederate government's increasingly authoritarian policies. As one dissatisfied Tar Heel complained to the *Standard*, "There is so much disaffection as to the manner in which the revolution has been conducted. Those late oppressive laws which have been passed have very much alarmed the people, they say we are tending to a perfect despotism."[71]

The influential editor of the *Standard*, William W. Holden, fanned the discontent. He thought Clark's policy to fight the enemy to the "last man and the last dollar" was a disaster, and he repeatedly criticized the governor and the "original secessionists" for their alleged mismanagement of the war. He blamed them for "neglecting the coast defences, injustice to the soldiers, advocating martial law, and abusing the privileges of office," and bluntly called them "traitors to the South."[72] Clark's seeming inability to check Union advances, combined with growing disaffection, high prices, and scarce goods, damaged the Democrats' political chances. Holden was convinced that they had driven the state to ruin and he encouraged disgruntled Unionists and former Whigs to form a new political coalition. This coalition was called the "Conservative Party" and it coalesced around the alleged ineffectiveness of the Davis and Clark administrations, calling for better management of the war effort at home.

The Democrats were alarmed at the speed with which the public accepted the Conservatives' message and as a result, they abandoned the name "Democrat" and called themselves "Confederates." The Confederate Party appealed to the voter's patriotism and the public's fear of partisan politics. Confederates also realized that the political battle to keep control of the state government would be difficult with Clark's name on the ballot. Clark had become a symbol of the state's problems, and accordingly, his party did not ask him to run for governor.[73]

The Confederates instead selected as their candidate William Johnston of Charlotte, president of the Charlotte and South Carolina railroad. Many Conservatives at first favored William A. Graham, but when he politely refused, they followed the urging of Holden and other party leaders and nominated the popular war veteran and Buncombe County native Colonel Zebulon B. Vance.

Neither candidate openly campaigned for the office. Vance remained in the field with his army regiment and Johnston stayed in the office managing his railroad, but both men allowed editors to conduct the campaign from the editorial pages of their newspapers. In a typical Holden editorial, he enthusiastically endorsed Vance, saying, "VANCE and VICTORY! Under that sign we will conquer, and partyism, favoritism, and inefficiency in office will give place to wiser, better, and more patriotic rule." The Confederate papers responded by blaming their opponents for "lashing the State into a bitter party contest" and questioned Vance's "moderate abilities" and loyalty to the Confederacy.[74]

A bitter partisan spirit characterized the elections and disaffected citizens threatened to disrupt polling stations, but when the final vote was counted, Vance had received over seventy-two percent and carried all but twelve counties. In fact, Vance had won by the largest margin of victory in a gubernatorial election since 1776. The Confederates had been soundly defeated, testifying to the high level of public discontent with the war's progress. Clark looked forward to returning to family life as he prepared to step down as North Carolina's Civil War governor and depart Raleigh for his beloved Tarboro home.[75]

6

"That Odious Constitution"

When Henry T. Clark's term expired he looked forward to returning home after a two-year absence, but he did not retire to a life of leisure. He continued to support North Carolina's war effort, but he did so at the local level, returning to his role as justice of the peace and Democratic Party leader. He spent the years after 1862 in Tarboro supporting his wife and five young children and, of course, dealing with the hardships created by the war. He wanted to make life as normal as possible for his family during these difficult times, living quietly and attending to his business and civic affairs, but he never really escaped the war or the public eye. He continued to be a notable presence in his community well after he left the Governor's Mansion.[1]

When the August 1862 election results became known, Clark was more than ready to leave Raleigh, but he remained dutifully at his post dispatching official business and fielding complaints. Many of the letters he received during his final weeks in office came from disgruntled citizens complaining about shortages and impressments. Democrats had lost the election because of their strong support of the Davis administration; its heavy-handed policies had turned the public against them. Some eastern planters had switched their allegiance to Vance and the Conservatives, in part because of their property losses at the hands of marauding Union and Confederate troops. Citizens looked to the governor for assistance, but Clark was unable to override Confederate authorities in the matter of impressments.

A typical letter concerning impressments came to Clark in late August. Brig. Gen. David Clark (no relation), a substantial planter from Halifax County serving in the state militia, complained about the "impressment of slaves [by the Confederate army] to work on the Fortifications in Virginia." The governor told him there was nothing he could do, that it was "a species of Martial law" and that "[Confederate] Officers resorting to these extreme measures are accountable to their superiors." As a slave owner himself, though, he certainly empathized with his fellow planters' frustrations, saying, "The means and propriety of enforcing such an order is a difficult question. After a community has freely sent forth all her citizens to the War, the slaves might reasonably be left to prepare a support for the soldiers on duty and their families at home. This view of the subject seems never to enter into the consideration of our Generals." He added, "It is an assumed authority only justified by the emergency of the case and citizens must decide for themselves how much aid they can contribute to it."² The governor was right: there was little he could do. But his inability to render assistance or his unwillingness to intercede for citizens in these matters hurt his party's chances for a second term.

Clark remained in Raleigh for several weeks after Vance's inauguration on September 8, tying up loose ends and making preparations for his return to Tarboro. His wife and children were at Monreath in Franklin County, a family home about thirty miles north of Raleigh. Its location near Louisburg was presumed healthier than the river lowlands around Tarboro. The Clarks enjoyed many summer days at Monreath over the course of their marriage, and Mary spent much of her time there during her husband's tenure as governor, but now she was ready to leave. She was tired, worried, and seven months pregnant with their sixth child. She told her sister, "You will be disturbed to see my letter dated from here [September 26] for I expected to have left a fortnight ago. It would be so tiresome going home from Franklin [County] in a carriage with children. Henry has been gone two weeks. The wagons came at that time for the servants and things and they have gone tonight. I hope Henry will come in time to go home [to Hilma] early in next week, but I don't know. I want to go [but] I hope we won't be troubled by the enemy."³

Clark was ready for home too. He wanted a break from the war, but "the enemy" was never far away. Federal troops remained in eastern North Carolina, launching raids and disrupting life for local citizens. New Bern and other coastal locations were home to thousands of Union soldiers, and their commanders often sent reconnoitering missions up local rivers and creeks, or sent raiding parties into the countryside. They often met with resistance and alarm from the locals, not least because their presence encouraged multitudes of slaves to seek freedom by fleeing to Union encampments. Larger battles fought at Plymouth, Washington, Kinston, and New Bern (though not always tactical Union victories) ensured Federal control of the region. Although physical damage was relatively light, the psychological effects of Federal dominance in eastern North Carolina greatly weakened the South's ability to fight effectively.

Confederate troops and state militia units traveled frequently through Edgecombe County. Tarboro was the staging area for a Confederate force of over eight thousand men before the Battle of Plymouth in April 1864. Afterwards the victorious Confederates marched 2,400 Union captives back to Tarboro and held them in a stockade built on the town common until they could be transported to prisons in Georgia and western North Carolina. However, the county was a choice target for Union raids. Its agriculture and manufacturing supported the southern war effort. The Rocky Mount Mills complex was the largest cotton mill in the state and local warehouses held considerable stores of supplies. A depot at Rocky Mount and a spur line connecting Tarboro to the Wilmington-Weldon railroad made the town strategically important. Federal troops raided the area several times from 1862 until the end of the war, usually burning bridges and destroying property, but the area remained in Confederate hands.⁴

The first raid on Tarboro occurred shortly after Clark's return home. On November 2,

6. "That Odious Constitution"

1862, five thousand men commanded by Gen. John Foster marched west from Washington, North Carolina, intending to surprise Confederate troops stationed at Fort Branch — about twenty-five miles east of Tarboro. The soldiers destroyed the small village of Hamilton and moved on Tarboro, but halted just short of the town, fearing that a larger concentration of Confederate forces might be arriving to flank them. Foster retreated to Plymouth having accomplished very little. His movements, however, attracted the attention of Governor Vance, who visited Tarboro the next day. Upon his arrival, he contacted Clark, and the two governors met with Gen. James Martin and "advised with [them] as to where the best position would be" to defend the town and prepare for any future Union demonstrations in the area.[5]

The second raid was more notable. A sizable cavalry force under the command of Union Brig. Gen. Edward E. Potter left New Bern for Rocky Mount on July 17, 1863, with orders to destroy a major rail bridge on the Wilmington-Weldon line. This lengthy bridge spanned the Tar River and its destruction would disrupt supplies desperately needed by Lee's recently defeated army returning from Gettysburg. While the main body marched on Rocky Mount, a detachment from the Third New York was ordered to Tarboro. The raiders arrived there on the morning of July 20. The soldiers charged into town and were greeted by a small force of local Confederates "who fired some shots and fled across the [Tar] River." The town was quickly secured. Facing no organized opposition, the Federals destroyed two steamboats, "an ironclad steamer of the Merrimac model, together with some railroad cars, 100 bales of cotton, quartermaster's subsistence, and ordnance stores." The unfinished ironclad was being built as a sister ship to the *Albemarle*. Its destruction ended major Confederate gunboat construction efforts in the Tar-Pamlico region.[6]

Potter's men swept through the town, burning government buildings and destroying private dwellings thought to contain military supplies. Shops were pillaged and houses plundered. Clark's home, Hilma, was only several hundred yards from the town limits and suffered the same fate. Clark himself was caught up in the action and was nearly captured by enemy soldiers. According to his nephew, who recalled the scene years later, Clark "was standing on his porch about eight o'clock in the morning, just after breakfast, when he was much astonished to see a column of Federal cavalry galloping rapidly by. [Hilma] stood back from the public road among shade trees and ornamental shrubbery. His riding horse 'Little Sorrell' stood for his morning ride, and [Clark] readily escaped into the woods behind the house." His mad dash must have frustrated his would-be captors, who returned to his home and looted it.[7]

The soldiers entered the house and treated the family "with brutal insolence." According to the *State Journal*, "Ex-Gov. Clark's residence was shamefully abused. Mrs. Clark and her niece were compelled to leave their house and take refuge in the kitchen. They ransacked the house from top to bottom, breaking open trunks, chests, and drawers." Jewelry and watches were stolen, their food was either eaten or thrown down the well, and his "stock of wines and brandies" plundered. The damage to his home and property was extensive, but the governor was pleased to discover on his return that the soldiers, many of

Hilma, ca. 1853. Clark purchased a modest plantation near the Tarboro town limits in 1850. The home was completed in 1853. This view is likely the one Federal soldiers would have seen when they spotted Clark on his horse during their raid of Tarboro in July 1863. (Courtesy Blount-Bridgers House Archives, Tarboro, North Carolina.)

whom who had been drinking heavily since leaving New Bern, had left "untouched several bottles of very fine old whiskey," which were labeled "Old Nick."[8]

Rebel troops from nearby Fort Branch had been alerted to the situation and were riding toward the town. They intercepted a contingent of raiders four miles east of the Tar River at Daniel's Schoolhouse and the two sides fought a hot skirmish for nearly two hours. Dozens of Federals were killed, captured or wounded before retreating back to Tarboro. They regrouped and prepared to rejoin the main body, which by now was returning to New Bern. Before departing at about five o'clock that afternoon, they fired the town and the

Opposite: Clark kept a healthy supply of wines and spirits at his home, some of which he distilled himself. When Hilma was looted by Federal soldiers in July 1863, Clark was pleased to discover that the marauding troops had left untouched several bottles of his "Old Nick" whiskey. (North Carolina Collection, University of North Carolina Library at Chapel Hill.)

ESTABLISHED 1768.

OLD NICK WILLIAMS' TEN YEAR OLD

KEEP CARD.

IN THREE CENTURIES.

Established in the 18th, covered every day of the 19th, and growing in popularity in this, the 20th, Century. That's the record of **The Old Nick Williams Whiskies**—133 years under the proprietorship of son, grandson and great-grandson of Col. Joseph Williams, the Revolutionary hero who began it when **quality not quantity was** their object. **No** other such record in the **World. No** other such Whiskey in the **World**—formula **150 years old. Not a minutes** headache in a barrel. With our reputation to protect we will not ship it until passed through nine immense and densely packed filterers which makes it today the finest whiskey in America. You can buy whiskey, **so-called,** for less than we offer it, but you **don't get what you expect.** If you care **nothing** for your health, then use **medicated** cheap stuff. **No brands** on packages, billed **as canned fruit** or merchandise if you prefer. One, two, three and five gallon packages in jug department, and nothing less than one gallon shipped from it. In case goods nothing less than (12) twelve full quarts though **they may be** an assortment of the varieties. A case is twelve quarts or twenty-four pints.

Name of Goods.	Price per Gal.	Price per Qt.	Price per Case	Name of Goods.	Price per Gal.	Price per Qt.	Price per Case
Rye, 10 years old	$4.70	1.25	15.00	Wheat, 6 years old	3.00	.82½	9.00
" 8 "	3.85	1.04	12.48	" 4 "	2.50	.70	8.40
" 6 "	3.20	.87½	10.50	Sour Mash, 8 "	4.00	1.07½	12.90
" 4 "	2.70	.75	9.00	" 6 "	3.00	.82½	9.90
" 3 "	2.40	.67½	8.10	Peach Bd'y, 10 yrs. old	7.00	1.82½	21.90
" 2 "	2.20	.62½	7.50	" " 4 "	3.50	.95	11.40
" 1 "	2.00	.57½	6.90	" " 1 "	2.50	.70	8.40
Corn, 10 "	3.75	1.01½	12.18	Apple " 10 "	6.00	1.57½	18.90
" 8 "	3.10	.85	10.20	" " 4 "	3.00	.82½	9.90
" 6 "	2.50	.70	8.40	" " 1 "	2.00	.57½	6.90
" 4 "	2.20	.62½	7.50	Blackb'ry Brandy	1.00	.34	4.00
" 3 "	2.00	.57½	6.90	" " extra fine	1.80	.52¼	6.30
" 2 "	1.80	.52½	6.30	Cherry Bounce, 8 yr old	4.00	1.07½	12.90
" 1 "	1.60	.47½	5.70	Rock and Rye	2.00	.57½	6.90
Bourbon, 10 yr's old	4.70	1.25	15.00	" " extra fine	3.00	.82½	9.90
" 6 "	3.00	.82½	9.00	Peach and Honey	2.00	.57½	6.90
" 4 "	2.50	.70	8.40	" " extra fine	3.50	.59	11.40

No extra cost for vessels or anything else.   Read carefully—Instructions in ordering.

Terms strictly cash with order or one dollar in part payment must be enclosed as evidence of good faith for payment of balance on a C. O. D. shipment; *though if good reference is* furnished we ship you goods direct. *If you remit full amount with order* we will allow *two per cent. discount* from above prices. Remit by New York exchange, post-office or express money order, or enclose currency or stamps in a registered letter. *If you prefer,* make your *money orders* or *checks payable* to or *address registered letters* to N. G. Williams, who is our president. Our goods are so securely packed that *they will ship hundreds of miles without breaking.* Shall we ship by *express or freight,* and to what place? With the very cheap through freight rates from our point your goods will not cost much. Mail us a list giving name and post-office of *every* person that uses whiskey in any shape and we will mail each one a *price list* in *plain* envelope without intimating where we got their names. Send in big orders. Costs no more to register one hundred dollars than ten dollars. Freight and express are cheaper on large lots.

Yours truly,   **THE OLD NICK WILLIAMS CO.**
         Or address **Lock Box, No. 11, Williams, N. C.**

References—Every bank in North Carolina, your bank or banker, R. G. Dun & Co., State officers at Raleigh, N. C., our postmaster and express agent, North Carolina Senators and Congressmen at Washington, D. C.

bridge, preventing the Confederates from crossing. Moving quickly, several rebel officers were able to ford the river and rally the townspeople to help douse the fires that threatened to overtake and destroy everything. Governor Clark was among the volunteer firefighters, and he "passed the first bucket to extinguish the blaze." By eight o'clock that evening, the fires were put out and the bridge hastily repaired. Although he did not engage in any fighting, this experience at Tarboro made clear to Clark, as a civilian, the war's destructive power.[9]

Most days in Tarboro, however, passed uneventfully. Clark spent much of his time at Hilma, farming and attending to business and his many local duties, including service as justice of the peace and chairman of the county court. Both were powerful positions. The county was the primary political unit of local government until the state was forced to revise its constitution in 1868. Until that time, there were no townships or municipal authorities such as mayor or city manager. The traditional structure of local government had changed very little since 1728, when seven of the eight lord proprietors sold their claims to the king. After American independence, the state governor appointed justices to each county — usually local men of property and standing. Justices held court several times a year, typically once a quarter, to transact official business, and they met as a body in January to plan the yearly calendar and select a chairman. The chairman was generally the most respected and experienced justice. The justices administered county affairs and appointed the sheriff, constable and coroner until these positions became popularly elected. However, they continued to appoint the clerk of court, register of deeds, county attorney and treasurer.[10]

The court performed other administrative functions, including assessing taxes, supervising internal improvement projects such as roads and bridges, granting licenses to taverns, and erecting and controlling mills (Clark owned at least one mill himself). It supervised local law enforcement and its own administrative officers, including the county surveyor and the wardens of the poor. In its judicial capacity, the court heard civil cases and was responsible for probate, guardianships, and the administration of estates. It had jurisdiction in most criminal cases, except murder and other major crimes. This system of local government was undemocratic, and voters had no direct control over the court or the appointment of the chairman.[11]

As court chairman, Clark once again enforced the law and supported state and Confederate directives when such cases fell under his jurisdiction. He jailed deserters in local stockades and turned over other violators of the law to the proper authorities. He also supervised the selling of bonds for the war effort. Neither the Confederacy nor the United States had a central bank to direct monetary policy; hence, local and state banks often issued their own bonds or currency no matter how insolvent they might be. Liquidity was a problem in much of the South and many local banks resorted to selling bonds, often payable in state or Confederate notes. On April 2, 1864, Clark supervised the selling of "Fifty Thousand dollars of Edgecombe County Bonds." As with many Confederate bonds, these were sold in five hundred dollar denominations at six percent interest, "payable in 15 to 20 years."[12]

6. "That Odious Constitution"

He also learned to live with shortages of basic commodities. Though comfortable before the war, the Clarks now felt its hardships. Mary complained to her sister of living "hand to mouth" and the former governor even took to wearing wooden shoes. Leather and cloth were scarce, and his nephew recalled his surprise at seeing his uncle "wearing a pair of 'wooden-soled shoes' [of the type] very considerably used for negroes whose work was in the fields." By this example, Clark "encouraged all efforts to find new means and sources for the supply of common wants." Though many necessities were difficult to procure, Clark's family was never hungry or destitute. He sold several slaves and prepared his family for possible financial ruin. As early as September 1862 he had asked R. R. Bridgers about the high prices slaves were bringing in the Richmond markets. But the war's effects on the economy touched everyone. Although his "means were greatly reduced," he was able to keep his home.[13]

His liquid assets, however, did not survive the war. For years Clark had managed "a trust fund belonging to citizens of Rhode Island." His connection to Rhode Island came from his Tarboro cousin John Mathewson, whose father, Nathan, was a native of Providence and had married into the Toole family in 1794. Nathan became very wealthy through investing heavily in slaves, and he established a trust fund.[14] The fund was turned over to Clark probably after Nathan's death in 1832 and under his management grew to fourteen thousand dollars by 1861. But soon after the war began the Confederate Congress passed the Sequestration Act, which seized all Union property "held, owned, possessed, or enjoyed by or for an alien enemy." As historian Daniel Hamilton has noted, "Families were required to offer up to court officers property belonging to children and siblings living in the North. Lawyers, bankers, brokers, and businesses were made to open their books to reveal any property located in the South belonging to Northern clients or partners." Clark obeyed the law. He informed the government and the entire fund was confiscated. Richmond, in effect, became "the new creditor for any debt owed by a Confederate citizen to an alien enemy;" thus, the fund was lost in the ruin of the South. To Clark's credit, he paid back every penny "to the Rhode Island creditors promptly" out of his own pocket, leaving his family "very limited and restricted" for many years after the war.[15]

The last major Civil War battle in North Carolina was fought March 19–21, 1365, at Bentonville. Three weeks later, Union forces marched into Raleigh. Governor Vance — who had fled the capital — would later be arrested and taken to a Washington, D.C., prison, where he would remain for several weeks. On April 26, seventeen days after the Battle of Appomattox in Virginia, Gen. Joseph E. Johnston surrendered his army to Gen. William T. Sherman and the Confederacy was no more. More than forty thousand North Carolinians were dead; the psychological and property damages were immense. Though Clark's children were too young for military service, several other family members had lost their lives on the battlefield or returned home wounded. His brother-in-law, Col. Francis Marion Parker of the Thirtieth North Carolina, saw heavy action and was wounded at Antietam. During the same battle, Clark's "cousin Larry" had been "shot by a sharpshooter through the head" and "died immediately in Cousin Joseph's arms — [he] never spoke."[16] The war was over, and much had changed.

Antebellum Edgecombe County had been one of the most prosperous and wealthy counties in the state. Tarboro was one of North Carolina's largest (and by some estimates the prettiest) of towns. It boasted a level of refinement and culture that rivaled or outdid other communities its size. The value of the county's lands and its agricultural output was the envy of the state. According to Alan D. Watson, "By 1855 Edgecombe's agricultural prosperity was such that only two counties in the state contributed more tax monies."[17] This wealth and culture, however, had been built upon slave labor, and the future of the county, and that of the Clark family, looked very different after 1865.

Ten thousand Edgecombe County slaves — three hundred and fifty thousand in North Carolina — were free. The Clarks, like many planter families, lost tens of thousands of dollars at the emancipation of their bondsmen. The social and economic bedrock of the Old South had been shattered forever. A white man's wealth and standing in the community — his "manhood"— had once been determined by his mastery of slaves and ownership of land, but now some land owners lost their farms at public auction while others sold their lands to northern businessmen. Property in man was abolished, and many of Edgecombe County's slaves responded to this change in status by walking away from their former masters. They took to the roads in search of loved ones who lived on other farms or plantations. Others left the county and even the state to find their wives, husbands, or children who had been "sold down the river." Some went north or west looking for work, escaping from their memories of bondage. For weeks scores of African Americans simply walked, experiencing the liberty to move about without the fear of an overseer's lash or harassment by an abusive slave patrol squad. Some freedmen settled near Union army camps where they might find protection or obtain food and other supplies. Others settled on uninhabited lands (often bottom lands near rivers prone to flooding) to start a new life.[18]

Residents at the time, both black and white, experienced a wide range of emotions: excitement and joy, fear and confusion, hatred, anxiety, and hope. Everything was in flux. The old social order, carefully constructed over two centuries and built upon slavery and its inherent racial caste system, had changed. Former masters did not understand why their slaves had rejected their "protection" and "care" by leaving them. They interpreted this abandonment as ingratitude and insolence. Freedmen, on the other hand, were eager to exert their newfound rights. They renamed themselves, got married, started their own churches and schools, and set to work rebuilding their lives. Though owners eventually accepted emancipation, they did not accept their former slaves as their social equals. Violent confrontations might erupt if blacks "talked back" or failed to defer to a white, and freedmen were sometimes jailed or whipped for the slightest breach of racial etiquette. As one authority on slavery, Ira Berlin, has noted, "The violence that accompanied emancipation led both black and white to withdraw into separate worlds."[19] Though whites and blacks attempted to separate themselves socially, economically their lives were bound together. The transition from slavery to freedom would be difficult as whites and blacks renegotiated their social and economic future.[20]

One of the first transitions to negotiate was labor. Seed needed planting. Fences and barns needed repair. Fields needed tending. Farms needed workers; but as free men, former slaves demanded public recognition of their manhood. They wanted cash payments for their labor. They wanted respect. Like their former white masters, black men too felt the need to protect their dependents. But the war's dislocations, shortages and economic hardships drove many of them back onto their old plantations and the mercy of their former masters.[21] Hopes of "forty acres and a mule" and all that it entailed — independence, land ownership, a new world order — came to nothing. Whites retained the land. They owned the tools, seed, animals, cash and access to credit. Freedmen had little choice but to leave or accept indenture.

The Freedman's Bureau — or more properly, the Bureau of Refugees, Freedmen and Abandoned Lands — was established in March 1865 to aid in the South's reconstruction. One of its many responsibilities included the supervision of labor contracts. These contracts, however, satisfied no one. As historian John David Smith has said, "The Freedmen's Bureau seemed to fit the bill in guiding the transition from slavery to freedom for both the former slaves and their ex-masters. Unfortunately, neither side found the government's involvement in economic Reconstruction satisfactory."[22] Many northern whites hoped to impose market-driven wage labor practices on the South, while white southerners sought to retain as much control as possible over their workers. Many whites doubted the efficiency of black workers, believing coercion was necessary to make them productive. As one correspondent bluntly told Clark after the war: "If they [the freedmen] are to be helpful to us, let us keep them in a state of bondage as their carelessness, shiftlessness, and want of desire to excel will certainly place them."[23] Former masters resented entering into contracts that limited their prerogatives (like whipping), while African Americans bristled at any restrictions to their freedom (like yearlong contracts). Neither side, however, had much choice but temporarily to abide by Federal government directives.[24]

Many of Clark's former slaves did just that. Several black families went to work for him but their condition was little improved from their slave days. The nearest bureau field office was in Rocky Mount — about twenty miles to the west — and as an attorney himself, Clark drew up his own contracts (and for other farmers too), though they were similar to others of the day. Typically the term ran from January to January and required workers "to remain till the expiration of the contract," a provision especially resented by the freedmen. Clark provided food, housing, and "half stock of mules and hogs," while "freedmen and women ... agreed to do all kinds of labor common to the farm, to obey all regulations proper for the government of the farm, to render the amount of labor cheerfully that is usual for their capacity." Wages were paid monthly, but laborers "agreed that one half of the amount due shall be retained till end of each year." However, if any terms of the contract were violated: "the amount due as wages at the time of the violation shall be forfeited." Any number of infractions could constitute a violation, and the contract favored the landowner. Its language was broad enough to ensure that laborers had as little bargaining power as possible. For example, terms like "the refusal to perform the proper amount of work" or a "failure to act faithfully and promptly" gave the hirer much latitude to withhold wages or void the contract if necessary. As in slave days, certain necessities were provided. Clark agreed to "furnish the men with four pounds of pork or its equivalent and one peck of meal a week." Women and children received slightly less. Clark generously allowed his workers "to get wood when needed" and granted them hunting rights as long as they did not "shoot about the house and yard."[25]

By the standards of the day, Clark was charitable in some ways. With emancipation, blacks could no longer count on receiving housing or food, but he provided these, and also allowed them the use of firearms to hunt game on his land. Five years after the war, according to the 1870 Federal Census, at least two black families still lived on his property, with one even assuming the Clark surname.[26] But however charitable he might have been, his contracts made no provision for medical care or clothing, nor did they specify dollar amounts or crop allotments in place of (or supplements to) cash wages. In these respects, his contracts differed slightly from indentures negotiated by the Freedman's Bureau. Bureau contracts varied widely, but might contain provisions that protected freedmen from abuse or prescribed a worker's monthly wage in a specific dollar amount or share of the harvest. There might be some provision for the elderly or infirm. Stipulations for medical care or clothing were not uncommon. Clark retained half the wages for the year, while other employers retained perhaps a third. He required laborers to "go to work in the morning halfway from sunrise," but set no quitting time. Though agricultural work demanded long working days, traditionally Sunday, at least a portion of it, might be reserved for rest, but Clark made no provisions for work stoppages or time off.[27]

Farmers and planters objected to the bureau, and they especially resented its efforts to enforce contract provisions that freedmen believed the planter may have violated. Bureau agents protected laborers from the exploitation which could occur, especially after the harvest. As one black politician testified to Congress, "The planters would make arrangements with [freedmen] and fail to perform their part of the contract. The contract specified that the planter should be allowed to retain one-half the monthly salary; they would retain it until the cotton was picked and then manage to get into a quarrel with them and drive them away without paying."[28] While Clark may or may not have "picked a quarrel" with his workers over wages, the practice obviously occurred with some frequency throughout the South.

Bureau agents, however, were not always sympathetic to the freedmen and their plight. Most of them were soldiers, not relief workers. They held racial prejudices common to most white Americans of the nineteenth century. Agents sometimes sided with farmers, or turned a blind eye to contract violations or physical abuses like whipping. Many freedmen, however, remained hopeful. They continued to hold on to the belief that the federal government would confiscate the lands of former Confederates and parcel it out to ex-slaves. President Andrew Johnson's Reconstruction plan should have divested them of these notions.

Johnson was a North Carolinian by birth but ran away to Tennessee in his youth. He was the same age as Clark (born in 1808) but unlike Clark, Johnson knew poverty and deprivation, and he worked hard to pull himself out of it. He showed talent as a stump speaker

6. "That Odious Constitution"

and entered politics in the 1840s as a Jacksonian Democrat, championing the common man and vilifying the planter aristocracy. He was the lone southern senator to remain in Congress after the Civil War began, and his loyalty to the Union was rewarded by the Republican Party, which nominated him for vice-president in 1864. Though he was not without intelligence or courage, many contemporaries described Johnson as obstinate and petty, and he rarely made concessions or took advice. He was sensitive to criticism and moved uncomfortably in the circles of high office and power. These character traits would prove his undoing as president.[29]

Like Lincoln, Johnson wanted to restore the southern states as functioning members of the Union as soon as possible, and his plan to do so did not include African Americans or certain former Confederates. He issued several proclamations outlining his reconstruction policy: the first came on May 29, 1865, and it applied to the whole South. He pardoned all ex-Confederates except for those who fell under fourteen exceptions, which included "all persons who held the pretended offices of governors of States in insurrection against the United States." He also denied amnesty to "all persons who have voluntarily participated in said rebellion and the estimated value of whose taxable property is over $20,000."[30] Clark could not receive a pardon on either of those two conditions (though he quibbled whether he fit in the latter category). He had lost his slaves, his real property was in jeopardy of seizure, and he might be arrested and charged with treason — without clemency he was outside of the law. Proscribed southerners "were without assurances that any civil rights would be allowed them.... He could neither acquire nor transfer property, and found it difficult to secure employment and otherwise engage in business."[31]

Middle-class and poor white southerners were relieved at Johnson's leniency, but men of property were nervous. Shortly before assuming the presidency, Johnson had condemned rich planters and secessionist politicians for starting a needless, criminal war, declaring, "I would arrest them — I would try them — I would convict them and I would hang them," and his first proclamation seemed to confirm a tough line on those two groups. For weeks, those excluded from Johnson's amnesty waited anxiously to see whether he would unsheathe the "avenging sword of the Republic" and have them condemned as traitors. They found some encouragement, however, from the final provision in the proclamation: "Special application may be made to the President for pardon by any person belonging to the excepted classes, and such clemency will be liberally extended as may be consistent with the facts of the case." As historian Dan T. Carter has noted, "Even as he threatened with one clause, the president offered clemency with the other."[32]

Subsequent presidential proclamations applied to each individual state and, like his pardon policy, were rather charitable. Johnson began with North Carolina. William W. Holden was appointed provisional governor and a convention was called to reorganize the state's government. Anyone who had been a voter before the war and had received a pardon could vote for convention delegates in a state-wide election. This provision in effect excluded African Americans from participation since they were previously disfranchised.[33] Johnson further required the ratification of the Thirteenth Amendment abolishing slavery, repudiating Confederate debts, and officially renouncing secession. Once these conditions were met, a state would be restored to the Union — with the final approval of Congress.[34]

North Carolina met the president's conditions, but not without strong debate among convention delegates who met in Raleigh in October 1865 and immediately clashed over Johnson's plan. Debt repudiation was hotly contested. Many delegates were opposed to repudiation because it would financially ruin many individuals, banks, and the state university, all of which had invested heavily in Confederate fortunes, but Johnson held firm. He told Holden that restoration was contingent on passage of all three requirements. Despite the president's tough reply, combative delegates argued over secession's repeal. Most of the delegates were former Whigs and Unionists who had originally opposed secession, but Edgecombe County sent Judge George Howard — an "original secessionist" — to Raleigh. Like Clark, he was a member of the old Edgecombe Democracy. He had voted to leave the Union at the 1861 convention and his mind hadn't changed after four years of war. Edgecombe was one of only seven counties to oppose secession's repeal. Less contentious was the decision to hold a November election to select an interim government staffed with (in theory at least) loyal Union men. These popularly elected officials would replace the president's provisional appointees and serve for one year until the next general election.[35]

The men elected to represent North Carolina, however, were many of the same who had served the Confederacy. Former slave owners and Confederate leaders (though few original secessionists) were sent back to the state legislature. Jonathan Worth defeated Holden for governor, and William A. Graham and John Poole were sent to Washington as senators. Without his pardon, Clark was unsure of his legal status and he remained at his Tarboro home, attentively watching from the sidelines at the political scene unfolding. Like virtually all white southerners, he supported Johnson's lenient, hands-off approach to reconstruction, and he also supported the state legislature's passage of the "Black Codes." Enacted in early 1866, these codes defined the legal status of the state's newly freed African Americans, which looked very similar to antebellum laws that had defined the free black population. North Carolina's codes were less harsh than those passed in other southern states, but as was the case in all of them, political and legal equality with whites was denied. Negroes and other "persons of color" could legally marry (but not with a white) and enter into other social contracts, but they could not vote or hold office. Slavery was abolished but African Americans were reduced to second-class citizenship and servitude.[36]

The post-war South had hardly reformed itself, and the 1866 November general election only confirmed the status quo. Edgecombe County returned Clark (unpardoned) to his old, familiar senate seat and Governor Worth easily won re-election. Though a former Unionist Whig, Worth's conservative approach to race and reconstruction was popular among Democrats and the state's middle-class white population. He cautiously opposed Republicans without arousing too much resentment, and he had formed a working relationship with President Johnson and Maj. Gen. Daniel E. Sickles, the commander of the Second Military District. Worth was a hard-headed businessman whose fiscal policies as both state treasurer and governor (save money, invest wisely, and avoid waste and unnecessary debt) had earned Clark's respect.

Worth was a Randolph County Quaker from a large family. Despite his taciturn, somber personality, he had found success in business and politics and had worked with some of North Carolina's most renowned figures over a career spanning four decades. He read law under Archibald D. Murphey and eventually married Murphey's niece, which enhanced his political standing in the Whig party. He served opposite Clark in the state senate for several terms and strongly denounced Democratic policies. Although they often disagreed politically, both men respected each other and remained friendly. After the war the two men united in their contempt for Holden and the Radicals, and Clark would call on Worth frequently for help in obtaining his pardon. This process proved to be a long and exasperating ordeal.[37]

Clark was one of an increasingly small number of ex–Confederates who had not been granted clemency by mid–1866. Other, more prominent rebel leaders "were pardoned by the scores" before the anniversary of Johnson's proclamation.[38] Indeed, the president's leniency toward proscribed southerners—with few exceptions—was well known. As early as June 1865 it was obvious that he had no intention of charging anyone with treason, and by September the White House began granting pardons "rather freely." Thus Clark thought it was odd that he had not received his. He had been seeking amnesty for some time, initially to protect his property from seizure and himself from prosecution, but as the battle for the future of Reconstruction escalated between Congress and the President, Clark became increasingly concerned about North Carolina's political future in the post-war nation. Clark was anxious to reenter politics, but he was unsure if he could legally take his senate seat without clemency.[39]

There was some confusion among those politically active former rebels who still had no presidential amnesty. William A. Graham had been elected to the state senate in November 1865, but "declined to be seated before his pardon." However, the state legislature didn't seem concerned about his unpardoned status and the next month nominated him to serve as North Carolina's senator in Washington (though Congress refused to seat him). Graham's disabilities would not be removed until 1873. Zeb Vance, who wouldn't receive clemency until March 1867, did not immediately seek political office because of his proscribed status as both a parolee and an unpardoned ex–Confederate. But there were other unpardoned rebels across the South who held public office or became politically active. Wade Hampton and other former Confederates in South Carolina sat as unpardoned delegates at that state's 1865 convention.[40]

Clark had applied for a pardon on July 17, 1865.[41] Applicants petitioned their state governor, who had the power to approve or deny the candidate. If the petition were approved, the governor forwarded the application to the attorney general in Washington, who recommended it to the president if he deemed the petitioner worthy. If the president agreed, he signed the pardon and returned it to the state governor, who forwarded it to the petitioner. The process was simple but not efficient, and the federal government's tiny bureaucracy was quickly overwhelmed by the many thousands of applications and throngs of supplicants desiring an audience with the attorney general or the president. Johnson never set up anything like a pardon bureau, or made any additional proclamations for two years; thus, his provisional governors were given much discretion in the approval process. Unionist governors sometimes rejected or delayed pardons or made petitioners wait anxiously for months, requiring them to write countless letters inquiring of their status or begging for mercy. Provisional governor Holden was one of the worst offenders, intentionally blocking pardons and often refusing to forward them to the president as an act of political revenge against his enemies, including Clark.[42]

Though friendly acquaintances before the war, they had become bitter enemies after Holden publicly questioned Clark's wartime leadership in the pages of the Raleigh *Standard*. The influential editor had initially advocated the "southern position" and opposed Congressional interference with slavery as early as 1840. Only months after the Civil War began, he broke from the Democrats and supported the Conservative Party, calling for better management of the war effort. He later led the state's peace movement and ran for governor in 1864 against Vance—the same man he had practically made governor two years earlier. Clark found Holden's political flip-flopping and naked ambition repugnant. Southern men like Holden, Clark told Worth, were "selfish, tyrannical, and Ishmaelitish, abandoned [and] devoid of even a pretense of virtue."[43] When Holden ran for governor in 1864 and again in 1865, Clark campaigned against him in Edgecombe County. Now it was Holden's turn at the screw and he suppressed Clark's pardon.

Clark, however, was "promised" his petition would be given the governor's "immediate attention." But several months passed and he had heard nothing of its progress. In December 1865, he wrote directly to North Carolina's Senator-elect John Poole asking about his petition. Poole replied, "I went to the Office of the Att[orney] General to look after your application for pardon ... hoping to find your name on [the list]. But not finding it there as I expected, I imagined why it was not." He told him that the president was not inclined to pardon him at the moment and suggested that he contact Worth, advising, "I have reason to believe that a recommendation from Gov. Worth would be of some service to you. Get him to push the matter for you, and I am satisfied I can have the case acted on very shortly."[44]

Governor Worth had come into office that December, replacing Holden, and he soon discovered a filing cabinet containing more than three hundred suppressed pardon requests.[45] He quickly forwarded them to the attorney general's office, where Clark's petition was officially filed on January 29, 1866. When Holden was asked about the pardon, he reportedly told Poole that it "was nothing against" Clark but rather, "he would never under no circumstances recommend Gov. Vance for clemency," and to approve Clark without also approving Vance "would expose him to the assault of Vance's friends." Clark thought this a poor excuse and believed Holden's actions were done in bad faith and "showed plainly that [he] was taking care of himself."[46]

Clark was convinced that his case had been "prejudiced" and that he was being punished by Johnson for Holden's misdeeds. He told Worth, "I can not believe that the President has designed my little property to the confiscator or my head to the block, yet such would seem the case.... As far as [he] knew I stood as one who declined or repelled his proffered amnesty."[47] Though Holden had doubtless injured his cause, the unrepentant attitude Clark expressed in his pardon letter probably had as much to do with the delay as anything else. In the letter which accompanied the original petition and explained why he sought amnesty, Clark told the president: "[I was] taught from my youth that the Declaration of Independence 1776 proclaimed the inalienable right of a people to alter, amend or abolish or institute anew their form of government." But only after the South had been "overcome by force" did he submit to the authority of the United States government. "If I have erred," he said, "the error was in behalf of liberty and my country."[48] His petition remained on file in the attorney general's office.

Six months passed. In June 1866, Worth wrote to a friend in the attorney general's office asking if there were anything he could do to expedite the pardon. Worth was told to "write a separate statement in respect to [Clark] and give such facts as would show the President that he is a worthy cause for clemency."[49] He did so, this time personally recommending him to the president, saying, "I have long known Gov. Clark, and though differing with him on national politics, I have always regard[ed] him as 'the noblest work of God,' an honest man. I have no doubt of his loyalty and I earnestly recommend that his pardon be granted."[50] The president, however, remained unconvinced.

The year 1866 passed into 1867 and Clark was beginning to think he might not ever get a pardon. "I am," he thought, "one of the few that the President seems to have censored for punishment as a public enemy.... To be singled out thus among so many more distinguished and eminent than myself to suffer the martyrdom for the 'lost cause' is a high and perhaps unmerited compliment."[51] The situation was becoming desperate for him and he feared that "any delay might throw [the President's] pardoning power into Radical hands." His senate colleague and member of the "North Carolina delegation," James Madison Leach, stepped in and wrote to the attorney general, Henry Stanbery, on January 21, 1867, saying, "I beg you to recommend [Clark] to the President for pardon. He is in the Senate, at least elected, and feels a delicacy in holding a seat unpardoned." Finally convinced (and exasperated), Stanbery approved Clark's petition two days later, and wrote to Johnson, "I heartily believe, Sir, that Mr. Clark deserves a pardon." But the president again refused him amnesty.[52]

If for no other reason, Clark needed a pardon to officially conduct personal business and execute his will. He pleaded to be "unshackled" so that his "little property might be secured" to his young children.[53] Worth tried one last time on his behalf in March 1867. "I mentioned to you when in Washington," he said to the president, "a subject about certain persons about which I may have troubled you too often—but so firm are my convictions that I trust you will pardon me for once more calling your attention to it." The governor said that he would be glad to see the "estimable" Clark pardoned, though he admitted that he was a "secessionist and favored the measures which led to the rebellion."[54] But Worth's entreaties were unconvincing. It would take a personal meeting between Johnson and Clark to finally convince the president of Clark's loyalty.

Johnson met Clark during his June 1867 visit to North Carolina. The president had been invited by the City of Raleigh to attend the dedication of a monument to his father, Jacob. His visit would coincide with graduation ceremonies at Chapel Hill, and the state university asked him to speak at their commencement exercises. He agreed to both invitations. In preparation for Johnson's visit, Worth asked Clark and other former executives to join an official state delegation to accompany the president on his tour; but Clark declined the invitation, saying it would be "indelicate" for him to greet Johnson in any capacity as an unpardoned ex-rebel governor. However, he did agree to meet Worth in Chapel Hill since he was required to attend commencement as a representative of the legislature, which had imposed upon him a public trust. Therefore, in that capacity he would "have the opportunity of witnessing the interesting scene of the President's visit."[55]

Commencement was held on Thursday, June 6, and Clark sat in front of the main stage along with his associates of the Legislative Committee. An imposing assembly sat before them, including the president, Secretary of State William H. Seward, Maj. Gen. Sickles, and other dignitaries. The event was filled with speeches, honorariums, and festivities, and was widely reported in the newspapers. Johnson met with Clark at some point — probably at Johnson's induction ceremony into the university's Dialectic Society — and what passed between them and other parties is unknown. But an impression was made and it was effective. Johnson departed Chapel Hill the next day arriving in Washington late on Saturday the Eighth. After a Sunday rest, he was back at work Monday morning and signed Clark's pardon. It was June 10, 1867.[56]

Although Clark thought it "a delicate matter" to serve in the senate unpardoned, his actions proved otherwise. He arrived at the Capitol on November 19, 1866, the first day the General Assembly convened, exhibited his credentials and was qualified according to the law. He accepted his senate seat and served for the five-month duration of the legislative session. If any "delicacies" remained, the legislature pardoned its own on December 22, 1866, granting amnesty to all Confederate civil and military personnel in the state, and authorized the governor to extend clemency to "such persons as in his judgment the peace, quiet and good order of the State of North Carolina may require."[57]

Clark was a very active senate member and, given his long experience and role as former governor, a natural leader for the other legislators. "In his addresses before the State Senate," it was recalled, Clark "drew the people to him and from his lips they heard words of wisdom."[58] As a veteran senator, he made motions and introduced legislation and amendments. For example, he proposed that the stealing of horses and mules be made a capital offense. The bill passed, to the approbation of the planters and the consternation of the northern press.[59] Clark also served on six committees. His committee assignments reflect his expertise: rules of order, corporations, agriculture, library, education, and amendment. Two of these committees — education and amendment — were joint assignments with the House of Commons. The first concerned the state university at Chapel Hill; the second the Fourteenth Amendment to the U.S. Constitution.

The General Assembly charged the six-member education committee to find solutions to the "state University's financial crisis."⁶⁰ The war had created hardships for the school and its future was uncertain. The university had invested heavily in Confederate fortunes and its endowment was rendered worthless after the war. Accounts were in arrears and faculty salaries could not be paid.⁶¹ Desiring to see his "old Alma Mater again in full sail," Clark (ever the businessman) suggested to Governor Worth that professorships and departments be combined to reduce expenses. He opposed a reduction in salaries and believed the school should avoid any assistance from religious sources, saying, "In a State University it is desirable by all means to avoid sectarianism — to steer clear of any Church influence." But no official report from the committee was ever prepared. The legislature was abolished by the 1867 Congressional Reconstruction Acts and the committee never met again. Clark wrote to inform Worth, "For want of another meeting of the Committee a report cannot be prepared." He added, "But your body has not a more devoted friend to the institution than myself." Despite this setback, he continued his efforts to help the school and encouraged William A. Graham to work diligently to reestablish Chapel Hill as a true university "*in fact* as well as name." "I feel a very great interest in our University," Clark admitted, "and I feel that its revival, if it ever succeeds, will owe it to your exertions." The university, however, closed in 1870 and did not reopen until 1875.⁶²

As a senator, however, Clark was more determined to resist at the state level a Congressional takeover of Reconstruction. He worried that "radical" Republicans in Washington might wrest control from the president and force a hard peace on the South. Indeed, by 1866 Congress was in open revolt against Johnson. They believed that the state governments supposedly restored under his policies remained disloyal; they refused to recognize his reconstruction plan without stronger safeguards to protect the freedmen. Johnson's refusal to cooperate with Congress drove many moderate Republicans into the radical wing of the party. Believing that Negro suffrage could be a bulwark against a recalcitrant white South, Congress drew up several laws, including the Fourteenth Amendment, to ensure the inclusion of African Americans in the American body politic.

The Fourteenth Amendment extended citizenship to African Americans, provided "equal protection of the laws," and prohibited states from abridging one's civil rights. It further stated that no person who had sworn an oath to uphold the United States Constitution and then supported the Confederacy could hold any civil or military office. That provision would turn out former Confederate leaders like Clark from state and local government, making them ineligible to officially participate in the process of reconstruction. Congress sent the amendment to the states for ratification in June 1866, over President Johnson's veto.

North Carolina legislators met in November and formed a joint select committee to evaluate the amendment and submit a resolution recommending its acceptance or rejection. Clark was appointed to this thirteen-member body and was a key committee member. He worked closely with its chairman, James Madison Leach, and on December 6 they presented to the Senate a lengthy, strongly worded, and unrepentant resolution that recommended rejection. They considered the Fourteenth Amendment illegal on the grounds that the "eleven seceding states" were "deprived of representation" in Congress and had "no voice" in the amendment's proposal. The amendment violated a state's right to regulate suffrage, argued the resolution, which added that "negroes can not wisely exercise the right" and "should not be allowed to vote." Legislators were angry that the amendment would take away their right to vote or hold office and declared that its ratification would impose a "deeper humiliation" upon North Carolina.[63]

After the resolution's reading, the document was printed and a copy given to each legislator. On December 13, a vote was called and the Senate rejected the Fourteenth Amendment by a vote of forty-five to one. Clark immediately motioned to "transmit the report and resolution to the House of Commons." It passed, and on December 14 the House likewise voted down the amendment and sent it back to Congress unratified. Like North Carolina, every former Confederate state, except Tennessee, had rejected the Fourteenth Amendment. Their refusal to accept it convinced Congress that stronger measures were needed.[64]

In March 1867 Congress passed the Reconstruction Acts, placing those states which had rejected the amendment under military rule. These acts invalidated state governments in the South and required two conditions to be met before they could be readmitted to the Union: ratification of the Fourteenth Amendment, and new state constitutions granting suffrage to all males over the age of twenty-one regardless of race. Once these two conditions were met, military rule would end and the state would be restored to the Union.[65]

Although regular state government continued to operate, the military held ultimate power and could override any directive from civilian authorities, including the state's courts and governor. Officials were appointed to fill vacant state offices and new voters were registered. Once their registration was complete, the military would order an election to be held to select delegates to serve in the state's constitutional convention. These acts immediately placed political disabilities on Clark—he could not vote for delegates or hold any political office until the state was readmitted to the Union. Though Clark was officially proscribed, he was consulted by both civil and military leaders to recommend appointees to state offices. The state's military leader, Maj. Gen. Sickles, made the final decision in all appointments but he was a cooperative man who permitted some latitude to the state's civilian authority, Governor Worth, in selecting qualified persons. Worth enlisted Clark's help to find eligible men to serve as registers, asking him to "try and find some men who will be more acceptable to your people than negroes or Yankees." Worth requested local men, or at least "some Northern men, who are not mean radicals" to serve, and especially asked Clark to not recommend any "Home Radical Confiscation Holden men."[66]

Clark obliged Worth but found it difficult to recommend anyone who met with Worth's (or his own) approval. He told the governor that no one who was a resident of Edgecombe County during the war was eligible to take a loyalty oath and serve as a register. Worth therefore did not make any recommendations to Sickles and thus the military stepped in and nominated three local black men—Simonton (no first name given), David Harris, and

6. "That Odious Constitution"

Thomas Newton — to fill a vacancy in the Tarboro precinct. Authorities sent a "Lieutenant Allison" to Tarboro to consult with Clark about the candidates. Clark told Allison that the "deportment and sentiments" of the three men recommended were "very fair and proper," and that they had not engaged in any "collisions" between the races. He added that the two races had "got along remarkably well" in Edgecombe County since the end of the war, and that "the colored are generally kept at work."[67]

The registration process was completed by October 1867 and the military ordered a November election for convention delegates. Every North Carolinian was anxious. Concerned citizens had been watching the political drama unfold since March when military rule began. Old Whigs and traditionalist Democrats like Clark joined together to resist congressional reconstruction and called themselves the "Conservative Party." African Americans, northern emigrants, and a significant minority of southern whites who opposed the established leadership of the planters came together to support the Republicans. Thousands of African Americans were registered to vote, but they never came close to holding a majority; there were thirty thousand more whites registered than blacks. Northern emigrants were influential beyond their small numbers. They were generally educated and politically experienced Republicans in areas where such traits were scarce.[68]

The Constitutional Convention of 1868 sat in session from January to March. Of its one hundred and twenty delegates, thirteen were Conservatives, fifteen were African-American, and eighteen were northerners. The vast majority of the delegates were native white Republicans, and the constitution they produced made significant changes to state and local government. The governor would hold the office for four years instead of two. It provided for a lieutenant governor elected by the people to succeed the governor in the case of death or disability. The lieutenant governor would also preside over the Senate, taking power away from its members to elect their own presiding officer. Senators would be elected from districts redrawn by population and not by wealth. The House of Commons was renamed the House of Representatives. The most significant proposal would alter the state's local government system, taking lawmaking power away from appointed justices and giving it to popularly elected boards of county commissioners. Townships were created in the counties. Judges would be elected and more cases would be tried in Superior Court. State schools were to be equal and open to the public — black or white — and interracial marriages were not officially proscribed. The 1868 state constitution was designed to give more power to more people.[69]

Clark despised the proposed constitution. He resented military rule and the reforms forced upon North Carolina by the Congressional Reconstruction Acts, and he opposed the racial equality and "northern ideas" that threatened to modernize the region's social, political, and economic traditions. He served on the executive committee of a local political group calling itself the "Conservatives of Edgecombe," dedicated to opposing the "odious [state] Constitution which the people will probably soon be called on to ratify." Clark and his committee pledged to "use every honorable means for the success of the party opposed to Radical rule in North Carolina."[70]

But his efforts failed. In April 1868 a general election was held to ratify the proposed constitution and select new state and national officers. Conservatives nominated Thomas S. Ashe for governor after Zeb Vance refused to run, while the Republicans nominated William W. Holden. Many Conservatives, however, did not vote. They believed Congress would propose an even tougher reconstruction plan if the constitution were defeated, and so many of them stayed away from the polls. Voters approved the new constitution and elected Holden by a wide majority. Republicans captured both houses of the General Assembly and won six of North Carolina's seven Congressional seats. Governor Holden called a special session of the legislature to approve the Fourteenth Amendment, which it ratified on July 4. Three weeks later Congress sat North Carolina's delegation and the state was officially restored to the Union.

The Conservatives lost the election but were not defeated. Many of them joined or supported the terror tactics of the Ku Klux Klan, which intimidated, threatened, and occasionally murdered Republicans and African Americans. There are no records that tell of Clark's thoughts or involvement (if any) with the Klan, but Col. William L. Saunders, the alleged leader and "Grand Dragon" of the North Carolina KKK, was his nephew by marriage. The two men corresponded, and given Clark's Democratic pedigree, racial views, and associations, it's very likely he supported the Klan to some degree. Governor Holden responded to the Klan with force in several counties, but he overreached his constitutional authority when he arrested political opponents and newspaper editors like Josiah Turner, who had criticized publicly Holden's tactics to suppress lawlessness. The results of the Kirk-Holden War aroused great interest for the 1870 elections, and many Conservatives thought they had a good chance to take control of the legislature. They believed a Conservative majority would impeach Holden for his alleged abuses of office and turn back the reforms initiated by the Republicans.[71]

Clark supported the overthrow of Holden and the "radical regime," and his local canvassing efforts against the Republicans were more successful in the next election. The Conservatives took control of the legislature in 1870 and Holden was impeached and turned out of office the next year. Clark proclaimed, "In the midst of bayonets and military prisons we have achieved a signal and bloodless victory with no crime on our hands and no blood on our flag. While we are proud of our people, we may safely trust them in the great contest for civil liberty."[72]

The Conservatives strengthened their legislative majorities in 1872 and the era of "redemption" was well on its way to completion. Clark continued to work with the Conservatives throughout this period from 1868 until 1872. He was elected to the board of county commissioners in 1868 and served as a local delegate to the state Conservative Party convention in 1871. As a delegate to that meeting, Clark supported the adoption of the party's slogan: "increased taxation and ruin."[73] Clark objected to increased taxation because landowners paid a disproportionate amount of the taxes that funded services which primarily benefited freedmen and poor whites. He also believed that these services — free public schools for both races, asylums and hospitals — fell outside the legitimate scope of government. He resented what he thought was "profligate spending" by a Republican state government allegedly awash in corruption and graft.

But by the 1870s, Clark's energy for political activity was flagging. The former governor spent most of his time after 1872 indulging his passions — history and genealogy. He corresponded about these subjects with his peers, including William A. Graham who, like Clark, spent his retirement years tracing his roots. Always an avid reader and fascinated by bloodlines, Clark was a "laborious and devoted student of the history of his state." He amassed historical records, memorabilia, and documents, and reconstructed in great detail over one hundred family tree charts — no small feat considering the poor quality of research technology and the absence of standardized records or repositories.[74]

He was also interested in writing North Carolina's history. He worked closely with John H. Wheeler, an early historian of the state and author of *Historical Sketches of North Carolina, from 1584 to 1851* (1851). Clark admired Wheeler's work (which was often pro–Democratic) and Wheeler wrote often to Clark asking him for help in tracing names and providing information about North Carolina's earliest settlers. Clark was more than happy to oblige and he told Wheeler that he was prodding the state legislature to establish a historical and genealogical register that would be the envy of the nation. "We will do everything," Clark said, "that is possible to do without money." He saved newspapers and his collection was donated to the state library. Several copies of the Raleigh *Standard* and many of the Tarboro *Free Press* and *Southerner* bear his signature. With Clark's encouragement, Wheeler established the North Carolina Historical Society in 1875, one year after Clark's death. Had he lived longer, his efforts in the field would likely have been significant. It had always been the "earnest wish of his heart to have printed the early journals of the [General] Assembly" and the early history of his state, and though he died before such works were published, Clark's nephew and secretary of state for North Carolina, Col. William L. Saunders, acknowledged his uncle's influence in preserving the state's past. He wrote in the preface to *The Colonial Records of North Carolina* that he was indebted to the influence of Clark "for the cultivation of a taste that has made bearable the years of sheer drudgery absolutely necessary to the preparation for publication" of his book.[75]

The old planter also longed for a fictional past. Drawing inspiration from Sir Walter Scott's *Ivanhoe*, Clark drafted a two-page document entitled "Regulations for the Tournament"— a medieval festival not unlike today's Renaissance fairs, complete with knights, ladies, and displays of sporting prowess. The event was held in Tarboro during the 1869 Christmas season and was a major social gathering, attended by "the fairest" spectators and participants alike from "all the adjoining counties." Fifteen men signed up for the riding competition, identifying themselves with elaborate titles such as "Knight of the Scarlet Plume" and "Knight of the Conquered Banner." The mounted "cavaliers" were given five opportunities to capture a ring with a pointed lance from a distance of ninety yards and a "time of running eight seconds." The knight who "takes the ring the greatest number of times" would win "the privilege of crowning the Queen of Love and Beauty." The "three next most successful Knights would select the 3 maids of honor." A ballroom coronation

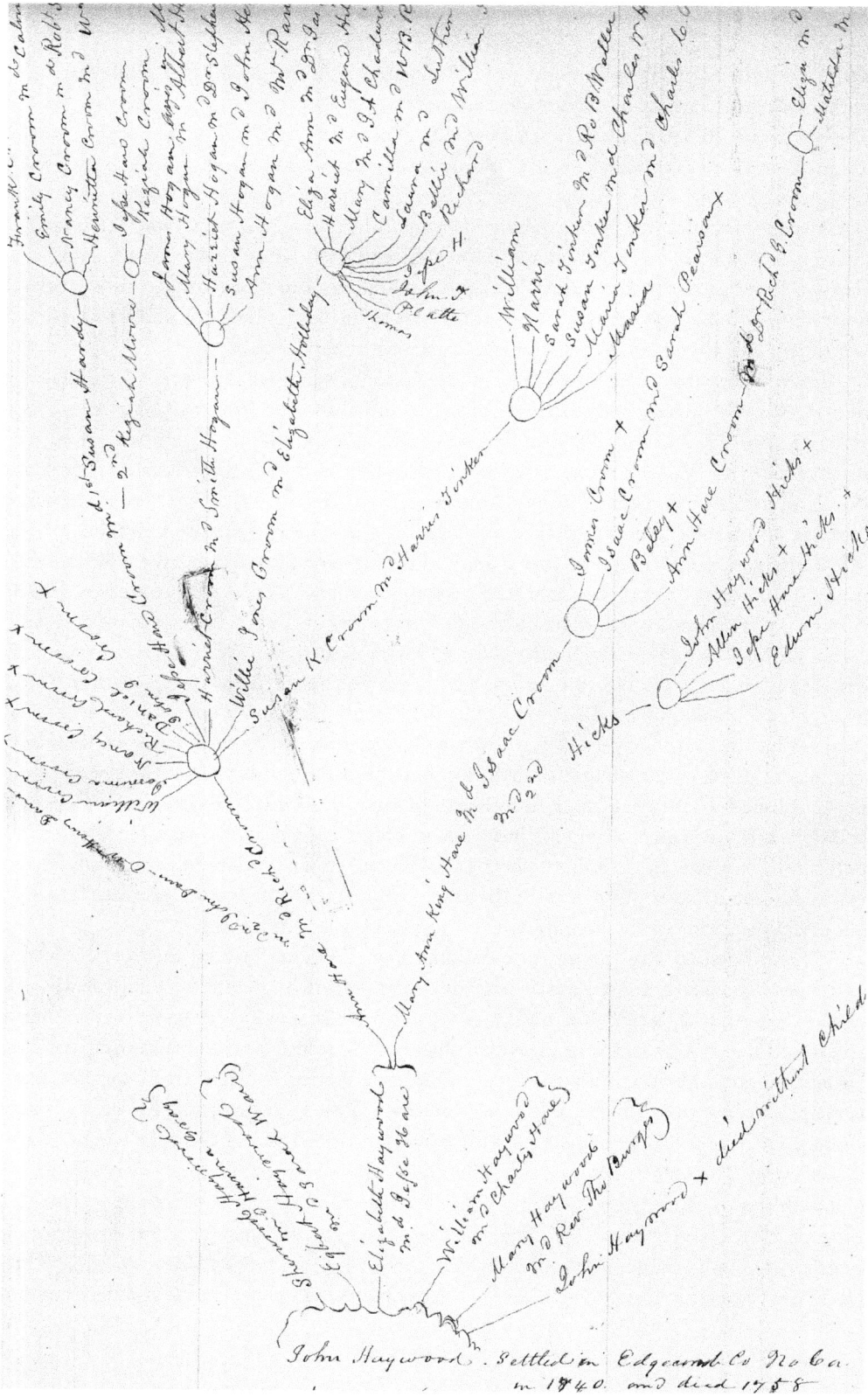

and dance was held later that evening where the "Knight of Stantonsburg" selected Clark's daughter, Laura, as First Maid of Honor. In celebration, town socialites danced the night away until "the wee hours."[76]

Although Clark may have played at enjoying the past, he lived in the present. He spent his days reading, riding horses, farming, and discussing current affairs, history and politics with friends and political leaders. He remained a respected figure both within the state and Edgecombe County, and was an active Freemason and leader in Calvary Episcopal Church. The Clarks were pious and devout people, and parishioners regarded Governor Clark as an "elder statesman" within the church. Indeed, the Clark, Parker and Toole families had been deeply involved in the life of the church since its revival in 1833. Clark's father was elected to its first vestry that year but declined to serve, having only recently returned to Tarboro from serving a two-year clerkship in Washington, D.C. There were few church members in the beginning and the congregation grew slowly from about a dozen regular communicants to thirty-three by 1858, when the church decided to erect a new building.[77]

Led by the venerable Rev. Joseph B. Cheshire, Calvary embarked on an ambitious project to build a church that would accommodate five hundred people (Tarboro's population at the time was 1,200). Parishioners elected to fund construction by subscriptions and, according to their terms, building would continue as long as the money lasted. No debt was to be contracted. Clark was one of the original subscribers and pledged two hundred and fifty dollars, which was slightly above the two hundred dollar average. By 1861 construction was nearly complete, but when the war began the windows and doors were boarded up and its bell was sent away and melted down for munitions. Building resumed in 1866 and was finished in 1867. The church and its grounds remain today as a stunning example of American Gothic.[78]

The war also divided the American Episcopal Church. As with other religious denominations, Episcopalians split along sectional lines into northern and southern branches, but the division was not lasting and the Episcopal Church was the first American church to reconcile after the war in the autumn of 1865. However, many southern Episcopalians remained skeptical of a quick reunion. Of all the southern dioceses only North Carolina and Virginia, and smaller "missionary districts" in Tennessee and Texas, sent delegates to the General Convention in Philadelphia and asked to rejoin. Cheshire was a member of the North Carolina delegation, but Clark begged him to not attend the convention. Clark encouraged caution and asked Cheshire to "at least wait until the other Southern Dioceses can act with us." Cheshire considered Clark's advice, but traveled to Philadelphia anyway and was welcomed by the northern church.[79]

Opposite: Clark created scores of similar family tree charts. The breadth, detail, number of families, and sheer volume of genealogical research completed by Clark is astounding. In an age before telephones, email, and official birth and death certificates, Clark would have had to travel and interview people, and recall data from an amazing memory, to obtain the level of detail that he recorded. (Courtesy of the North Carolina Office of Archives and History, Raleigh, North Carolina.)

Calvary Episcopal Church, Tarboro, North Carolina. Clark was a devout Episcopalian and regular member of Calvary. He was involved in the construction of the present church building, which began in 1859 and was completed in 1867. The Clark family, including their relatives from the Parker and Toole families, were prominent church members and leaders. The Rev. Joseph Blount Cheshire (1814–1899) and his son, Clark's nephew and future bishop of North Carolina, Joseph Blount Cheshire, Jr. (1850–1932), served in this church. (Photograph by the author.)

Clark never relished the glare of the public spotlight that the war turned upon him. He preferred the life of the dignified country squire, and in many respects he ran the executive department much as he would run his plantation — issuing orders and expecting them to be carried out with alacrity. Though he met with political failure as governor, Clark did find success as a businessman and father. He lost much of his income with the abolition of slavery, but he was able to keep his farm. Like all North Carolinians after the war, his means were limited, but he made sacrifices to educate his children privately.[80] His son Haywood was sent to Cape Fear Academy in Wilmington and Irwin trained for the medical field. All of his children seem to have done well in later life. Their success is due in part to their father, a dedicated family man who stressed good character and industrious habits. In a

6. "That Odious Constitution"

rare personal letter to his eldest son, Haywood, in 1873, Clark, less than a year before his death, advises the teenager about the value of honorable employment:

> Your letter was unusually interesting from the information given me of a prospect of increased duties and pay in your official connection with the R[ail] R[oad]. I know you have the capacity for business and I think your habits of punctuality and industry will qualify you for any duties you may think proper to undertake. And I will take an early opportunity to thank Col [Sewall L.] Fremont [superintendent of the Wilmington and Weldon railroad] for his kind consideration of you. Col F[remont] acquired in his early military education strict discipline and he is sometimes rough, but not unkind in his administration of business and control of subordinates and I trust you have learned to understand and appreciate such conduct and feeling. I am glad you have the offer of more employment. Take all you can possibly do. If it is not immediately profitable to you, it will ultimately prove of great profit in schooling you into industrious habits and give you the reputation of attention to business which will always avail you great profit hereafter. And employment is not only the school of good habits and the source of prosperity, but contributes to your happiness and gives you that independence of feeling and character which constitutes true manhood. So I say take any honorable position and employ-

Clark family gravesite. Governor Clark is buried (center left) next to his wife and parents in the Calvary Episcopal churchyard. His tombstone reads, "a good name is better than precious ointment." (Photograph by the author.)

ment. Get full and just compensation for your services. But if you get little, still accept that little. It will prove more profitable hereafter. The formation of little good habits will spread into a general character of usefulness. The utterance of little kind words will [be] heard and felt far beyond the place and occasion of the utterance. You are too young to know these things and must therefore heed the experience of others. If I had the wealth of the Indies, I could not give you a richer legacy.

Clark concluded by reassuring his son, "If I don't write to you often, it is not from neglect or want of love and consideration for you. You know my habits and this is one of my bad ones." There are few such personal letters in Clark's collection, and none that voice so clearly his appreciation of a good name.[81]

The former governor fell ill from the effects of cancer in early 1874 and his health declined quickly. He suffered a "painful illness" for three months, which "was borne with patience and Christian fortitude." He died at home at age sixty-six on April 14, 1874—the first warm day after record spring frosts. R. R. Bridgers wrote that when he last saw him, "I felt it was our last meeting and parted with him in a feeling of sadness.... I feared he would never recover." Edgecombe County honored him on the day of his burial by closing all businesses and shops. Commenting on his death, the local newspaper editor said, "His name was never once connected with aught that savored of corruption, he never betrayed a public trust, and he leaves the scenes of life with an untarnished [reputation] beloved by friends, respected by acquaintances, and honoured by all." Bridgers agreed and told his son, "I have met with but few his equal and none his superior." Clark is buried in the Calvary Episcopal churchyard in Tarboro where his tombstone reads, "A good name is better than precious ointment."[82]

Epilogue

Henry Toole Clark was more than a figure who simply occupied the governor's chair. He assumed the governorship at the most crucial period in North Carolina's history and served thirteen months as the state's chief executive. Despite overwhelming difficulties, he achieved some remarkable administrative results. He built a successful powder mill, managed efforts to supply essential salt, and established a Confederate prison. He mobilized and equipped thousands of troops for Confederate service. He sent agents to England and throughout the Confederacy to locate guns and the supplies needed to wage war, and contracted with manufacturers to supply what could not be readily found at home or abroad.

Clark worked diligently for the cause of Southern independence. His performance as governor belies the claim that "probably no state raised more obstacles to the execution of policies of the central government [in Richmond] than North Carolina."[1] Even though Clark voiced his disagreements to the Davis government, and raised objections to some of its demands, he usually supported Confederate policy. He was a committed Confederate nationalist who showed no hesitation in prosecuting the war effort. Clark clearly understood that Confederate defeat would result in the end of slavery and thus the end of the social, economic, and political world dominated by the planter class to which he belonged. Unlike some white southerners, he never expressed doubts or ambivalence concerning secession or the war—even after the South's defeat. He was sure of his course and acted as a man sure of his duty. While he did not articulate his vision to the public, he knew that his political career, as well as his personal fortunes, rested with Confederate success on the battlefield, and so he supported unpopular measures like conscription.

Historians have speculated about why Clark left office without seeking his party's nomination for the governorship. Previous accounts have focused on the planter's "lack of ambition," or his supposed "limited experience and ability." Similar misjudgments have also been applied to his earlier political career, which has likewise been dismissed as lightweight. Scholars have continually repeated the mistaken assumption first given by historian John H. Wheeler in 1884 that: "Neither did [Clark] take much interest in politics until 1850, when he was elected to the state Senate."[2] Such pronouncements reveal an ignorance of Clark's long political experience as a local party chairman, national convention delegate, and party writer, and give insufficient weight to his extensive business and social network,

Epilogue

which inevitably involved him in political issues. In truth, Clark was always interested in political matters, though he never considered himself a "politician."

He was a skilled businessman and planter, and those skills helped him towards administrative success as governor. His official papers reveal that he acted with authority. He was an assertive and at times aggressive executive, but his ability to intervene directly in the declining military and home-front situation by 1862 was constrained by state law, Confederate policy, and the realities of war. He was not authorized by the legislature to provide poor relief to citizens, and he was legally bound by the May 20, 1861, decision of the state convention to raise, equip, and transfer state troops out of North Carolina and to the Confederacy. He executed that duty with energy and dedication. As he told President Johnson, he "endevoured to sustain the course and cause" of his state "with zeal."[3] Though his relations with Richmond authorities were usually cordial, Clark showed little hesitation in confronting Jefferson Davis, his cabinet officials, or Confederate generals in matters of policy and military strategy, especially in relation to North Carolina's defense. But given the realities of his situation, there was little he could do beyond begging Richmond for more soldiers.

Clark did fail, however, as a political leader. He never managed to overcome the blame for the Federal military advances in eastern North Carolina and the hardships caused by the increasingly protracted conflict. He also failed to communicate effectively with the people of North Carolina. He responded with force when opposition arose to Confederate policy. His willingness to send troops, what few he had available, to quell disturbances was only marginally effective and it did little to improve his public image. He was disinclined to manipulate the newspapers to his advantage, or to make direct appeals to the public. He considered such tactics vulgar, dishonest, and ineffective. He remembered the lesson learned from his cousin's partisan battles in the 1840s. Henry Irwin Toole had suffered through an acrimonious Democratic party nomination process that led to rumors of nepotism and secret deals, casting aspersions on Toole's character. Toole's public pleas in defense of his reputation had fallen on deaf ears, and permanently damaged his political career.

Clark's father had taught him lessons too. James West Clark served one term in Congress and later as chief clerk of the Navy department. James West did what he considered his duty, but he disliked the partisan atmosphere of Washington politics and so retired to his home, content to manage his business interests and participate in local affairs. James West was a quiet and thoughtful man who set a lasting example for his son. Indeed, many of Henry's leadership skills and character traits were formed at an early age. As governor, Henry Clark would recall the old adage his father had taught him: "You have two ears and but one mouth. Hear twice as much therefore as you talk."

Clark was unwilling to adapt his conservative leadership style to the new political realities of the Civil War, which required finesse, flexibility, and a willingness to form and manipulate political coalitions. Antebellum southern politics often encouraged the appearance of disinterestedness and aloofness, while disapproving of the public displays of ambition that were becoming necessary in the new political world ushered in by the Civil War.

Clark's successor, Zeb Vance, had no such reticence. He was successful in keeping his state committed to the war effort, largely because he communicated more fluently with both Richmond and the people of North Carolina; in substance, his firm approach to specific problems, especially conscription, was not very different from Clark's.[4]

Historians have so far neglected the importance of viewing Clark within his cultural and social context: he was a planter-politician of the old order. He was a member of that generation of boys in the early republic raised as both "American" and "Southern." They were under tremendous pressure from their fathers to uphold not only the family's reputation, but also that of their state and the South. Honor, duty, and "manliness" were central to their defense of the "southern way of life" as its "peculiar institution" (slavery) came under increasing criticism, and they bristled at what they perceived as an encroaching, centralized federal power increasingly controlled by abolitionist "radicals."

Like so many of his peers, Clark had learned from the "school of states' rights." He considered himself first a "citizen of North Carolina," and was taught from childhood that "the several States were sovereign and exclusively charged" with the protection of life, liberty and property. When his state left the Union in May 1861, Clark "felt it his duty" to "follow her fortunes." He stated in his pardon appeal to President Johnson in July 1865 that he had done what any "good and loyal citizen" would have done. Like other southern men of his time and place, Clark had studied Thomas Jefferson's Virginia and Kentucky Resolutions, and was familiar with John C. Calhoun's defiant rhetoric. If he was mistaken in his political views, Clark told the President, it was only because "that mistake" had been taught to him "by the greatest and purest statesmen" of America.[5]

At first glance, Clark might be considered one of those Southern leaders described by historian William C. Davis as "pretend republicans," leaders who paid lip service to republican values which "allowed them a cover for instincts so aristocratic that such men decried real democracy. If they mouthed the platitudes of democracy, it was only because a system that ostensibly kept everyone equal at least prevented anyone from becoming superior to themselves. These men were oligarchs in all but open avowal."[6] For slave-owning planters like Clark, values of liberty and freedom often came second to obedience and loyalty.

But Davis's characterization, while accurate, does not fully explain Clark's views. Clark never sought the lofty heights of power and he turned down legitimate opportunities for higher office. The Edgecombe planter believed in and usually practiced republican values of transparency, simplicity, and honesty in his daily life, and he expected the same from others. After repaying a large debt after the war, Clark was proud to say that he felt "like a man" for doing it.[7] His ambition came not from any inherent desire for power, per se, but from a sense of *noblesse oblige*. He believed it was his responsibility to hold public office and to sustain for future generations the conservative, compact theory of government, albeit one that protected slavery. He could be rigid and uncompromising in his beliefs, and he did not easily accept opinions different from his own. Clark did not seek his party's nomination partly because by 1862, neither the Confederacy, nor his party, had the political unity or integrity he felt were necessary to support his efforts as a war governor.

Hilma, ca. 1900. The old house suffered fire damage in the 1890s and was renovated and enlarged by Clark's eldest daughter, Laura (seen standing), and her husband, John L. Bridgers. After her death in 1933, the house fell into disrepair and was torn down in 1957. (Courtesy Blount-Bridgers House Archives, Tarboro, North Carolina.)

He also fell victim to Richmond's "Virginia first" policy. At the outbreak of the war, Confederate authorities had placed him in a difficult, if not untenable, position. President Davis and the War Department failed to support Clark militarily, and their neglect of North Carolina frustrated and angered him. It is true that the Confederacy's resources were stretched thin, and Clark was not alone in making fruitless requests for help. Other state governors were desperately pleading with Richmond for assistance. However, in failing to respond to Clark's modest and intelligent requests for assistance in a theater of war near Virginia, Richmond squandered early opportunities to fortify strategic locations such as Hatteras Inlet or Roanoke Island. After these defenses fell, Confederate authorities failed to act promptly on Clark's advice to retake those locations before Union forces could secure their positions. A determined attempt to recapture Hatteras, or at least properly fortify Roanoke Island, might well have altered the war's course in North Carolina along with Clark's political fortunes. The Confederacy's inaction meant that the governor never pos-

Epilogue

Most of Clark's lands were willed to his son-in-law, John L. Bridgers, at the former governor's death in 1874. A large subdivision, hotel, and a nine-hole golf course and country club now occupy the former site of Clark's Hilma plantation. Clark's grandson, Henry Clark Bridgers, started the first golf team at UNC and the game was first played on this land in the 1890s, making it one of the oldest golf courses in the state. (Photographs by the author.)

sessed enough men or arms to check the Federal occupation and raids in his state, and he was unable to control the public's increasing disaffection with the war's prosecution. He was also constrained by the state's constitution in the traditionally weak political role assigned to the North Carolina executive. Furthermore, as an un-elected governor, he operated without the benefit of a public mandate or clear historical precedent to support and guide him.

Clark was also a realist. He saw that he had little chance of being elected governor in his own right, and that his apparently blind support of Confederate war policies had damaged him politically. As state senator in the 1850s, he had fought to retain traditional values and a limited government. As governor, he sought to maintain the antebellum world of slaves and masters to "the last man and the last dollar."[8] From the time he left the governor's office, and again during his brief appearance as a state senator after the war when members of the old order came back into power, he never really changed his deep-seated white-male republican vision of society and politics.

Clark's accomplishments and significance have been overlooked partly because the source material that documents his life is thin. Very few letters survive to give us intimate details of his life and mind, and what does survive has not been edited or published. There has hitherto been no monograph dedicated to his life. His successor Vance lived longer and was able to trumpet his accomplishments over a longer period of time. Vance remained in the public eye long after the war, returning to the governor's mansion in 1876 and later, serving as a United States senator from 1879 until his death in 1894. Clark, however, retired from the larger public view, refusing to answer his critics or to stoop to the level of "stump politics."

Other historians have not taken into account how heavily Clark's personal responsibilities weighed on him as he decided whether to seek another term as governor. During the summer of 1862, just before the general election, Clark was fifty-four years old with four small children and a pregnant wife (Mary was forty years old during her last pregnancy). He was an attentive parent, a concerned husband, and like his father before him, a family man who enjoyed being at home. Political duties had kept him away from Hilma and in Raleigh for two years from 1860 to 1862 as the escalating secession crisis turned to armed conflict. His wife and children spent some of that time at Monreath, a country home closer to Raleigh, and he wanted to take them back to Edgecombe County and secure his property from the ravages of war. His finances crumbled after the Confederate government confiscated a valuable trust fund he managed, which he paid back to his creditors in good faith from his own funds. His decision to do so was honorable, but of course it imposed a tremendous financial burden to his family. "Enemy raids" in July 1863 had severely damaged his property and "reduced his means." The emancipation of his slaves, though he claimed to be "contented" by their release, nearly ruined him.[9] His tenuous financial situation, coupled with his responsibilities as a father to five small children, likely kept him from participating in a more prominent, statewide political role after 1862. He slowly rebuilt his fortunes, and in a few years was able to live in relative comfort until his death in April 1874.

Clark's wife and five children survived him, and his real and personal property was valued at over twenty thousand dollars. Mary was left "property enough" to "support herself and two little girls comfortably." Some of the land was bequeathed to his sons, Haywood, only nineteen years old, and Irwin, aged seventeen; but most of it, including the house, was left to his son-in-law, John L. Bridgers.[10] Bridgers had married Laura, and Clark had hoped that Mary would be allowed to remain with them at Hilma. This decision was not without some debates. The will was filed nine days after Clark's death as family members worked out its details. As the eldest son, Haywood, who lived in Wilmington, haggled over the future of the estate, but not rancorously. He told Bridgers that "you know I am anxious for you to get the place," and suggested selling Hilma and investing the money to support his mother. Given the stagnant agricultural situation at the time, it might have seemed a good idea; but a wiser and slightly older Bridgers rejected the proposal and kept the land intact. He was a large Tarboro cotton planter, while Haywood spent the rest of his life in New Hanover County, working for the Wilmington-Weldon railroad.[11]

Mary lived at Hilma for the rest of her life with the Bridgers. Her younger daughters, Maria and Arabella, aged fifteen and twelve at their father's death, respectively, remained at Hilma until they married. Maria became the first president of the Tarboro chapter of the United Daughters of the Confederacy, honoring the legacy of her father. Clark's second son Irwin went on to work in medicine. Like Haywood, he never entered the political world. Mary died in 1896, aged seventy-four, leaving $4,300 in personal property to her children.[12] She was buried next to her husband in the Calvary Episcopal churchyard. The Bridgers renovated and enlarged Hilma in the 1890s after the home suffered fire damage; but following the death of John in 1932, and Laura in 1933, the house fell into disrepair. Portions of the property were sold in 1957 and Hilma was torn down. Today the land is home to a small motel, a nine-hole golf course and country club, and a large subdivision. The family still retains about eighty acres of the original property.

In the final analysis, Clark was an honest and capable man in both his private and public life. He deserves credit as a wartime leader, but truly great statesmen grow and adapt to changing conditions, while Clark clung to the old republican ideas that had shaped him from his youth. According to historian J. Rufus Fears, all great statesmen possess four virtues: "a bedrock of principles, a moral compass, a vision, and the ability to build a consensus to achieve that vision." Clark possessed all but the latter of these virtues. It was his misfortune to encourage and support a cause that was difficult to sustain once the war turned sour, and in the end, supporting the Confederacy was a struggle against the odds and the tide of history. Governor Zeb Vance observed in 1864 that the southern heart was never truly in the war for the long haul: rather, "It was a revolution of the politicians; not the people."[13] Clark was one of the hundreds of politicians and administrators who made the revolution of 1861 happen. They executed the orders of their superiors and issued commands of their own to their subordinates. They made decisions and proclamations from the capital, and passed laws from the halls of state legislatures which affected the lives of hundreds of thousands of people. Their legacy would resonate through southern history for the next century, and into our own.

Appendix A:
The James West Clark Letters
(1822–1827)

These sixteen letters from James West Clark to his only son, Henry, represent the thoughts of a concerned father as his son left home for the first time, and Henry was only fourteen years old when he left home to attend the University of North Carolina at Chapel Hill. James West was a university graduate of Princeton and was well aware of the dangers and pitfalls a young teenaged boy would face as he entered college. In these letters, he gives Henry instructions and timeless advice about his studies and the world. The original letters are owned by the Blount-Bridgers House in Tarboro.

Tarboro, July 10th, 1822[1]
My dear Boy,

This letter will be handed [to] you by Mr. Wilson. And the opportunity being a good one, I write to inform you that [your sister] Laura is much better. She was dangerously sick the day you left home and for two days afterwards, and not until yesterday was there any decided change for the better. The rest of the family [are] well. I shall certainly expect to hear from you at the earliest possible day, and in order for the letter to reach me by the time I expect it, it must be in the office at [Chapel] Hill by the 14th or 15th of the month. Write me again as soon as you join your class, stating their number etc. Be diligent, be moral, and frugal and in due season you will meet with your reward. Mother and sister unite in precatory their best wishes and love for you.

Your father,
JW Clark

Tarboro
July 14th, 1822
[Dear Henry]

Altho I have not been informed of the fact, yet from your qualifications, I have no doubt, [?] this can reach you, that you are a member of the University of North

Carolina. This new station requires from you the exertion of <u>all</u> your <u>talents</u> and <u>all</u> your <u>virtue</u>. A fondness for study will early attract the notice of your preceptors[2]; and while it acquires for you their esteem, and will also insure their support.

You are now a candidate for the first degree that universities confer. But I hope and believe that while you are receiving it, you will also be ambitious of deserving it. For you know a horse may be led thro' college and be nothing the wiser for the trip.

The Temple of [?] is erected on the summit of a mountain, the ascent to which is difficult on all sides, tho' it is possible, less so in one direction than another. The path chose for you, though rough and winding, will certainly conduct to this fair structure. Every step gained will reward your exertion and facilitate your advances. If new obstacles arise, you will have new strength to surmount them. The great object will brighten as you approach it, and I would hope that the rewards of the scholar will even surpass the expectations of the pack when he said, "sublimi feriam sidera vertice."[3]

You have enclosed a letter of introduction from Mr. [?] to R. H. Booth or Mr. Davie. Mr. Landers for yourself and Henry Hodge.[4] Look for Mr. Booth and deliver the letter yourself. If you can't find him or he is not on the Hill,[5] search for Mr. Landers and give it to his heirs.

Write to me immediately on the reception of this letter and let me know what books you were examined on, and by whom, where you board and at what price and who are your mess mates and of what class, and how many members there are in the freshman class. The family are all at present in tolerable health.

Y[ou]r father,
JW Clark

Tarboro, 24th July 1822
[Dear Henry]

Your letter of the 19th inst. announcing your examination and admittance into the freshmen class is at hand. Be assured I was pleased to learn you were admitted. Of which, however, I never entertained a doubt. All my anxiety arose from the desire of your acquitting yourself. You state the authors you were examined on, but not the places, nor do you inform me how often you were at a loss. Give me this information in your next letter and also how many were examined at the same time as their performances.

Henry Hodge wrote his uncle that some difficulty had arisen about your entering one or the other of the Societies. On this subject although a member of the Dialectic Society myself, I had not, nor have I now any wish to control you in your choice. Had you, however, followed my advice you would have been in no difficulty yourself nor cause any uneasiness to others.

I placed you fully on your guard as to the polite treatment you would receive from the members of both Societies until you entered one. In order that you might follow my advise more effectually which you must remember was this — to become well acquainted with the standing and merits of the members of both and then join that Society, which in your opinion had the greatest number of respectable members that would remain at college the longest time with you. That in the name of Societies there was nothing to lead you one way or the other but that you were to judge from the members. Although you have not followed my advice, yet if you have made a choice and have given assurances in consequence thereof that you would join either society, adhere to your word; don't waver. It is a case of conduct which will neither gain you friends at the University nor any where else. But hereafter remember to take time before you determine on anything of importance, and then act consistently with your cool and deliberate determination. In the present instance if you have promised to join the Philanthropic Society although the promise might have been given hastily and without proper deliberation, adhere to that promise unless there is something to prevent which I know nothing of. I am decidedly of the opinion that a young man should be constant and firm in his conduct and strict in the performance of his promises. This is the advise of a father who has witnessed scenes such as now happening before you. Enter either Society your judgment or inclination prompt you to enter, but be firm and decided. When you [act] prudently and with due deliberation, you need never apprehend either a parent's censure or that of your own conscience.

I will give you another piece of advise which I strictly require you to keep always in view. Beware of forming or contracting intimate acquaintance with any one at first sight or first interview. Be familiar and polite to all but for your father's sake and your own welfare and happiness be <u>intimate</u> but with a <u>very few</u> and not with <u>them</u> until you <u>know</u> them <u>well.</u> This advice, if followed will save you many an unhappy moment.

We are tolerably well and join in love to you.

Your father,

J.W. Clark

[P.S.] What are the cities on the Elbe [River] for I cannot answer your question, Sir.
[P.S.] Tell me who Samuel Hinton is and of what class.[6] Say to Henry Hodge that your mother [and the] children desire to be remembered to him and that I will write to him shortly. I shall certainly expect a letter from you once a fortnight and on the receipt of this letter write me directly and let me know which Society you are going to join [torn] your own choice   J.W. Clark

Tarboro August 9th 1822

[Dear Henry,]

By the last mail I received a letter from you and one from Mr. Booth. I answered Mr. Booth but had not time to write to you. You informed me that you were examined on certain parts of the books which you mentioned, but did not inform me as I requested you how often you were corrected or at a loss in your translations in Greek and Latin. I am afraid in Ovid you made badly out as the part you had to translate was somewhat difficult. In next letter inform me whether you missed as much or not as much as the boys who were examined with you and whether you stand well in your class in Greek and Latin and what number of your classmates you consider good scholars. Also what house you board at and the price, and as you must have paid before this time for your board and tuition and gotten your receipt. Write me after paying how much money you have left.

In the second [passage] on which you were examined is the following line of which you have often heard me speak as confirming an excellent advise which will be of infinite service to you if attended to this life. "O formose puer, nimium ne crede colori."[7] My son do not trust too much to appearances they will often deceive you to your cost and sorrow. Weigh with any and every matter before you and keep a still tongue in relation to your companions, and tell no person not even your most intimate friend every thing you think. Act towards him as if he might by chance one day be your enemy. I mean in regard to telling him every thing you think and know. Avoid this <u>bane</u> of [?] A disposition to study will early attract notice of your instructors and whilst it gains their esteem will secure their assistance.

If you have leisure, and I presume you will, to read history let me recommend first Millot's "Elements of General History." But Millot only furnishes the elements of history. To obtain a clean and comprehensive view of ancient and modern events, you must have recourse to other writers. You have read Rollin, when you have leisure after Millot, read "Gillies's [History of] Greece" and "The Travels of Anacharsis."[8] Then Russell's "Ancient and Modern Europe." Hereafter, I will give the names of other historians. Learn your college lessons first. If you have time to spare read, but do not read before you have your lessons at command. Do not put off for tomorrow what you can and should do today. Pay the utmost attention to Mr. Booth's advice. He has promised to advise and befriend you.

Write by the first mail after you receive this.

Your father,

J.W. Clark

[P.S.] Don't forget to answer all my enquiries. Do not write in such hurry. The family are all tolerably well.

[P.S.] Take care of your umbrella. Although old it will answer you a valuable purpose in rainy weather, in going to prayers and to meals, as you have no great coat.

Tarboro
August 24th, 1822
D[ea]r Henry,

It is indeed surprising how soon we learn to do the things we ought not to do, and omit those we are in duty bound to do.

When you left home I strictly required of you to write to me once in two weeks, and you faithfully promised to do so. But now six weeks have passed. You are verifying the old adage — out of sight, out of mind — not only of your parents, but of their advice and best consuls. Three weeks have elapsed and I have not heard from you. Altho' I have not been as yet informed where you board, what you give for your board, how many board with you and whether you have paid your tuition money and board and gotten your receipts. Regard your promises more, and perform them more punctually in [the] future.

We are at present in tolerable health at present. Mother and children say howdie.
Your father,
JW Clark
Your [sister] Mary Sumner went to the office to day for a letter but there was none.

Tarboro
August 31st, 1822
[Dear Henry]

I received your last letter by the Warrenton mail on Sunday night last and I had written to you the day before by the Raleigh mail. I was much pleased at receiving this letter, in as much as it convinced me you had not been so much wanting in your duty towards me, as I had expected yet according to promise the letter should have been written a week sooner. For I was anxious to hear from you, where you boarded and whether you had paid for your board and tuition, etc. You inform me you have paid all except $11. And why not pay this also? You state that 10 or 12 out of 36 this number your class consists of, are aiming for the first distinction. I hope you have enrolled your name with the chosen few. The prize is worthy the struggle.

Statues of brass and marble <u>may decay</u>, but the <u>virtues</u> of the <u>heart</u> and the <u>endowments</u> of the <u>mind</u> will be <u>immortal</u>. Winds and rain may beat, barbarians may assail, adversity may beset them, yet they are still fresh and unhurt. but <u>bear in mind</u> that <u>success</u> attends him <u>alone</u> who holds out to the end. Start therefore as you can and will hold out. History and philosophical reading generally make the amusement of your leisure hours. Do not sacrifice to your love or desire for reading your classical or collegiate studies. In your compositions do not aim at bombastic style. Let your language be selected for its neatness and perspicuity. In letter writing aim at a familiar style, as much as approaching to conversation as possible.

How does young Norfleet stand in your class, the [?] sons, and a young man from Williamston by the name of Watts?[9]

I saw him as he passed thro' and from his chat I inferred he thought himself equal to the best he might have to encounter.

Have you entered one of the Societies? How do you like it? Pay strong attention to the performance of the duties which may be assigned you. If you excel there it will be of great use to you at College and in after life. Be not forward in your expression of opinion in any situation. You have two ears and but one mouth. Hear twice as much therefore as you talk. The family are tolerably well. They are all up and desire to be remembered to you. After you answer this letter, which you must do by the first mail, you may write but once in three weeks to me.

    Yr father,
    JW Clark

Keep my letters. They may be of service for you to read.

Conetoe [plantation]
Oct 11th, 1822
My dear Henry,

    Your letter, together with the catalogue, were duly received. I have thus long deferred writing to you that you might experience some degree those feelings which arise from the disappointment of hearing in due season from those we greatly regard and esteem — feelings which you have more than once given rise to in the breasts of your parents by not writing in [?] since you have been at the Hill.

    After this exordium, I will observe that there is one remark I must make on your writing to which your attention must in future be directed, as it may save you from some <u>severe criticisms</u> from your literary associates. Be it remembered therefore that in all heads of writing the <u>first word</u> of a <u>sentence</u> must begin with a <u>capital</u> letter. That the names of persons and places must also commence with a capital letter as John, Philadelphia, Father, Wake County, etc. And in poetry, the beginning of every line, as well as every sentence and every proper name, must be with a large letter. Another remark I will make. Write in less haste and do not leave out words least you should have done so, read over whatever you have written and insert in its proper place the word omitted. But less hurry will prevent these omissions and your performance of whatever kind, will look much better without interlineations or erasures. Attend to these remarks and you will greatly improve in your writing. You have with great propriety omitted on the back of your last letter the ugly [seal flourish]. If the letter be sent by a private hand, just write the person's name straight without a flourish.

    You have not mentioned for some time a word about your studies or private reading. What have you read, and what are you reading? Inform me when you again write to me.

    If you are not perfect — I say perfect in vulgar and decimal fractions and square root — you had better review them in you leisure hours. Otherwise you will <u>greatly regret</u> not having done so. When you get some what advanced in Algebra and Geometry, remember this advice. My family have been a good deal sick this fall, but none so sick as Laura when you left home. I have been a good deal unwell but not confined. We are all about at present but none of us in perfect health. Your grandmother returned from the Springs a week ago. Mr. Parker's family are in pretty good health. Apply yourself to your studies and remember that he alone is safe who holds out to the end.

    JW Clark

Mother and children desire to be remembered to you.

Conetoe
Nov[embe]r 8th 1822
Dear Henry,

    I have been to bed and have arisen again being not inclined to sleep, and having nothing particularly to engage my attention, my thoughts insensibly roved until they reached Chapel Hill, having arrived at this spot, dedicated to virtue and to science. My mind was quickly engaged in eager contemplation on the passing scenes, and various actors. But it soon singled out an individual, in no unusual manner distinguished from his companions, and on him it dwelt with intense interest. The more I viewed and thought and reflected from some cause or other, the more uneasy I became, until at last I became fully impressed with the idea that something or other was wrong with you. And why Father, you would ask, were you induced to arrive at this conclusion to form this opinion? I can't tell, Henry; but such is the fact. Yet I will endevour to place before you the train of my reflections, by means of which I have brought my self to my present way of thinking.

    I have often told you, my son, how heedless you were in most of your conduct; and how soon the best advice would be disregarded and forgotten by you.

    I had hoped, however, that altho' young, and as thoughtless as ever, that on reaching the University, and becoming a member thereof, you would, for character sake, if for no other motive, become more thoughtful, more firm and less fickle; and more steady and manly and dignified in your conduct and deportment. Quitting those little trifling ways and actions and amusements, which boys too frequently and too readily contract. By trifling ways, I mean an undue desire to see and know <u>little</u> things <u>unworthy</u> your notice, etc., etc. I still hope and believe that you have done so. I know nothing to the contrary. But then I reflected, that for want of one moments thought, and by permitting my advice to be forgotten, you might, in the crowd of young men and boys who surround you, differing in disposition, in talents, in character, in their pleasures of amusements — <u>some</u> of them being <u>worthy</u> of being <u>members</u> of a Seminary founded with the most beneficent views and calculated to impress its inmates with the most manly and virtuous feelings — others totally <u>unfit</u> for such a place and whose views and feelings and conduct are calculated to bring before you, that you might answer for yourself, and I hope with candour and relieve my anxious mind. Sooner would I see you following the meanest, if honest, occupation in life, than such companions as I have described. Yet a ray of hope bursts in and cheers me well [in] the belief that all is well, that you are doing as I have advised you.

    I shall be at Raleigh on the 16th or 17th of the month and shall expect a letter from you by that time directed to me at Raleigh and sent by the mail. I will then inform you how you are to get home.

    Your affectionate father,
    JW Clark

Raleigh
Nov[embe]r 18th 1822
[Dear Henry]

I arrived here yesterday. When I left home your mother was a good deal unwell with the ague and fever but I heard from her to day and she is much better. Mama also has the third day ague and fever. I wrote to you by the last mail and requested you to answer me at this place. I presume I shall get the letter tomorrow.

On the receipt of this letter, I wish you immediately to write to me, directed of course to Raleigh, where I shall continue during the sitting of the assembly, and inform me on what day of the next month yourself and Henry Hodge will be ready to leave the University. My object in writing to know the <u>day precisely</u> is, in order that I may be able to have a horse and chair at the Hill by the day so as not for you to be delayed, or the horses detained.

If you have not the necessary information you can obtain it from some of the Faculty. Remember I wish to know the day you will be ready to start that the horses may be there the night before, and you must let me know by the return of the mail to this place, as I must write home by the next mail to give orders when the horses are to start. Henry Hodge will come with you. If you have any thing new or worthy of notice let me have it. Don't fail to give me the information I want as soon as possible.

Y[ou]r father,
JW Clark

Raleigh
Dec[ember] 3rd 1822
Dear Henry,

It is now near eight o'clock at night and Sam[10] has not yet arrived as I expected, most certainly, he would have done. What has detained him I can't tell. I hope however he will arrive in time to get to the [Chapel] Hill tomorrow. Henry Hodge's trunk is large, and you both have some clothes you will want to have. And only bring such clothes as may be necessary to wear & your summer clothes and such as want mending or are worn out. These if you can, you had better put in your trunk and bring down. And put what you want to leave in Henry Hodge's trunk to remain at the Hill, and bring yours to leave both and to bring such books as you may have done with.

Your examination no doubt is over and both yourself and Hodge know your fate. I mean the standing, which, in the opinion of your teachers and the Faculty, your acquirements entitle you to, which I hope is such as will do credit to your preceptors, to yourself, and anxious friends. I had hoped to have heard from you to day but was disappointed. I heard from home to day. Your mother has been seriously sick but is now much better. My regards to Hodge and tell him I sent him $20 by the last mail which I hope has arrived safely.

Y[ou]r father,
JW Clark

If Sam does not come by the time Mr. Stephen Haywood's son leaves the Hill, and he will be sent for tomorrow write to me by him and tell me the [?] of the report of the Faculty.

Tarboro
26th Jan[uary] 1823
Dear Henry,

   Your letter of the date of the 16th inst. was received today. Why it has been 10 days coming I can't tell. The receipts were enclosed, except your receipt for board, washing and bed the last session. I am pleased to learn you have Mr. Croom[11] for a roommate, and have no desire you should change you room this session, as you have changed your roommate. On the contrary, I wish you to remain where you are and at the end of this session when the seniors are going off and the new building coming in play, you can get choices of rooms.[12] I hope you are studious and attentive to your college duties, but I fear not. As I have understood, you have already been called on publickly for absence from prayer. Inattention to one part of your duties necessarily leads to neglect of others, and so on, till you will become perfectly idle. The two years I spent at college I was never absent from prayers after the first week. I entreat you therefore as you regard your own character and my advice, attend strictly to every part of your prescribed duties, confine yourself strictly and closely to your room during such hours as you are required to be there, nor let any idle curiosity or any such motive induce you to violate this injunction. When you finish [John] Gillie's "History of Greece," read Plutarch's "Lives" attentively and minutely. In your next letter, which I shall expect in promised time, tell me what you are studying and what you are reading and whether you have any addition to your class, and how many there are, and if the young men in the class stand nearly as they did the last session.

   We are all nearly as you left us as to health. Tell [William Henry] Hodge he is a sorry hand for not writing to me, and that if he does not write quick I shall count him out.

   Your father,
   JW Clark

See how soon news when it is bad spreads? You know when you were called on about your absence from prayers, and it is known here already. Let my bird, I pray you, bear me better news hereafter.

Tarboro
March 27th 1823
Dear Henry,

   Your letter of the twenty second is at hand, and I am much gratified in having it in my power to say that your letters become monthly more interesting, not because my feelings for your welfare and well-being increase, for they are already sufficiently intense; but from the arrangement of the materials of your letters, being more easy and suitable to the occasion, and from your indulging yourself in a wider range in the selection of the subjects which you bring under review. In other words, you have given in your last letter more escape to your feelings, and presented to my view a greater variety of subjects than formerly, and served them up to me in better style. Go on —*perseverantia vincit*— and you will be well rewarded.[13]

You state that one of your class of first standing has withdrawn. Tell me in your next [letter] who he is, and also how many are left in your class, and how you succeed with Geometry, that noble science, which promising but little, performs a great deal; whether your recitations in Geography are too long for you to become master of them, and also how you are to get on in reviewing your [Greek], having sent yours to [?] If Algebra is to be examined on at the close of the session. Also I entreat you review it well, if you have to steal some moments from sleep. Be perfect also in Geometry, and when called to the black board, demonstrate slow and distinctly. There is a great advantage in it. In regard to money, I would cheerfully fill your purse, had I the ability to do so. I enclose you $15 and will try to make good the balance say $15 in time.

Your mother tho' not yet perfectly recovered, goes about the house and attends to her concerns. The children are not well but going about. My best respects to Henry Hodge. Tell him I have had so much distress and uneasiness of mind, that I had not the [inclination] to take up my pen to write, but will try to do so shortly. You say your master quoted Horace's "Art of Poetry." I will now draw from the same fountain in the hope of exciting you to excel. "*occupet extremum scabies*," says the Poet.[14] In the hope that although you may see others infected, you will not be contaminated yourself. I remain,
Your father,
JW Clark

Don't neglect to write. Be punctual to a day. I am uneasy when you fail. Acknowledge the receipt of this letter as it contains money.

Tarboro
9th April 1823
[Dear Henry]

Your long expected letter came to hand by the last mail, but was not received early enough to return an answer by the same mail.

You attribute my silence to every thing but the real cause: your own neglect in writing to me. And I was not disposed to urge you by writing, to do that, which you had been enjoined to perform, and had promised not to neglect. Nothing, I repeat again, will have a more unfortunate tendency in your intercourse with the world than a non-performance of an engagement, where nothing intervenes to prevent. Remember to promise only when it becomes absolutely necessary, and then make it a point of honor to comply.

I have often, nay repeatedly represented to you the necessity of attention to Arithmetic, Vulgar and Decimal fractions, and square and cubic root particularly. You can't know them too well. From your observations in your letter I should judge that you are now convinced of the correctness of my advice, but not until the time is passed when you could have mastered it at your leisure. Thus it will be, in relation to much of the advice I have given you. You will appreciate its value I am fearful when it is too late to profit by it. I will, however, continue to give it, altho' it may be lost or unheeded.

I recommended to you to read Plutarch and nothing else this session. But you say you shall commence [John] Gillie's [History of Greece] shortly. <u>Listen to me — lay history aside</u> for the <u>present,</u> and the moments you would have to spare to the reading of it, devote to the reviewing of your Collegiate studies, particularly <u>Algebra and Arithmetic</u>. Without any intimate acquaintance with these branches of study, you will be greatly beset in the higher and more difficult parts of the mathematics. Conic sections, for example. Familiar[ize yourself] with Algebra and Arithmetic and they are comparatively easy. Again, in your Latin you are certainly so well prepared as to be equal to any of your class. If you have more time, which I greatly doubt, that will enable you to prepare yourself for the approaching examination. Let it be given together with the studies I have mentioned to the Elements of Geometry. You will see the value of this advice, sooner or later.

If you must read, for the present read a chapter in the Spectator or Looker-on, but never until you have perfectly mastered your recitation. Hereafter I will say more on this subject. Think of nothing the balance of the session, but your approaching examination. The family are well. Tell Hodge I am astonished he will not write to me. Do write certainly in due time and let me know how algebra comes on and how the members of the class stand, if the same as before or not.

Your father,
JW Clark

Tarboro
20th May 1823
Dear Henry,

Your mother received your letter by the last mail and was much pleased with it. Doctor Robert Williams Jr., by whom this is written, is just starting for the university. Your grandmother sends you 4 dollars to bear your expenses and do you be <u>certain</u> without fail to write to her, directly on receiving this letter. Bring down as many of your things as you can your mother says. My pen is so intolerably bad I can't write, and I have no knife to mend it. Pack your trunk snugly. At the examination read and speak slow and loud and distinctly. There is much to be gained by it. Your grandmother is sick. She cryed because you did not write, therefore don't fail to write to her.

I am well, be at Raleigh on Friday night the 6th of June. Your mother requests me again to say bring your trunk and as many clothes as you can. If you have time write to me the Sunday after the examination commences. Be of good courage, and maintain your standing.

In haste
Your father
JW Clark

Tarboro
21 July 1823
Dear Henry,

    I called a few moments past for pen and well. Your mother asked to whom I was going to write? I answered to Henry. Do says she "write to the poor little fellow and give him some advice, it is a shame you don't write oftener." Thus, my son, while you are indulging yourself, probably, in youthful frivolities, or in unprofitable amusements, your parents, ever anxious for your welfare, are attempting to discover what advice or assistance you may need. For they view you, as you really are, but a child, placed on an extensive theatre to act your part without prompter before a giddy but censorious audience.

    Permit, therefore, the language of <u>experience</u> to reach you, thro' the only channel which absence will admit of, and not only to reach you; but also to be received with willing ears. Determined to profit thereby, let me, then impress on your mind, the necessity of, and the happy consequences which will result from a <u>firm, manly</u> and <u>courteous</u> deportment. Laying aside, as much as possible, with a determination also to keep it there, that <u>levity</u> which too frequently attends youth, and is always accompanied with a hundred nameless <u>littlenesses</u>, if I may be allowed the expression, which sink a Boy, altho' slowly, yet most surely in the estimation, not only of his superiors in years, but also of his equals.

    Remember you have two ears and but one mouth. Be therefore more reserved than communicative. Hear twice as much as you speak yourself, even in company of with a single individual. Be polite and respectful in your deportment to all, with whom you may have occasion to associate, using at the same time, much caution and circumspection in the choice of your companions. For it is an adage, the truth of which time and experience have long since confirmed, "tell me what company you keep and I'll tell you who and what you are." "Evil communications corrupt good manners." Altho' you may not be sensible of the influence of your companions on your conduct and disposition in a week or a month, yet at the end of the year, the alteration will confound yourself and place you infinitely below your former standing. I pray, therefore, to look before you leap, think before you act, and act at all times, as becomes yourself, and the high and dignified calling, that of <u>virtue</u> and <u>science</u> in which you are engaged.

    I would say much more on this subject, but not "the mail is ready to start" [rather] it is my paper which is giving out. A word or two about your studies. Have you finished Gillie [History of Greece] and Plutarch? If you have, and will follow my advice, I would recommend to you to turn your attention exclusively to your collegiate course; you are now able from being a little before hand with your Latin course to look in private at Arithmetic, Algebra and <u>Geometry</u>, to enable you to be at least on an equality with your competitors. To algebra, pay particular attention. If you do not understand it well and are not able to work it readily, it will make some parts of the Mathematicks, conics for example, very hard to learn. Write to me, in due time and state what you have read in

History, whether you have spoken again in public, whether you improved. My paper [is] gone. Love to [Henry] Hodge. He is a sorry chance.

JW Clark

[P.S.] Begin your sentences with a large letter

[Addressed to Mr. Henry T. Clark, Care of A. H. Vanbokkiln, New York]

July 29th 1827

Dear Henry,

    Mr. Hamilton will start in the morning for New York and altho' I have but little to communicate, as there will be no postage to pay, I have taken up my pen to write to you. I regret the low state of your funds because I can't at present day say when I shall be able to replenish them as it depends on entering upon my time and means of collection. Husband therefore what you have, but pay your board regularly at the end of the week or month as may be the custom. We start for Franklin tomorrow to return about the tenth or fifteenth of October. Address your letter, therefore to Louisburg until 5th October. Our Congressional election has been close in the county. Both candidates fell short a few votes of their former number. The increase of [Richard] Hine's votes was seven only. I mean that [Thomas H.] Hall's majority was seven less than as the former election. Only Hall gained 109 votes. The other counties have not voted. [Benjamin] Wilkinson and [Benjamin] Sharp for the Commons.[15]

    Your grandmother is at [?] with Mr. [Theophilus] Parker.[16] It is at present tolerably healthy here. The weather sultry with much rain. Our corn crops good, but the cotton is indifferent. There will not be to exceed 2/3 of a crop made in no event. It is the same thing I am informed through this state and Tennessee and more or less so in Georgia and South Carolina. Let me hear from you frequently and regularly and state your progress in French. Mr. Floyd brought home his wife on the 23rd instant. Remember that diligence and perseverance are the surest pledges of success in any undertaking, and that a penny saved is a penny gained.

    We are all well.

    Your father,

    J. W. Clark

Appendix B:
"On the English Character,"
Clark's University Oration

This essay was Clark's "Intermediate Oration" given at his graduation from the University of North Carolina, June 1826. The original is in Clark's papers at Duke.

The character of a people is closely interwoven with the history of their country; and in the events in that history are we accustomed to discover the spirit and ruling passion of a people. When a country has occupied a conspicuous place in history the predominate trait in the character of that people become strongly marked and is known to everyone: hence we speak of the Roman for his valour; the Greek for his learning and heroism; the Spaniard for his ~~pride~~ haughtiness; the Turk for his self-conceit and self-esteem; or the Frenchman for his vanity and politeness. But we do not propose to consider or compare these different characteristics; our business is to exhibit the character of the English; a people who have occupied a large space in the various transactions of Europe and the world; a people who by their intelligence and enterprize have extended their power and authority to the most distant quarters and by their vast resources have taken the most conspicuous stand among the nations of these modern times.

A nation never rises at once to greatness. The march is slow and gradual. It requires time to settle and mature its principles and policy: to throw off the incumbrances of those measures which were adapted to its early state, to widen its views, to put its constitution to the test of time and to improve it to the condition required.

Tho' England hold[s] such an important station at present, it is equally as interesting to consider what she has been. The Gaul, the Roman and the Saxon have all held the sway over that little island, and other nations too have shared with them to power and dominion of that territory. But it is to the Saxon race that the English look up with proud satisfaction and recognize in that hardy and valiant race those cardinal and fundamental principles upon which their liberties have been built. From them they first learnt to consult and respect the voice of the people and derived those ideas of freedom which are contained in Magna Charta. When they felt the force of feudal tyranny under the Norman kings....

Can a nation be great without being free? History indeed can furnish instances when nations have risen to exclusive power under arbitrary governments. But they have only manifested any true greatness at long and distant intervals under some fortunate and illustrious reign when the mighty genius of some chief has been actuated by patriotic motives and his ambitions restrained and guided by his regard for the welfare of his subjects. But to advance constantly and uniformly in the great road of improvement the rights and privileges of the people must be ascertained by the laws of the land, and so secured as to be beyond the grasp of human ambition. Such a steady march is seen in the history of the English people, and the first trait in their character which demands attention is their steady adherence to liberty. Kings have a natural fondness for power, and the long line of English kings exhibits many who were disposed to tyrannize over the rights of the subject until they were controlled by proper restraints. The free-minded Briton could not brook the oppression of feudal power, and their contests for freedom commenced under the Norman kings and did not end till the full confirmation of Magna Charta and the further improvement in the laws of Edward I.

Watchful of the stretch of power from whatever source they had to resist the encroachments of the papal dominion which was spreading its malignant influence throughout Europe. And although they contended against the most deep-rooted prejudices apparently under the awful sanction of religion and enforced with superstitious fury, yet their love of liberty finally prevailed. And the conduct of kings, barons and people plainly prove that the errors and encroachments of popery no where met with such spirited opposition. After this their history affords repeated instances of their struggles for freedom. At one time the country is distracted between the interests of two leading families. At another the kingdom is subjected to all the multiplied evils of civil war, from the ambition of a single individual. These instances afford high proof of the spirit of a nation, and although their liberty was often oppressed by these struggles, yet like the flower which droops from a heavy rain the returning sunshine of peace and prosperity adds fresh brilliancy to its former lustre.

No nation has fought so much and so long for liberty as the British. Those with less perseverance have bowed to the tyrants nod. The English too, have submitted, but it was only for a time. Afterwards as soon as opportunity offered they rose in their might and dared to be free. A favorable combination of circumstances has sometimes swelled the royal prerogative beyond the just rights of the people, but time has never failed to reduce it to the proper level of justice and liberty.

Has England deviated from this character in times more recent? She indeed became a party to the Holy Alliance; but it was a case of peculiar exigency.[1] England roused by uninterrupted success of Bonaparte and dreading his vast resources accumulated by [the] spoils of Europe, was compelled to seek aid from the continent to preserve those liberties she so dearly prized, on the other hand the monarchies of Europe unable to resist his overwhelming power turned their eyes anxiously to England to stem the mighty current of his victories and support their falling thrones.

After having reserved to herself the triumph and the infamy of chaining that modern Alexander on the barren rock of St. Helena, She withdrew from their <u>unholy</u> councils under the conviction that the people were better judges of their rights than kings.

[omitted] ~~Touch our sacred soil, says the Englishman, says to the slave, and your shackles fall to the ground. They were the first to lead the way in abolishing that abominable traffic in human flesh and in recognizing the rights of the oppressed and unfortunate Africans~~.

What shall we say of her judiciary establishments, of the far famed independence and impartiality of her judges, of her ancient trial by jury, of her habeas corpus and the great statutes of her parliament which form the security of the peoples' rights. England is the great fountain of justice and from that fountain flow those pure streams which enrich our own happy land.

This attachment to wise and good institutions has been the exaltation of England. Her love of Law and Liberty has been extended to considerations of Charity and beneficence. Out of the abundance of her wealth, millions go to supply the poor. And numerous institutions and establishments adorn her land to relieve the wretchedness and miseries of humanity. View her immense possessions and see an evidence of the charity and enterprize of her population — in America, in Asia, in the islands of the Atlantic and Pacific. See her ~~immense~~ extensive trade, her extensive territories, terminated only by the bounds of the ~~Universe~~ globe.

H. T. Clark

[Note from professor to Clark:] The long and determined struggle for the abolition of the slave trade which was maintained by Wilberforce and his associates, and finally terminated with success in spite of the array of disparate opposition of so many who were growing rich by this horrible traffic, proves the strong spirit of liberty which pervades and animates the British nation. (G[reat] Britain was not the first to abolish the slave trade. <u>We</u> led the way.)[2]

Mr. Clark is late in handing in his speech. I hope he will be particular in committing it to memory, remembering his embarrassment on a former occasion.

Appendix C:
A Poem Describing Members of the North Carolina Senate, 1861

2ND EXTRA SESSION, AUGUST 15–SEPTEMBER 23

Clark penned this witty poem while sitting as both governor and speaker of the state senate. He was a lover of poetry and a quiet observer of people. The original is found in his private papers in the State Archives, Raleigh.

A line or two
Will inform you
Of our grave Senate
Here is Speaker Clark
I would remark
Is now double prelate

Here the first honest Outlaw
That you or I ever saw
In his biting strain
Slays many Bills
Which would cause ills
Tabling them again

There is a Brown
Of great renown
As a ready debater

And enigma Joe
Turned you know
A secessionist hater

Gaither from Burke
Who has a smirk
And manners extremely fine
Then mountain Candler
The waxen handler
Also balsom & quinine

Who sounds his horn
To sagely warn
The coming of Jubilee
In a prophetic strain
Says he now I ordain
That you all must take al tree

Appendix C

Here is lawyer Stubbs
Not ranked with scrubs
In debate no defaulter
Our kind little friend Eure
Who is very demurr
Walkup, Stub & twast Slaughted

Next in play
The Gents sway
Such as Simpson & Dowd
They need fly around
But are always found
In a genteel crowd

Here is friend Sharpe
Who plays the harp
Sweetly & softly on a thousand strings
Next I must rhyme
To be in time
You want to be speaker Humphry he sings

Now follows the retinue to cure ills
Copeland, Dickson, Ramsey, Whitaker, pills
Soft soda Arendell being left out
Wild Doctor Blount of Pitt
Gave him a severe hit
Grimly says you're always on the scent

There is the Greene Speight
Who did refuse to wait
To end our legislation
Did you call on me
Twould be him or Whidbee
As a dandy for the occasion

Friend Lincoln Stowe
Made a loud blow
On the subject of taxation
But master Winstead
Was not to be lead
On this matter of vexation

Adams ought to be first
But being on a burst
And carrying such as Burton
I was forced to leave him out
On the dreary lonesome route
And take /only/ Staylaw Watson

There is Mosy Bledsoe
Whom you very well know
As /quite/ full of advalorem
Pitchford came in
Up to his chin
Says darky is the theorem

Barringer of Cabarrus
Often times enlivens us
With figures of rhetoric
He brings to his call
The fanciful Hall
And Dobson the plethoric

The farmer of Wayne
Travels a broad Lane
Attended by old man Worth
They oft times meet
With my short friend Street
Who was always fond of mirth

My Captain General Dockery
With his heavy crate of crockery
Went after for his Grist
Come in dear Spenser
The feminine fencer
And be [illegible]

There is old Captain Walker
The game, coarse, and fine talker

A Poem Describing Members of the North Carolina Senate

Of Mecklenberg declaration
And the Jackson Junnaluskee
Who is quite a faithful trustee
On Internal Corporation

Here are the three great Taylors
In number they are whalers
When they vote on a Bill
One with an iron face

A second with good grace
The third certain to kill

Thomas of the Hogpen Bank
Surely didn't intend to prank
With the confederate nation
But simply make his jack
Out of an old knapsack
This surely is adoration.

Appendix D: Maps

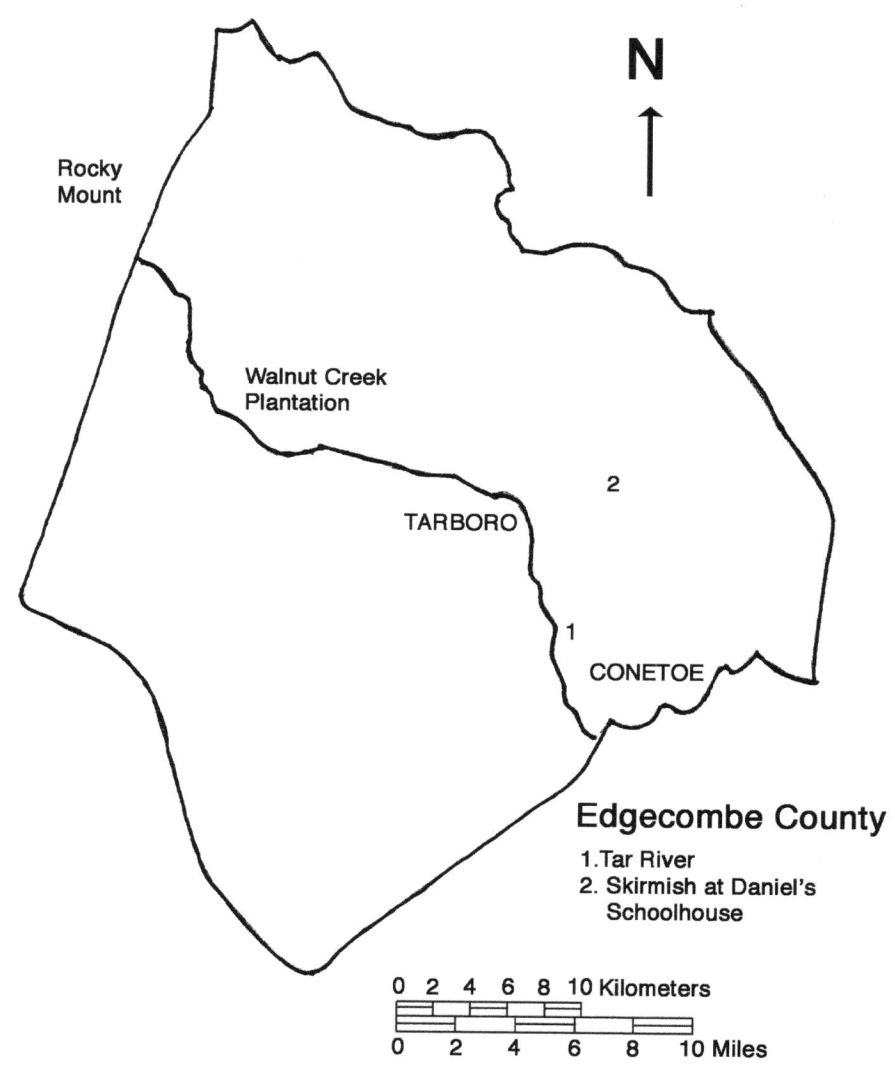

Maps

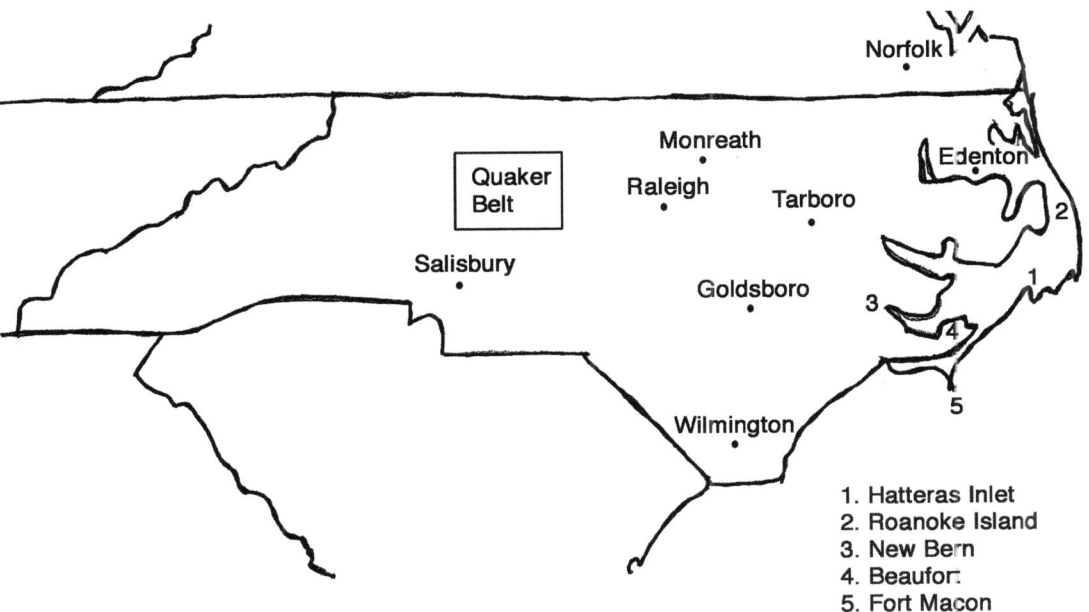

Map of Civil War locations in North Carolina.

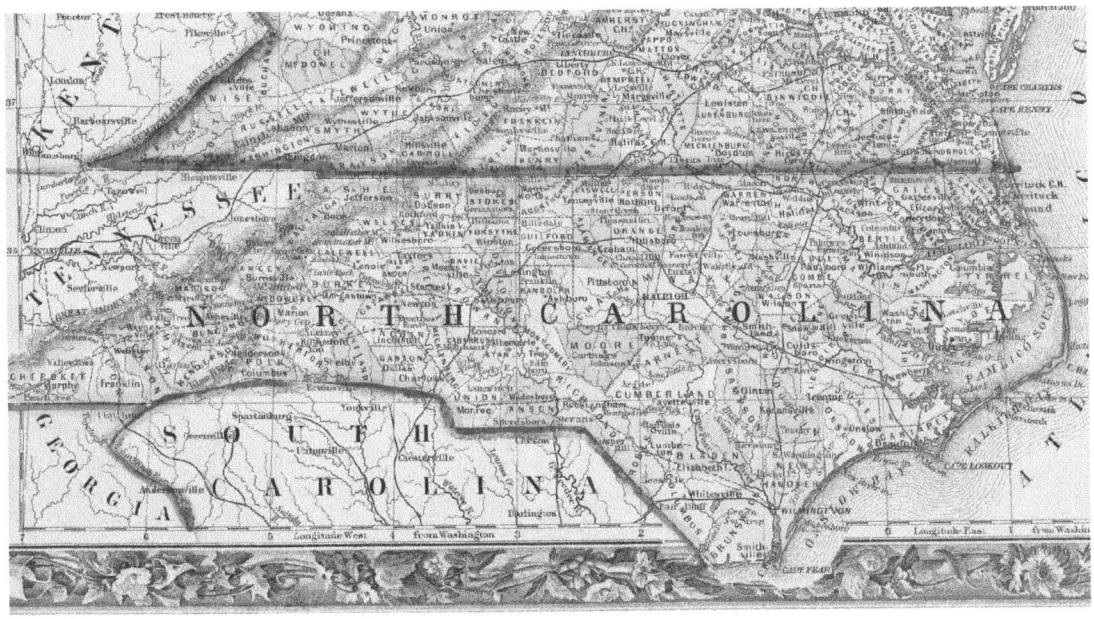

County Map of North Carolina, 1860. Courtesy David Rumsey Map Collection, http://www.davidrumsey.com.

Appendix D

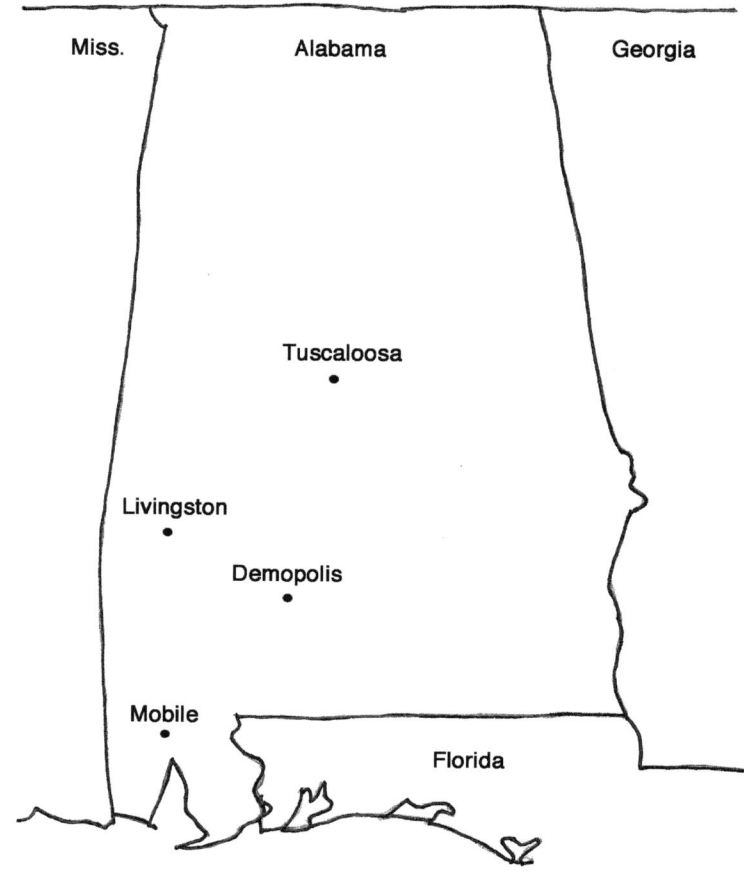

Map of Alabama

Opposite: This portion of a larger 1882 map of Tarboro depicts the town much as Clark would have known it. Clark's eldest son, Haywood, owned the land adjacent to Hilma (center left).

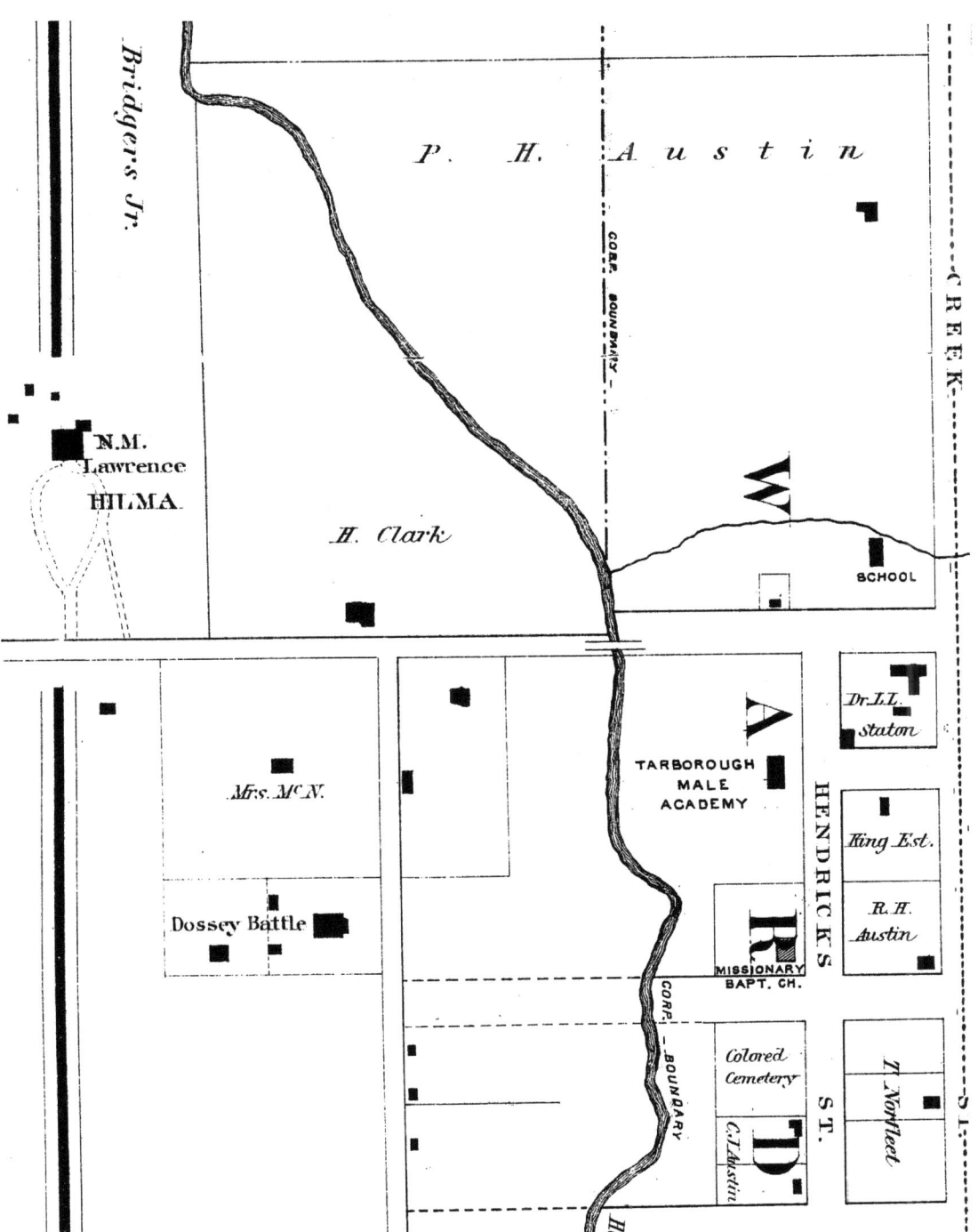

Chapter Notes

Abbreviations Used in the Notes

CGL — Clark, Governors Letter Books, State Archives, North Carolina Office of Archives and History, Raleigh.

CGP — Clark, Governors Papers, State Archives, North Carolina Office of Archives and History, Raleigh.

DNCB — William S. Powell, ed. *Dictionary of North Carolina Biography*. 6 vols. Chapel Hill: University of North Carolina Press, 1979–1996.

HTCBB — Henry Toole Clark Papers, Blount-Bridgers House, Tarboro, North Carolina.

HTCD — Henry Toole Clark Papers, William R. Perkins Library, Duke University Manuscript Collection, Duke University, Durham.

HTCUNC — Henry Toole Clark Papers (microfilm), Davis Library, University of North Carolina, Chapel Hill.

ORA — *Official Records of the Union and Confederate Armies in the War of the Rebellion*. 31 vols. Washington, D.C.: Government Printing Office, 1894–1927.

ORN — *Official Records of the Union and Confederate Navies in the War of the Rebellion*. 31 vols. Washington, D.C.: Government Printing Office, 1894–1927.

PC — Private Collections, State Archives, North Carolina Office of Archives and History, Raleigh.

SHC — Southern Historical Collection, University of North Carolina Library, Chapel Hill.

Introduction

1. John W. Ellis to Christopher G. Memminger, June 20, 1861, General Orders of Warren Winslow, July 9, 1861, Noble J. Tolbert, ed, *The Papers of John W. Ellis*, 2 vols. (Raleigh: Office of Archives and History, 1964), 2: 851, 886; *Standard* (Raleigh), July 13, 1861; *Journal* (Wilmington), July 11, 1861; *Daily Progress* (New Bern), July 11, 1861. The office of "speaker of the senate" is sometimes referred to as "president of the senate" though the original 1776 state constitution says that "the Senate and House of Commons, when met, shall each have power to choose a speaker." Red Sulphur Springs is now located in West Virginia, near the town of Beckley.

2. Paul D. Escott, "Unwilling Hercules," in *The North Carolina Experience: An Interpretive and Documentary History*, Lindley S. Butler and Alan D. Watson, eds. (Chapel Hill: University of North Carolina Press, 1984), 267. Approximately 125,000 North Carolinians served in Confederate armies. Though the state had one-ninth the white population of the South, it produced one-sixth of its soldiers — no other state had a higher percentage of its men under arms. For this reason, the state was called the "Hercules" of the Confederacy.

3. Wayne K. Durrill, *War of Another Kind: A Southern Community in the Great Rebellion* (Oxford: Oxford University Press, 1990). Durrill's analysis of this political coalition between planters and small farmers in Washington County, North Carolina, is particularly useful.

4. *Ibid.*, 14.

5. The "twenty slave rule" in defining membership

to the planter class is traditional, though historian Walter Johnson argues effectively that in truth, ownership of nine or more slaves represented a significant and an uncommonly large investment. Walter Johnson, *Soul by Soul: Life Inside the Antebellum Slave Market* (Cambridge: Harvard University Press, 1999), 79; George Brown Tindall, David E. Shi, *America: A Narrative History*, sixth edition, vol. 1 (New York: W.W. Norton and Co., 2004), 581.

6. Bertram Wyatt-Brown, *Southern Honor: Ethics And Behavior in the Old South* (New York: Oxford University Press, 1982); Lorri Glover, *Southern Sons: Becoming Men in the New Nation* (Baltimore: Johns Hopkins University Press, 2007).

7. Glover, *Southern Sons*, 1.

8. Gary Mercer, "The Administration of Governor Henry Toole Clark, 1861–1862" (master's thesis, East Carolina University, 1965).

9. *Ibid.*, 80; Alan D. Watson, *Edgecombe County: A Brief History* (Raleigh: Office of Archives and History, 1979), 41.

10. John G. Barrett, "North Carolina" in W. Buck Yearns, ed., *The Confederate Governors* (Athens: University of Georgia Press, 1985), 140–149; Glenn Tucker, *Zeb Vance: Champion of Personal Freedom* (New York: Bobbs-Merrill Co., 1965), 132.

11. Mercer, "The Administration of Governor Henry Toole Clark," abstract page.

12. *Free Press* (Tarboro), July 20, 1850; Mercer, "The Administration of Governor Henry Toole Clark," 69–70.

13. Barrett, "North Carolina," 149.

14. *Ibid.*, 148.

15. *Ibid.*, 148.

16. Glenn Tucker, *Zeb Vance: Champion of Personal Freedom* (New York: Bobbs-Merrill Co., 1965), 164; Gordon McKinney, *Zeb Vance: North Carolina's Civil War Governor and Gilded Age Political Leader* (Chapel Hill: University of North Carolina Press, 2004), 80.

17. Barrett, "North Carolina," 149; William S. Powell, *North Carolina: A History* (Chapel Hill: University of North Carolina Press, 1988), 134.

18. Marc Kruman, *Parties and Politics in North Carolina, 1836–1865* (Baton Rouge: Louisiana State University Press, 1983), 230–233; Barrett, "North Carolina," 148.

19. Powell, *North Carolina: A History*, 106–107; Michael Albert Powell, "Confederate Federalism: A View from the Governors" (Ph.D. diss., University of Maryland, College Park, 2004), 1–7.

20. Joe A. Mobley, *War Governor of the South: North Carolina's Zeb Vance in the Confederacy* (Gainesville: University Press of Florida, 2005); Frank L. Owsley, *State Rights in the Confederacy* (Chicago: University of Chicago Press, 1925); H.T. Clark to William S. Ashe, April 24, 1862, CGL; Richard Franklin Bensel, *Yankee Leviathan: The Origins of Central State Authority in America, 1859–1877* (Cambridge: Cambridge University Press, 1990); Louis B. Hill, *State Socialism in the Confederate States of America* (Charlottesville, Va.: The Historical Publishing Co., 1936).

21. For an extended discussion on the development of republican and Confederate revolutionary thought in early America, see Drew R. McCoy, *The Elusive Republic: Political Economy in Jeffersonian America* (Chapel Hill: University of North Carolina Press, 1980); Emory M. Thomas, *The Confederacy as a Revolutionary Experience* (Englewood Cliffs, N.J.: Prentice-Hall, 1971).

22. McCoy, *The Elusive Republic*, 7; Samuel A. Ashe, Stephen B. Weeks, and Charles L. Van Noppen, eds., *Biographical History of North Carolina*, 8 vols. (Greensboro: Charles L. Van Noppen Publishers, 1905–1917), 4: 291–305; *DNCB*, s.v. "Nathaniel Macon," s.v. "Willie Jones."

23. George C. Rable, *The Confederate Republic: A Revolution Against Politics* (Chapel Hill: University of North Carolina Press, 1994), ix; William C. Davis, *Look Away: A History of the Confederate States of America* (New York: Free Press, 2002).

24. H.T. Clark to Leroy P. Walker, September 2, 1861, *ORA*, ser. 1, 4: 638.

25. Michael Albert Powell, "Confederate Federalism: A View from the Governors," 1.

26. Donald C. Butts, "The 'Irrepressible Conflict': Slave Taxation and North Carolina's Gubernatorial Election of 1860," *The North Carolina Historical Review* 58 (January 1981), 45; Ralph A. Wooster, *Politicians, Planters, and Plain Folk: Courthouse and Statehouse in the Upper South, 1850–1860* (Knoxville: University of Tennessee Press, 1975), 40; Kruman, *Parties and Politics in North Carolina*, 47–49; Drew Gilpin Faust, *The Creation of Confederate Nationalism: Ideology and Identity in the Civil War South* (Baton Rouge: Louisiana State University Press, 1988), 15.

27. Paul D. Escott and Jeffery J. Crow, "The Social Order and Violent Disorder: An Analysis of North Carolina in the Revolution and the Civil War," *Journal of Southern History* 52 (August 1986), 373–402; Durrill, *War of Another Kind: A Southern Community in the Great Rebellion* (Oxford: Oxford University Press, 1990); Robin E. Baker, "Class Conflict and Political Upheaval: The Transformation of North Carolina Politics during the Civil War," *The North Carolina Historical Review* 69 (April 1992), 148–178.

Chapter 1

1. Approximately $1.5 million (year 2005 dollars); Eighth Census of the United States, 1860: Edgecombe County, North Carolina, Population Schedule, National Archives, Washington, D.C. (microfilm, State Archives, Office of Archives and History, Raleigh). Clark owned twenty-five slaves, but his widowed mother Arabella lived with him and owned eight.

2. "Henry Toole Clark," February 1908, Joseph Blount Cheshire Papers, SHC. Text of a speech given by Joseph Blount Cheshire to the Edgecombe County chapter of the United Daughters of the Confederacy.

Notes — Chapter 1

Joseph Blount Cheshire (1850–1932) was a nephew of Governor Clark and the Episcopal bishop of North Carolina from 1893 until 1932.

3. *Ibid.*; Clark Family Bible, 1766, Dr. Henry T. and Mrs. Blanche Clark, Jr., family records, Chapel Hill.

4. Invoice of Christopher Clark, November 11, 1783, HTCD.

5. Thomas Jefferson to John Adams, November 27, 1783, *The Adams-Jefferson Letters: The Complete Correspondence Between Thomas Jefferson, Abigail and John Adams*, edited by Lester J. Cappon (Chapel Hill: University of North Carolina Press, 1987), 100–103.

6. Seth Sothel was one of the most corrupt governors in American colonial history. His crimes and high adventures are too numerous to retell here. There is speculation that he is buried at Elmwood. Michael Hill, ed., *The Governors of North Carolina* (Raleigh: Office of Archives and History, 2007), 131–132.

7. Dr. Henry T. and Mrs. Blanche Clark, Jr., family records.

8. William H. Nelson, *The American Tory* (Oxford: Oxford University Press, 1961), 91.

9. "An Act for Improving the Navigation of Albemarle Sound, 1788," Walter Clark, ed., *The State Records of North Carolina*, vol. 24, 965; Dr. Henry T. and Mrs. Blanche Clark, Jr., family records.

10. Second Census of the United States, 1800: Bertie County, North Carolina, Population Schedule, National Archives, Washington, D.C. (microfilm, State Archives, Office of Archives and History, Raleigh) 34; *Southerner* (Tarboro), February 27, 1908; Receipt from Dr. James Norcom to James W. Clark, September 1801, HTCD. James Norcom (1778–1850) graduated from the medical college of the University of Pennsylvania in 1797.

11. Ronald David Kerridge, "Answering 'The Trumpet to Discord': Southerners at the College of New Jersey 1820–1860, and Their Careers." Senior thesis, Princeton University, 1984.

12. "James West Clark," Undergraduate Alumni Files, Mudd Manuscript Library, Princeton University. The Whig Society later merged with the Cliosophic Society, Princeton's other student debate club in 1928, to become the American Whig-Cliosophic Society, and it remains active today.

13. James West Clark to H.T. Clark, January 23, 1823, HTCBB.

14. "James West Clark," Undergraduate Alumni Files, Mudd Manuscript Library, Princeton University.

15. James West Clark letters, HTCBB; *DNCB*, s.v. "James West Clark"; James West Clark, Undergraduate Alumni Files, Mudd Manuscript Library, Princeton University.

16. Edgecombe County deed books, DB 11, 221.

17. *DNCB*, s.v. "James West Clark"; Fifth Census of the United States, 1830: Edgecombe County, North Carolina, Population Schedule, National Archives, Washington, D.C. (microfilm, State Archives, Office of Archives and History, Raleigh), 264; *Southerner*, February 27, 1908; Edgecombe County deed books, DB 12, 122; Monika S. Fleming, *Edgecombe County: Along the Tar River*, part of the Making of America Series (Charleston, S.C.: Arcadia Publishing, 2003), 26.

18. Edgecombe County deed books, DB 17, 69.

19. Kemp P. Battle, *History of the University of North Carolina: From its Beginning to the Death of President Swain, 1789–1868*, (Raleigh: Edwards and Broughton Printing Co., 1908–1912), 280; Unknown to H.T. Clark, December 22, 1843, HTCD.

20. "A Commemoration of the Death of George Washington," February 22, 1800, HTCD.

21. Alan D. Watson, *Edgecombe County: A Brief History* (Raleigh: Office of Archives and History, 1979), 60; Edgecombe County deed books, DB 17, 539.

22. Alan D. Watson, "Battling 'Old Rip': Internal Improvements and the Role of State Government in Antebellum North Carolina," *North Carolina Historical Review* 77, April 2000, 180.

23. Business receipts, HTCD; William S. Hoffmann, "John Branch and the Origins of the Whig Party in North Carolina," *The North Carolina Historical Review* 35 (July 1958), 299–315. Antebellum North Carolina held elections for state offices in August, not November.

24. Harry L. Watson, *Liberty and Power: The Politics of Jacksonian America* (New York: Noonday Press, 1990), 125.

25. James West Clark to Arabella Clark, August 10, 1829, HTCD.

26. *Ibid.*

27. James West Clark to Arabella Clark, September 7, 1829, HTCD.

28. James West Clark to Arabella Clark, January 26, 1830, HTCD.

29. *Ibid.*

30. Turner and Bridgers, *History of Edgecombe County* (Raleigh: Edwards and Broughton Printing Co., 1920), 136.

31. Daniel E. Parker to H.T. Clark, March 26, 1850, HTCUNC.

32. T. De Graffenried to James West Clark, January 8, 1831, HTCD.

33. Edmund Ruffin, *The Farmer's Register*, vols. VI and VII (1838, 1839).

34. Albert Luther Hume, *A Compilation of the History of Dyer County* (Dyersburg, Tenn.: the complier, 1960).

35. Daniel Parker to H.T. Clark, June 27, 1847, HTCD.

36. "Henry Toole Clark," February 1903, Joseph Blount Cheshire Papers, SHC.

37. Alan D. Watson, *Edgecombe County: A Brief History* (Raleigh: Office of Archives and History, 1979), 43–45; Fleming, *Edgecombe County: Along the Tar River*, 29–30.

38. Oliver Wolcott Treadwell came from a distinguished Connecticut political family, and Erasmus

Darwin North (d. 1858) received bachelor's and master's degrees from the university in 1826 and 1829 respectively and an M.D. from Yale in 1833. North became a professor at Yale. Both men served as tutors at UNC for a few years after their graduation. Battle, *History of the University of North Carolina*.

39. Glover, *Southern Sons*, 56; Robert A. Margo and Georgia C. Villaflor, "The Growth of Wages in Antebellum America: New Evidence," *The Journal of Economic History* 47 (December 1987), 873–895; Ronald Story, "Harvard Students, the Boston Elite, and the New England Preparatory System, 1800–1876," *History of Education Quarterly* 15 (Autumn 1975), 281–298.

40. Eugene D. Genovese, *The Slaveholders' Dilemma: Freedom and Progress in Southern Conservative Thought, 1820–1860* (Columbia: University of South Carolina Press, 1992), 4–5; Battle, *History of the University of North Carolina*, 1: 94–95; Davis, *Look Away*, 1–34.

41. Wyatt-Brown, *Southern Honor*, 92; Glover, *Southern Sons*, 57.

42. Battle, *History of the University of North Carolina*, 463.

43. Ibid.

44. Richard H. Lewis to Exum Lewis II, March 5, 1825, electronic edition, John Francis Speight Papers (#3914), SHC; *Register* (Raleigh), March 8, 1825.

45. Battle, *History of the University of North Carolina*, 461.

46. Glover, *Southern Sons*, 60.

47. E. Merton Coulter, *College Life in the Old South* (Athens: University of Georgia Press, 1928), 89; Battle, *History of the University of North Carolina*, 281.

48. Battle, *History of the University of North Carolina*, 281.

49. Battle, *History of the University of North Carolina*, 72; http://honor.unc.edu/honor/code_history.html.

50. James West Clark to Henry T. Clark, July 24, 1822, HTCBB.

51. Battle, *History of the University of North Carolina*, 464.

52. Ibid., 465.

53. Ibid.

54. Ibid., 452.

55. Ibid., 200.

56. James West Clark to H.T. Clark, January 26, 1823, HTCBB.

57. James West Clark to H.T. Clark, November 8, 1822, HTCBB.

58. Ibid.

59. James West Clark to H.T. Clark, August 24, 1822, HTCBB.

60. James West Clark to H.T. Clark, May 20, 1823, HTCBB.

61. James West Clark to H.T. Clark, August 31, 1822, May 20, 1823, HTCBB.

62. James West Clark to H.T. Clark, July 14, August 9 and 31, 1822, HTCBB.

63. James West Clark to H.T. Clark, April 9, 1823, HTCBB.

64. Battle, *History of the University of North Carolina*, 1:315; "On the English Character," HTCD; Herbert Snipes Turner, *The Dreamer: Archibald DeBow Murphey, 1777–1832* (Verona, Va.: McClure Press, 1971), 177.

65. James West Clark to H.T. Clark, July 29, 1827, HTCBB.

66. *Southerner* (Tarboro), February 27, 1908; *Alumni Directory of the University of North Carolina at Chapel Hill* (Chapel Hill: Alumni Office of the University of North Carolina, 1954), 161; Admittance to serve as counselor, February 15, 1833, HTCD.

Chapter 2

1. *Southerner* (Tarboro), ca. 1909; John H. Wheeler, *Reminiscences and Memoirs of North Carolina and Eminent North Carolinians* (Columbus, Ohio: Columbus Printing Works, 1884), 158–159.

2. Receipts, January 26, 1797, August 17, 1802, HTCD.

3. Johnson, *Soul by Soul: Life Inside the Antebellum Slave Market*, 82–83.

4. Federal Census of the United States, 1810, 1820, 1830, 1840, Edgecombe County, North Carolina; James Steer quoted in Jonathan D. Martin, *Divided Mastery: Slave Hiring in the American South* (Cambridge: Harvard University Press, 2004), 17.

5. Constitution of the United States, Article I, Sec. 9. The Constitution prohibited Congress from banning the importation of slaves before 1808. In 1807, Congress passed the bill "An Act to Prohibit the Importation of Slaves," which was signed by President Jefferson. The law came into effect on January 1, 1808.

6. Nelle Morris Jenkins, *Pioneer Families of Sumter County, Alabama* (Livingston: University of West Alabama Livingston Press, 1961); Powell, *North Carolina: A History*, 105.

7. Federal Census of the United States, 1840, Greene County, Alabama, "John H. Parker."

8. Ibid.; Louis Roycraft Smith, "A History of Sumter County, Alabama, Through 1886," Ph.D. dissertation, University of Alabama, Tuscaloosa, 1988, 79–122.

9. Walter Johnson, *Soul by Soul: Life Inside the Antebellum Slave Market* presents one of the best accounts of the conditions of the second middle passage; Ira Berlin, *Generations of Captivity: A History of African-American Slaves* (Cambridge and London: Belknap Press of Harvard University Press, 2003); James Benson Sellers, *Slavery in Alabama* (Tuscaloosa: University of Alabama Press, 1950), 150–152.

10. Slave inventory, ca. 1835–1840, HTCD.

11. *Voice of Sumter* (Livingston), August 15, 1837, January 2, 1838; *Journal* (Livingston), March 24, 1871; John Haywood Parker to H.T. Clark, March 12, 1842, HTCD.

Notes — Chapter 2

12. Johnson, *Soul by Soul*, 131, 146; Receipts, 1836, HTCD.
13. Receipts, 1836–1840, HTCD.
14. James Hair to H.T. Clark, May 31, 1854, HTCD.
15. H.T. Clark to Maria Clark, December 25, 1836, HTCD.
16. H.T. Clark to Bia and Sumner Clark, December 27, 1840, HTCD.
17. *Ibid.*
18. Haywood Parker to H.T. Clark, March 12, 1842, HTCD; Martin, *Divided Mastery*, 12–13.
19. *Ibid.*
20. James Hair to H.T. Clark, December 20, 1858, Henry Toole Clark Papers, PC; Robert D. Spratt, *A History of the Town of Livingston, Alabama* (Livingston, Ala.: University of West Alabama, Livingston Press, 1928, reprint, 1997), 75.
21. James Hair to H.T. Clark, October 9, 1844, HTCUNC.
22. James Hair to H.T. Clark, November 12, 1847, HTCD.
23. Martin, *Divided Mastery*, 160–187; Account ledger, n.d., HTCD.
24. James Hair to H.T. Clark, October 9, 1844, HTCD; Receipts, 1847, HTCD.
25. James Hair to H.T. Clark, December 20, 1858, Henry Toole Clark Papers, PC.
26. James Hair to H.T. Clark, May 22, 1849, HTCD.
27. *Ibid.*
28. Robert R. Bridgers to H.T. Clark, September 6, 1862, HTCD; *DNCB*, s.v., "Henry Clark Bridgers."
29. *Southerner*, February 27, 1908; McCoy, *The Elusive Republic: Political Economy in Jeffersonian America*, 250–251.
30. "Jackson Addresses the People of South Carolina, December 10, 1832," in *Major Problems in the Early Republic 1787–1848*, Sean Wilentz, ed. (Lexington, Mass.: D.C. Heath, 1992), 381–384; Lefler and Newsome, *North Carolina*, 328–329); Michael F. Holt, *The Rise and Fall of the American Whig Party: Jacksonian Politics and the Onset of the Civil War* (Oxford: Oxford University Press, 1999), 20.
31. Holt, *The Rise and Fall of the American Whig Party*, 24.
32. H.T. Clark to Willie P. Mangum, March 12, 1834, Henry Thomas Shanks, ed., *The Willie Person Mangum Papers, 2 vols.* (Raleigh: Office of Archives and History, 1952), 2: 120–121. The Latin phrase "et id omne genus" translates to "and that whole class, or sort." The "K. C. Regency" perhaps refers to Jackson's Kitchen Cabinet. Mangum also served as president pro tempore of the Senate, and later as vice president of the United States upon the death of Whig President William Henry Harrison in 1841.
33. Turner and Bridgers, *History of Edgecombe County*, 128–129; *Free Press*, June 24, 1848. Clark had previously served as an adjutant in company C of that regiment.
34. *Ibid.*

35. *Free Press*, July 9, 1842; Fleming, *Edgecombe County*, 37; Joe Gray Taylor, *Eating, Drinking, and Visiting in the South: An Informal History* (Baton Rouge: Louisiana State University Press, 1982), 53–67.
36. *Free Press*, July 9, 1842.
37. *Free Press*, November 9, 1844, March 15, November 26, 1845; Toole and Clark's grandfather was the namesake of both men. The first Henry Irwin Toole was a Revolutionary War officer and hero and a member of the state General Assembly.
38. Turner and Bridgers, *History of Edgecombe County*, 129.
39. Joseph Blount Cheshire, *Nonnulla: Memories, Stories, Traditions, More or Less Authentic* (Chapel Hill: University of North Carolina Press, 1930), 15–16.
40. John L. Cheney, ed., *North Carolina Government 1585–1974: A Narrative and Statistical History* (Raleigh: Department of the Secretary of State, 1981).
41. *Free Press*, March 8, April 26, 1845; Turner and Bridgers, *History of Edgecombe County*, 130.
42. Henry Irwin Toole to H.T. Clark, May 17, 1845, HTCUNC.
43. *Free Press*, May 10, 1845.
44. *Free Press*, May 24, 1845.
45. *Free Press*, July 9, 1845.
46. Watson, *Edgecombe County*, 35.
47. *Free Press*, August 26, 1848; "Speech to the Returning Veterans," n.d., HTCUNC.
48. *Journal* (Wilmington), February 11, 1848.
49. *Standard* (Raleigh), February 21, 1848; *Free Press*, February 19, 1848.
50. *Free Press*, March 18, 1848.
51. *Free Press*, April 22, April 29, 1848.
52. *Free Press*, June 3, 1848; William C. Harris, *William Woods Holden: Firebrand of North Carolina Politics* (Baton Rouge: Louisiana State University Press, 1987).
53. Glover, *Southern Sons*.
54. Will of James W. Clark, November 1, 1843, Record of Wills, Edgecombe County 1810–1885 (microfilm), State Archives, Office of Archives and History, Raleigh; Reel Index, HTCUNC, 1–2; Unknown to H.T. Clark, December 22, 1843, HTCD.
55. Receipts, n.d., HTCD.
56. Mary Weeks Parker to H.T. Clark, May 12, June 28, 1849, Henry T. Clark Papers, PC; *Free Press*, February 23, 1850; *DNCB*, s.v. "Henry Toole Clark."
57. Mary Weeks Clark to Catherine Drane, ca. 1851, Robert Drane Papers, SHC.
58. Edgecombe County deed books, DB 30, 63; "Concentration of Agriculture in Edgecombe County, Table 4," in Paul D. Escott, *Many Excellent People: Power and Privilege in North Carolina, 1850–1900* (Chapel Hill: University of North Carolina Press, 1985), 14.
59. James Hair to H.T. Clark, January 27, 1854, HTCD.
60. Federal Census of the United States, 1850 and 1860: Edgecombe County, North Carolina. Clark's mother died in 1860. She lived at Hilma and owned eight slaves, but only two would have been old enough

to work as field hands. The others were children, two adult females, and one male over seventy years old.

61. Fleming, *Edgecombe County*, 45–47.
62. Turner and Bridgers, *History of Edgecombe County*, 333; Watson, *Edgecombe County*, 59–61.
63. James Hair to H.T. Clark, September 1, 1848, HTCUNC; Clarence Gohdes, *Scuppernong: North Carolina's Grape and Its Wines* (Durham, N.C.: Duke University Press, 1982).
64. *Standard*, March 27, 1850; *Free Press*, March 16, 1850.
65. *Free Press*, March 16, July 13, 1850.
66. Herschel V. Johnson to Mississippi Senator H.S. Foote, January 19, 1850, Percy Scott Flippin, ed., "The Hershel V. Johnson Correspondence," *North Carolina Historical Review* 4 (April 1927), 199.
67. *Standard*, January 23, 1850.
68. W.W. Holden to H.T. Clark, June 21, 1849, Horace Raper and Thorton W. Mitchell ed., *The Papers of William Woods Holden*, 1 vol. to date (Raleigh, N.C.: Office of Archives and History, 2000), 28.
69. *Standard*, January 16, 1850; Gail O'Brien, "Power and Influence in Mecklenburg County, 1850–1880," *North Carolina Historical Review* 54 (April 1977), 131(n). One hundred seventy-six delegates from Virginia, South Carolina, Georgia, Alabama, Mississippi, Texas, Arkansas, Florida, and Tennessee convened at McKendree Methodist Church in Nashville for nine days.
70. *Free Press*, July 20, 1850.
71. Ibid.
72. Ashe, *Biographical History of North Carolina*, 6: 171–175. Dancy died in 1860 at age forty-one, having served two terms in the state House.
73. *Free Press*, July 20, 1850.
74. *Free Press*, July 27, 1850; Ashe, *Biographical History of North Carolina*, 6: 171–175.
75. *Southerner*, August 21, 1858; Turner and Bridgers, *History of Edgecombe County*, 451; Wyatt-Brown, *Southern Honor*.
76. *Free Press*, August 17, 1850; *Standard*, August 10, 1850.
77. *Southerner*, January 17, 1857.
78. *Journal of the Senate of North Carolina, 1854–1855*, 149, 305.
79. The completed 223-mile railroad opened in January 1856. Lefler and Newsome, *North Carolina: History of a Southern State*, 348–349.
80. *Journal of the Senate of North Carolina, 1854–1855*, 295–296. The "falls" of the Tar River are located in Rocky Mount, northwest of Tarboro, bordering Nash and Edgecombe counties.
81. Hugh T. Lefler and William S. Powell, *Colonial North Carolina: A History* (New York: Charles Scribner and Sons, 1973), 285–286.
82. *Journal of the Senate of North Carolina, 1852*, 80, 424; Turner and Bridgers, *History of Edgecombe County*, 351; Kruman, *Parties and Politics in North Carolina*, 81.
83. H.T. Clark to Willie P. Mangum, March 12, 1834; Shanks, *The Willie P. Mangum Papers*, 2: 120–121; William Freehling, *Prelude to Civil War: The Nullification Controversy in South Carolina, 1816–1836* (New York: Harper and Row, 1966) offers an excellent discussion of state rights and how federal intrusion during the nullification crisis was perceived as a threat to slavery.
84. Butts, "The 'Irrepressible Conflict': Slave Taxation and North Carolina's Gubernatorial Election of 1860," 44–45; Cheney, *North Carolina Government, 1585–1974*, 812–813, 820.
85. Kruman, *Parties and Politics in North Carolina*, 87; *Standard*, May 17, 1848.
86. *Free Press*, August 17, 1850; *Journal of the Senate of North Carolina, 1850–1851*, 117; Kruman, *Parties and Politics in North Carolina*, 95.
87. Kruman, *Parties and Politics in North Carolina*, 94; Paul D. Escott and Jeffery J. Crow, "The Social Order and Violent Disorder: An Analysis of North Carolina in the Revolution and the Civil War," *Journal of Southern History* 52 (August 1986), 375.
88. *Journal of the Senate of North Carolina, 1850–1851*, 111.
89. *Free Press*, August 9, 1857.
90. *Journal of the Senate of North Carolina 1850–1851*, 299; Kruman, *Parties and Politics in North Carolina*, 92.
91. Genovese, *The Slaveholders' Dilemma*, 10–11; Edmund S. Morgan, *American Slavery, American Freedom: The Ordeal of Colonial Virginia* (New York: Norton, 1975), 295–337; *Free Press*, March 17, 1849; *Journal of the Senate of North Carolina, 1850–1851*, 42.
92. *Journal of the Senate of North Carolina, 1858–1859*, 3–6; *Standard*, November 17, 24, 1858.
93. *Southerner* (Tarboro), ca. 1909; Wheeler, *Reminiscences and Memoirs of North Carolina and Eminent North Carolinians*, 158–159.
94. *Standard*, November 21, 1860. The quote is the speech as reported in the newspaper. Clark's words were not reprinted verbatim because of the amount of space dedicated to the national election.
95. William C. Harris, *North Carolina and the Coming of the Civil War* (Raleigh: Office of Archives and History, 1988), 30; Ralph A. Wooster, *The Secession Conventions of the South* (Princeton: Princeton University Press, 1962), 191; Butts, "The Irrepressible Conflict," 44–67.
96. Kruman, *Parties and Politics in North Carolina*, 196–197; Harris, *North Carolina and the Coming of the Civil War*, 30; J. Carlyle Sitterson, *The Secession Movement in North Carolina* (Chapel Hill: University of North Carolina Press, 1939), 72–99; *Register* (Raleigh), July 25, August 22, October 24, 1860.
97. *Southerner*, November 10, 1860. Clark's own district of Tarboro voted 196 for Breckinridge and 53 for Bell and Douglas combined. Edgecombe County voted 1789 for Breckinridge, 213 for all other candidates.
98. John Hill to H.T. Clark, October 22, 1860, HTCUNC.
99. David Potter, *Lincoln and His Party in the*

Secession Crisis (New Haven, Conn.: Yale University Press, 1942), 208; Barrett, *The Civil War in North Carolina*, 4.
   100. *Journal of the House of Commons of North Carolina, 1860–1861*, 592; *Southerner*, February 23, 1861.
   101. *Ibid.*
   102. Thomas L. Clingman to James M. Mason and James Seddon, March 22, 1861, HTCD.
   103. The "right of secession," as opposed to the "right of revolution," as a basis for a state to leave the Union was a point of serious legal contention among secessionists and Unionists. The issue, as revealed in the Badger Amendment, would become more pronounced in the secession convention of May 1861. See Wooster, *The Secession Conventions of the South*, 198–199.

Chapter 3

   1. The term "His Accidency" is usually associated with Vice President John Tyler, who became president upon the death of William Henry Harrison in 1841. The comparison was not lost on some North Carolina observers in 1861.
   2. John L. Sanders, "The Constitution of North Carolina," *The North Carolina Encyclopedia*, November 2007, http://statelibrary.dcr.state.nc.us/nc/stgovt/Preconst.htm (June 4, 2008).
   3. *Ibid.*; North Carolina Constitutional Convention http://docsouth.unc.edu/nc/conv1835/menu.html; Powell, *North Carolina: A History*, 117.
   4. Michael Hill, ed., *The Governors of North Carolina* (Raleigh: Office of Archives and History, 2007).
   5. Brian G. Walton, "Elections to the United States Senate in North Carolina, 1835–1861." *North Carolina Historical Review* 53 (April 1976): 168–92; Hill, *The Governors of North Carolina*.
   6. Cheney, *North Carolina Government*, 813.
   7. *Journal of the Senate of North Carolina, Second Extra Session, 1861*, 8; DNCB, s.v. "Josiah Turner, Jr."
   8. Clark served as senate speaker, which met in regular session from November 19, 1860, to February 25, 1861, and continued as speaker in the first extra session (May 1–13, 1861) and second extra session (August 15–September 23, 1861). He remained in Raleigh serving as governor until September 1862.
   9. *Journal of the Senate of North Carolina, Second Extra Session, 1861*, 5–8; *Journal* (Wilmington), August, 17, 1861. Mr. Speight was the senator from Greene County.
   10. *Standard*, August 17, 1861.
   11. Cheney, *North Carolina Government*, 829.
   12. *Standard*, July 17, 1861; *Journal*, August 17, 1861.
   13. *State Journal* (Raleigh), July 10, 1861.
   14. *Journal of the House of Commons, Second Extra Session*, 1861, 77.
   15. *State Journal*, July 10, 1861; *Daily Progress*, July 11, 1861; David H. McGee, "A Revolution in Raleigh:

The Early Transformation of a Confederate State Capital, 1861," in *Inside the Confederate Government: Essays in Honor of Emory Thomas*, ed. Lesley J. Gordon and John C. Inscoe (Baton Rouge: Louisiana State University Press, 2005), 41–54.
   16. *State Journal*, July 17, 1861; Telegraph to Graham Lawes, July 10, 1861, CGP; Cheney, *North Carolina Government*, 605–612. The executive mansion, or "Governor's Palace" as it was called, was then located at the foot of Fayetteville Street on the site of the present day Memorial Auditorium.
   17. Turner and Bridgers, *History of Edgecombe County*, 230–231.
   18. Kenneth Rayner to Thomas Ruffin, July 18, 1861, J.G. de Roulhac Hamilton, ed., *The Papers of Thomas Ruffin*, 4 vols. (Raleigh: Publications of the North Carolina Historical Commission, 1920), 3: 237. Rayner was from Bertie County and both men were educated at the Tarboro Academy. Though an old Whig, he was a strong state rights supporter and secessionist. DNCB, s.v. "Kenneth Rayner."
   19. Kenneth Rayner to Thomas Ruffin, July 18, 1861, *The Papers of Thomas Ruffin*, 3: 237.
   20. ORA, ser. 1, 3: 691; William B. Hesseltine, *Civil War Prisons: A Study in War Psychology* (New York: Frederick Unger Publishing, 1930), 55.
   21. Sgt. W.D. Bishop to Susan Bishop, July 18, 1861, R. Matthew Poteat, ed., "Dear Mother: The Papers of Sergeant William D. Bishop, Co. L 22nd North Carolina Troops," unpublished manuscript, State Archives, Raleigh, 4.
   22. *Standard*, July 24, 1861.
   23. Brig. Gen. John H. Winder to Lt. D.H. Todd, July 13, 1861, CGL.
   24. Kenneth Rayner to Thomas Ruffin, July 18, 1861, Hamilton, *The Papers of Thomas Ruffin*, 3: 237; *Standard*, July 24, 1861; *Register*, July 24, 1861; Elizabeth Reid Murray, *Wake: Capital County of North Carolina*, 1 vol. to date (Raleigh: Capital County Publishing Co., 1983), 460, 619. The local church was "Neville's Church," a "stone building located in the eastern suburbs" between E. Cabarrus Street and E. Lenoir Street, near Swain Street.
   25. Sgt. W.D. Bishop to Susan Bishop, July 18, 1861, Poteat, "Papers of Sgt. W.D. Bishop," 4; *Standard*, July 24, 1861; *Register* (Raleigh), July 24, 1861.
   26. H.T. Clark to D. H. Todd, July 18, 1861, CGL.
   27. H.T. Clark to Leroy P. Walker, July 10, 1861, Military Board Letter Book, State Archives, North Carolina Office of Archives and History, Raleigh.
   28. H.T. Clark to Leroy P. Walker, July 26, 1861, CGL; Leroy P. Walker to John W. Ellis, July 8, 1861; Tolbert, *The Papers of John W. Ellis*, 2: 884. Walker had contacted the governor's office in July the day after Ellis' death about the possibility of building a prison and suggested Alamance County, near Greensboro. Clark and his administration located the Salisbury property.
   29. William Johnston to H.T. Clark, July 25, 1861, CGL.
   30. H.T. Clark to Leroy P. Walker, July 10, 1861,

ORA, ser. 2, 3: 682; Hesseltine, *Civil War Prisons*, 56.

31. Leroy P. Walker to H.T. Clark, July 30, 1861, CGL.

32. *Ibid.*, 46; ORA, ser. 4, 1: 130, 126–127, 827.

33. H.T. Clark to Leroy P. Walker, July 26, 1861, CGL.

34. Leroy P. Walker to H.T. Clark, July 27, 1861, CGL.

35. Louis A. Brown, *The Salisbury Prison: A Case Study of Confederate Military Prisons 1861–1865* (Wendell, NC: Avera Press, 1980); Braxton Craven to Judah P. Benjamin, December 20, 1861, ORA, ser. 2, 3:758; Judah P. Benjamin to Braxton Craven, December 24, 1861, ORA, ser. 2, 3:758, 760.

36. Hesseltine, *Civil War Prisons*, 57.

37. Brown, *The Salisbury Prison*, 2.

38. HT Clark to Judah P. Benjamin, March 22, 1862, CGL.

39. *Journal of the Senate of North Carolina, First Extra Session 1861*, 61; Barrett, *Civil War in North Carolina*, 32; *State Journal*, July 17, 1861.

40. "An Act to Create a Military Board," Minutes of the Military Board, Governor's Office Records, State Archives, Office of Archives and History, Raleigh; Barrett, *Civil War in North Carolina*, 32.

41. *Standard*, July 24, 1861.

42. *State Journal*, June 26, 1861.

43. *State Journal*, August 14, 1861.

44. McKinney, *Zeb Vance*, 111; Kruman, *Parties and Politics*, 231.

45. W. Buck Yearns and John G. Barrett, eds., *North Carolina Civil War Documentary* (Chapel Hill: University of North Carolina Press, 1980), xii–xiii; Walter Clark, ed, *Histories of the Several Regiments and Battalions from North Carolina in the Great War, 1861–1865*. 5 vols. (Raleigh: State of North Carolina, 1901), 5:4; Brian Holden Reid, *Robert E. Lee: Icon for a Nation* (London: Orion Publishing, 2005), 66–67.

46. HT Clark to Jefferson Davis, August 6, 1861, CGL.

47. Lefler and Newsome, *North Carolina*, 442.

48. Barrett, *The Civil War in North Carolina*, 17.

49. William C. Harris, *North Carolina and the Coming of the Civil War* (Raleigh: Office of Archives and History), 1988.

50. Drew Gilpin Faust, *The Creation of Confederate Nationalism: Ideology and Identity in the Civil War South* (Baton Rouge: Louisiana State University Press, 1988), 34.

51. *Journal of the House of Commons, First Extra Session, 1861*, 34–38; "An Act to raise 10,000 State troops," May 8, 1861, ORA, ser. 4, 1:402–404; "An Act to raise provisional forces for the Confederate States of America, and for other purposes," February 28, 1861, ORA, ser. 4, 1:117; Louis H. Manarin and Weymouth T. Jordan Jr., comps, *North Carolina Troops, 1861–1865: A Roster*, 15 vols. to date (Raleigh: Office of Archives and History, Department of Cultural Resources, 1979), 1:xi–xii; Barrett, *The Civil War in North Carolina*, 14–15; Eric McKitrick, "Party Politics and the Union and Confederate War Efforts," in *The American Party Systems: Stages of Political Development*, ed. William N. Chambers and Walter Dean Burnham (New York: Oxford University Press, 1967), 134; *Standard*, May 1, 1861.

52. "An ordinance to provide for the disposition of the state troops and volunteers," *Ordinances of the State Convention*, June 27, 1861, (Raleigh: State of North Carolina, 1863), 8–10; *The Journal of the House of Commons*, Second Extra Session, 1861, 11; *Journal*, August 15, 1861; Sitterson, *The Secession Movement in North Carolina*, 72–99; Barrett, *The Civil War in North Carolina*, 14–15; Wooster, *The Secession Conventions of the South*, 190–203.

53. *The Journal of the House of Commons*, Second Extra Session, 1861, 9–15.

54. *The Journal of the House of Commons*, Second Extra Session, 1861; *Journal*, August 22, 1861.

55. *State Journal*, August 21, 1861.

56. *Public Laws of the State of North Carolina, Second Extra Session, 1861*, 15; "Militia Bill," September 20, 1861, *Public Laws of the State of North Carolina, Second Extra Session, 1861*, 18–46.

57. *Standard*, August 17, 1861.

58. Clark, *Histories of the Several Regiments*, 1:25; Barrett, *Civil War in North Carolina*, 27.

59. Bezer Blundell, *The Contributions of John Lewis Peyton to the History of Virginia and of the Civil War in America, 1861–65*, (London: John Wilson, 1868), 27–28.

60. *Daily Examiner* (Richmond), November 29, 1861; John L. Peyton to HT Clark, December 31, 1861, CGP; John L. Peyton to William A. Graham, September 28, 1861, Max R. Williams, J. G. de Roulhac Hamilton, and Mary R. Peacock, eds., *The Papers of William Alexander Gra*ham, 8 vols. (Raleigh: Office of Archives and History, 1957–1992) 5:297; John L. Peyton, *The American Crisis: Pages from the Notebook of a State Agent during the Civil War* 2 vols. (London: Saunders, Otley, and Co., 1867), 1:112–113, 195; DNCB, s. v. "John Lewis Peyton"; Bezer Blundell, *The Contributions of John Lewis Peyton*, 27–28, 35.

61. John L. Peyton to HT Clark, December 31, 1861, CGP; *Public and Private Laws of North Carolina, 1862–1863*, 136; Clark, *Histories of the Several Regiments*, 1:42; "Estimate of the cost of an armory," *Executive and Legislative Documents*, Document 29, January 10, 1861.

62. Blundell, *The Contributions of John Lewis Peyton to the History of Virginia and of the Civil War in America*.

63. John L. Peyton to HT Clark, December 31, 1861, CGP; Powell, "Confederate Federalism: a view from the governors."

64. HT Clark to George Randolph, April 23, 1862, CGL.

65. Chris E. Fonvielle, Jr., "'Never Suffer for Machines' of War: Louis Froelich as Arms-Maker to North Carolina and the Confederacy," *North Carolina Historical Review* 84 (July 2007), 300–325.

66. *Ibid.*

67. *Ibid.*
68. HT Clark to General Richard C. Gatlin, March 24, 1862, CGL.
69. HT Clark to Jefferson Davis, April 3, 1862, CGL.
70. Jefferson Davis to HT Clark, April 15, 1862, CGL.
71. *Public and Private Laws of North Carolina, 1862–1863*, 131–214; Clark, *Histories of the Several Regiments*, 1:43.
72. *Standard*, April 5, 1862; *DNCB*, s. v. "William Shepperd Ashe." In the spring of 1862, when much of the eastern portion of the state came under attack, Ashe (1814–1862) pressed his long-time friend President Jefferson Davis for a commission. He was killed in a train accident in September.
73. *Public Laws of the State of North Carolina, Second Extra Session, 1861*, 124–125; Quartermaster-General Circular, November 1861, *ORA*, ser. 4, 1:767; Special Orders No. 86, Adjutant and Inspector General's Office, April 15, 1862, *ORA*, ser. 4, 1:1059–1060; Frank E. Vandiver, "Makeshifts of Confederate Ordnance," *The Journal of Southern History* 17 (May 1951), 183; Charles W. Ramsdell, *Behind the Lines in the Southern Confederacy* (Baton Rouge: Louisiana State University Press, 1944), 93, 117; Bensel, *Yankee Leviathan*, 135.
74. *The Journal of the House of Commons, Second Extra Session*, 1861, 13.
75. "To the People of North Carolina," April 15, 1862, CGL.
76. Clark issued "500 flint and steel muskets" to Florida troops. Madison Stark Perry to HT Clark, July 21, 1861, CGL.
77. HT Clark to William S. Ashe, April 24, 1862, CGL.
78. Ibid, 26–28; McKinney, *Zeb Vance*, 111.
79. Clark, *Histories of the Several Regiments*, 1:25–27.

Chapter 4

1. *The Journal of the House of Commons, Second Extra Session*, 1861, 12–13; Barrett, *Civil War in North Carolina*, 25.
2. *Ibid.*
3. Trotter, *Ironclads and Columbiads*, 16.
4. William Morrison Robinson, *The Confederate Privateers* (New Haven: Yale University Press, 1928), 101–115; David Page, *Ship Versus Shore: Civil War Engagements Along Southern Shores and Rivers* (Nashville: Rutledge Hill Press, 1994), 59; James M. Merrill, "The Hatteras Expedition, August, 1861," *North Carolina Historical Review* 29 (April 1952), 201–219.
5. *Journal* (Wilmington), July 11, 1861; Robinson, *The Confederate Privateers*, 101–115; Barrett, *Civil War in North Carolina*, 35; Clark, *Histories of the Several Regiments*, 5: 299–301; John W. Ellis to Jefferson Davis, April 25, 1861; Ellis to Marshall Parks, April 25, May 9, 1861, Ellis to Walter Gwynn, June 6, 1861, Tolbert, *The Papers of John W. Ellis*, 2: 618, 678, 733–734, 826. The *Winslow* was captured and sunk in Ocracoke Inlet in November 1861.
6. Gideon Welles to Silas Stringham, August 20, 1861, *ORN*, ser. 1, 6: 100–101. There is some dispute over the actual number of guns aboard the *Winslow*. Some primary sources say one, others two.
7. William Morrison Robinson, Jr., "Admiralty in 1861: The Confederate States District Court for the Division of Pamlico of the District of North Carolina," *North Carolina Historical Review* 17 (April 1940), 132–138.
8. Robinson, *The Confederate Privateers*, 110; *Journal*, August 24, 1861.
9. Trotter, *Ironclads and Columbiads*, 33–41.
10. Report of Major General Benjamin F. Butler, August 29, 1861, *ORA*, ser. 1, 4: 583–586; Merrill, "The Hatteras Expedition," 201–219; Ivan Musicant, *Divided Waters: The Naval History of the Civil War* (New York: Harper Collins, 1995), 76–89; Barrett, *Civil War in North Carolina*, 36–49; Trotter, *Ironclads and Columbiads*, 33–41.
11. Trotter, *Ironclads and Columbiads*, 41; Page, *Ship Versus Shore*, 63.
12. *Times* (London, U.K.), September 13, 23, 1861; *Journal*, July 16, 1861; Robert M. Browning, Jr., *From Cape Charles to Cape Fear: The North Atlantic Blockading Squadron During The Civil War* (Tuscaloosa: University of Alabama Press, 1993), 7–8.
13. H.T. Clark to Leroy P. Walker, September 2, 1861, *ORA*, ser 1, 4: 638; Trotter, *Ironclads and Columbiads*, 56–57.
14. H.T. Clark to Judah P. Benjamin, September 25, 1861, *ORA*, ser. 1, 4: 658.
15. H.T. Clark to Leroy P. Walker, September 8, 1861; S. Cooper to Brig. Gen. Joseph R. Anderson, September 3, 1861, *ORA*, ser. 1, 4: 639.
16. "An Act to Provide Additional Defences for the Coast of North Carolina," September 20, 1861, *Public Laws of the State of North Carolina, Second Extra Session*, 1861, 53–54.
17. H.T. Clark to Jefferson Davis, December 16, 1861, *ORA*, ser. 1, 1: 711–712.
18. *DNCB*, s.v. "Marble Nash Taylor;" Governor's Scrapbook, Henry T. Clark Papers, PC; Alex Christopher Meekins, "Unionism and the Arcane Origin of 'Buffalo,'" *The North Carolina Historical Review* 85 (July 2008), 305.
19. Neptune was the Roman god of the sea and Boreas the Greek god of the north wind. Beth Crabtree and James W. Patton, eds., *Journal of a Secesh Lady: The Diary of Catherine Ann Devereux Edmondston, 1860–1866* (Raleigh: Office of Archives and History, 1979), 86.
20. Louis M. Goldsborough to Gideon Welles, February 1, 1862, *ORN*, ser. 1, 6:540.
21. H.T. Clark to Judah P. Benjamin, September 24, 1861, *ORA*, ser. 1, 4:657.
22. H.T. Clark to Judah P. Benjamin, September 24, September 25, 1861, *ORA*, ser. 1, 4: 657–658;

Cheney, *North Carolina Government*, 825–826. State law defined treason as "levying War against [North Carolina], or in adhering to her enemies; giving aid and comfort."

23. Judah P. Benjamin to H.T. Clark, September 27, 1861, *ORA*, ser. 1, 51: 319.

24. John W. Graham to William A. Graham, September 22, 1861; Williams, Hamilton, and Peacock, *Papers of William Alexander Graham*, 5: 296; David Schenck Papers, September 11, 1861, SHC.

25. *Journal*, September 15, 1861.

26. William J. Clarke to Mary Bayard Clarke, September 21, 1861; Terrel A. Crow and Mary M. Barden, eds., *Live Your Own Life: The Family Papers of Mary Bayard Clarke, 1854–1886* (Columbia: University of South Carolina Press, 2003); Meekins, "Unionism and the Arcane Origin of 'Buffalo,'" 307–309.

27. "Report of the Commissioners sent by the Convention to confer with the President of the Confederate States in regard to the transfer of the troops raised by North Carolina to that Government, June 1861," *Documents of the Convention of 1861*, North Carolina Collection, University of North Carolina at Chapel Hill.

28. H.T. Clark to Judah P. Benjamin, September 27, 1861, *ORA*, ser. 1, 4: 660.

29. H.T. Clark to Judah P. Benjamin, October 26, 1861, CGL.

30. Diary of Thomas Bragg, entry of February 14, 1862, SHC.

31. Proclamation, Henry T. Clark Papers, PC.

32. H.T. Clark to Jefferson Davis, December 16, 1861, *ORA*, ser. 1, 1: 711–712.

33. *Ibid.*

34. Barrett, *Civil War in North Carolina*, 74–84; Browning, *From Cape Charles to Cape Fear*, 24–27; Trotter, *Ironclads and Columbiads*, 64–65; Page, *Ship Versus Shore*, 65.

35. L.O.B. Branch to H.T. Clark, September 17, 1861, CGL.

36. William J. Clarke to H.T. Clark, March 1, 1862, CGP.

37. "An ordinance to provide for the disposition of the state troops and volunteers," *Ordinances of the State Convention*, June 27, 1861 (Raleigh: State of North Carolina, 1863), 8–10; William T. Auman and David D. Scarboro, "The Heroes of America in Civil War North Carolina," *North Carolina Historical Review* 58 (October 1981), 333; Clark, *Histories of the Several Regiments*, 1: 8.

38. *New York Times*, May 2, 1862; Barrett, *Civil War in North Carolina*, 66–130.

39. *Ibid.*, 107–120.

40. *Ibid.*, 133, 149. Lee told Gen. Longstreet, "The enemy's positions in North Carolina have always appeared to me to be taken for defense."

41. *Journal of the House of Commons, Second Extra Session*, 1861, 14–15.

42. Stephen R. Wise, *Lifeline of the Confederacy: Blockade Running During the Civil War* (Columbia: University of South Carolina Press, 1988), 105–106;

Clark, *Histories of the Several Regiments*, 5: 358–363; "Henry Toole Clark," February 1908, Joseph Blount Cheshire Papers, SHC. Cheshire claims that James G. Martin told him that "this scheme for the purchase and use of a blockade-running steamship was suggested and taken up by Governor Clark's administration." Therefore, I contend that the idea was not wholly Vance's and that Clark had some input into its conception.

43. Michael Powell, "Confederate Federalism: A View from the Governors," 1–7.

44. Frank Lawrence Owsley, *King Cotton Diplomacy: Foreign Relations of the Confederate States of America* (Chicago: University of Chicago Press, 1959).

45. H.T. Clark to Robert M. Hunter, October 15, 1861, HTCUNC.

46. Christopher Ewan, "The Emancipation Proclamation and British Public Opinion," *The Historian* 67 (Spring 2005), 1–19; R.J. Blackett, *Divided Hearts: Britain and the American Civil War* (Baton Rouge: Louisiana State University Press, 2001).

47. H.T. Clark to Jefferson Davis, September 14, 1861, *ORA*, ser. 2, 3: 720; *Journal*, August 1, 8, 1861; Milledge L. Bonham, Jr., *British Consuls in the Confederacy* (New York: Columbia University, 1911), 97.

48. McRae appears not to have been British. Clark said, "Vice-consul D. MacRay [sic] of Wilmington, I only know as a citizen of North Carolina." H.T. Clark to Robert M. Hunter, October 15, 1861, HTCUNC; Bonham, *British Consuls in the Confederacy*, 97.

49. Robert Bunch to H.T. Clark, August 29, 1861, *ORA*, ser. 2, 3: 721.

50. Robert Bunch to H.T. Clark, September 11, 1861, *ORA*, ser. 2, 3: 721; Bonham, *British Consuls in the Confederacy*, 101.

51. H.T. Clark to Robert Bunch, October 4, 1861, CGL. Bunch did press the claim for damages to the Confederate government, but to no avail. H.T. Clark to Robert Hunter, October 15, 1861, HTCUNC.

52. Bonham, British Consuls in the Confederacy, 99(n).

53. Browning, *From Cape Charles to Cape Fear*, 12; H.T. Clark to Leroy P. Walker, September 8, 1861; S. Cooper to Brig. Gen. Joseph R. Anderson, September 3, 1861, *ORA*, ser 1, 4: 639. Civil War-era military organization was not an exact science. A Confederate artillery "battalion" usually consisted of three to five batteries of about three to six guns each. An infantry battalion was made up of a few companies, ideally 100 men per company. A regiment usually consisted of 1000 men (ten companies), but a full complement of men was rarely achieved. The seven forts mentioned are Oregon, Hatteras, Clark, Ocracoke, Macon, Johnston, and Caswell. There were other numerous other "forts" and batteries along the state's rivers and inland waters.

54. H.T. Clark to Leroy P. Walker, September 7, 1861, *ORA*, ser. 1, 4: 643.

Chapter 5

1. *Journal of the House of Commons, Second Extra Session, 1861*, 14; Barrett, *Civil War in North Carolina*, 182.
2. Mark Kurlansky, *Salt: A World History* (New York: Walker and Co., 2002); Ella Lonn, *Salt as a Factor in the Confederacy* (Tuscaloosa: University of Alabama Press, 1965).
3. Lonn, *Salt as a Factor in the Confederacy*, 87, 98–99; McKinney, *Zeb Vance*, 118; David D. Scarboro, "North Carolina and the Confederacy: The Weakness of States' Rights During the Civil War," *North Carolina Historical Review* 56 (April 1979), 140–141.
4. H.T. Clark to Ebenezer Emmons, November 7, 1861, CGL; "Manufacturing of Salt from Sea Water," *Documents of the Convention, 1861–1862*, North Carolina Collection, Chapel Hill; *DNCB*, s.v., "Ebenezer Emmons."
5. H.T. Clark to John M. Worth, July 21, 1862, CGL; "An Ordinance to Encourage the Mining and Manufacture of Salt in the Interior of the State," *Ordinances of the State Conventions*, January 30, 1862, 28–29; An Ordinance in Regard to the Supply of Salt," December 6, 1861, *Ordinances of the State Conventions*, 15–17; Lonn, *Salt as a Factor in the Confederacy*, 98.
6. H.T. Clark to N. W. Woodfin, July 5, 1862, CGL; Contract with N. W. Woodfin, July 1, 1862, CGL.
7. Lonn, *Salt as a Factor in the Confederacy*, 104–105; H.T. Clark to John M. Worth, August 31, 1862, CGL; "An ordinance for enabling the governor to regulate the price of provisions and clothing, and to cause them to be seized for public use," April 1862, Henry T. Clark Papers, PC.
8. H.T. Clark to John M. Worth, June 16, 1862, CGL; Tinsley Lee Spraggins, "Mobilization of Negro Labor for the Department of Virginia and North Carolina," *North Carolina Historical Review* 24 (April 1947), 160–197.
9. H.T. Clark to John M. Worth, August 31, 1862, CGL.
10. Z.B. Vance to the North Carolina General Assembly, November 17, 1862, *ORA*, ser. 4, 2: 182.
11. *Journal of the Senate, Second Extra Session*, 1861, 74; *Public Laws of the State of North Carolina, Second Extra Session*, 1861, 3.
12. Z.B. Vance to the General Assembly, November 17, 1862, *ORA*, ser. 4, 2: 184.
13. *Standard*, June 11, 1862; Clark, *Histories of the Several Regiments*, 1: 44; Barrett, *Civil War in North Carolina*, 25; H.T. Clark to Josiah Gorgas, January 10, 1862, CGL; Murray, *Wake: Capital County of North Carolina*, 469.
14. William T. Auman and David D. Scarboro, "The Heroes of America in Civil War North Carolina," *The North Carolina Historical Review* 58 (October 1981), 333; James H. Moore to H.T. Clark, July 18, 1861, CGL.
15. Federal Census of the United States, 1860: Davidson County, "John Helton." There is no John "Hilton" listed in the 1860 census for North Carolina.
16. Ibid.
17. H.T. Clark to James H. Moore, July 19, 1861, CGL.
18. Paul D. Escott, *Many Excellent People: Power and Privilege in North Carolina, 1850–1900* (Chapel Hill: University of North Carolina Press, 1985), 59–60; David Schenck Books, Diary (May 25, 1861, to December 15, 1861), entry for Tuesday, August 6, 1861, entitled "Disturbance in Davidson County," SHC.
19. The Quaker Belt included the counties of Davidson, Forsyth, Guilford, and Randolph. William T. Auman, "Neighbor against Neighbor: The Inner Civil War in the Randolph Area of Confederate North Carolina," *North Carolina Historical Review* 61 (January 1984), 60. For a discussion of disaffection see Georgia Lee Tatum, *Disloyalty in the Confederacy* (Chapel Hill: University of North Carolina Press, 1934); William W. Freehling, *The South vs. The South: How Anti-Confederate Southerners Shaped the Course of the Civil War* (New York: Oxford University Press, 2001).
20. Auman, "Neighbor against Neighbor," 65.
21. Proclamation, March 4, 1862, CGL.
22. H.T. Clark to Spier Whitaker, March 6, 1862, CGL; Mobley, *War Governor of the South*, 42.
23. Durrill, *War of Another Kind: A Southern Community in the Great Rebellion*, 49–56.
24. Ibid.
25. Meekins, "Unionism and the Arcane Origin of 'Buffalo,'" 312–313.
26. Henry M. Earle to H.T. Clark, March 8, 1862, CGP.
27. Alex J. Cansler to H.T. Clark, August 20, 1861, CGP; Federal Census of the United States, 1860: Polk County, "A.J. Cansler."
28. Martin Crawford, *Ashe County's Civil War: Community and Society in the Appalachian South* (Charlottesville: University of Virginia Press, 2001), 86; H.T. Clark to Judah Benjamin, November 16, 1861, CGL; Barrett, *Civil War in North Carolina*, 181; John C. Inscoe and Gordon B. McKinney, *The Heart of Confederate Appalachia: Western North Carolina in the Civil War* (Chapel Hill: University of North Carolina Press, 2000), 107.
29. Barrett, *Civil War in North Carolina*, 197.
30. E. Stanly Godbold, Jr., and Mattie U. Russell, *Confederate Colonel and Cherokee Chief: The Life of William Holland Thomas* (Knoxville: University of Tennessee Press, 1990), 97–105.
31. Richard H. Garrett to Charles Garrett, February 6, 1862, Miscellaneous Papers, 1861–1912, series 1, vol. 4, p. 9, State Archives, Raleigh. Garrett was an Edgecombe County native and a first lieutenant in the 30th Regiment of state militia.
32. Confederate military strategy, often described as "offensive defense," combined elements of European-Napoleonic tactics with American combat experience in the Mexican War. Jomini advocated the use of large land forces, speed, maneuverability, and the

Notes — Chapter 5

capture of strategic points during battle. Clausewitz pressed the need for a mobile defense that could move against an enemy's flank or rear. He is credited with the concept of "total war." See Antoine Henri Jomini, *The Art of War*, trans. G.H. Mendell and W.P. Craighill (Westport, Conn.: Greenwood, 1971); Carl von Clausewitz, *On War*, edited and translated by Michael Howard and Peter Paret (Princeton: Princeton University Press, 1976); Richard E. Beringer, Herman Hattaway, et al., *Why The South Lost the Civil War* (Athens: University of Georgia Press, 1986), 39–52; Frank E. Vandiver, *Their Tattered Flags: The Epic of the Confederacy* (New York: Harpers Magazine Press, 1970).

33. Joseph L. Harsh, *Confederate Tide Rising: Robert E. Lee and the Making of Southern Strategy, 1861–1862* (Kent: Kent State University Press, 1998), 14; E. Merton Coulter, *The Confederate States of America, 1861–1865* (Baton Rouge: Louisiana State University Press, 1950), 308–332; Paul D. Escott, "Unwilling Hercules," 267; Barrett, *Civil War in North Carolina*, 183, 234. Incomplete reports show that 81,993 conscripts were drafted in the Confederate states east of the Mississippi from April 16, 1862, until early 1865.

34. Sgt. W.D. Bishop to Susan Bishop, April 4, 1862, Poteat, "Papers of Sgt. William D. Bishop," 23–24.

35. There is controversy over the length and purpose of desertions in Southern armies. Though some deserters simply quit the army, many returned to the ranks after a visit home. See Richard Reid, "A Test Case of Crying Evil: Desertion Among North Carolina Troops During the Civil War," *North Carolina Historical Review* 58 (July 1981), 234; Ella Lonn, *Desertion During the Civil War* (Gloucester, Mass.: Peter Smith, 1966); Richard Bardolph, "Inconstant Rebels: Desertion of North Carolina Troops in the Civil War," *The North Carolina Historical Review* 41 (April 1964), 163–189; Inscoe and McKinney, *The Heart of Confederate Appalachia*, 143; Barrett, *Civil War in North Carolina*, 182; Bell Irvin Wiley, *The Life of Johnny Reb: The Common Soldier of the Confederacy* (Indianapolis: Bobbs-Merrill, 1943), 143; Escott, "Unwilling Hercules," 267.

36. George W. Randolph to H.T. Clark, July 17, 1862, CGL.

37. H.T. Clark to the Council of State, March 18, 1862, CGP.

38. H.T. Clark to Jefferson Davis, July 31, 1862, HTCD.

39. H.T. Clark to the People of Randolph, August 4, 1862, CGL.

40. H.T. Clark to George W. Randolph, April 24, 1862, CGL.

41. H.T. Clark to Jefferson Davis, April 23, 1862, CGL.

42. H.T. Clark to Jefferson Davis, August 22, 1862, *ORA*, ser. 4, 2: 67–68.

43. Albert Burton Moore, *Conscription and Conflict in the Confederacy* (New York: Macmillan, 1924), 16; David Donald, "Died of Democracy," *Why the North Won the Civil War*, 90.

44. H.T. Clark to Rev. I.G. Whitfield, July 14, 1862, CGL; H.T. Clark to Col. Sol Williams, July 14, 1862, CGL.

45. H.T. Clark to Col. Williams, July 11, 1862, CGL.

46. "An Act to Organize Bands of Partisan Rangers," *ORA*, ser. 4, 1: 1094; Coulter, *The Confederate States of America, 1861–1865*, 338; Patricia L. Faust et al., eds., *Historical Times Illustrated Encyclopedia of the Civil War* (New York: Harper Collins, 1986), 561.

47. H.T. Clark to George W. Randolph, August 28, 1862, *ORA*, ser. 4, 2: 71–72.

48. H.T. Clark to Robert Bunch, March 24, 1862, CGL; D.M. Barringer to Col. J.C. Barnhardt, March 25, 1862, CGL; Bonham, *British Consuls in the Confederacy*, 104. Alfred G. Crate, another Englishman, was also drafted and appealed his impressment. Lt. Col. A.S. Holton to H.T. Clark, March 20, 1862, CGP.

49. Moore, *Conscription and Conflict in the Confederacy*, 27.

50. *ORA*, ser 4, 1: 694–695, 975, 1099. Substitution was allowed by most states early in the war before the draft law was enacted. The infamous "Twenty-Negro rule" that exempted one white man for every twenty slaves was not passed until October 1862, and therefore was not an issue Clark faced. See "An Act to Exempt Certain Persons from Military Duty," *ORA*, October 11, 1862, ser. 4, 2: 162.

51. H.T. Clark to James F. Oliver, Esq., May 26, 1862, CGL; *Standard*, June 25, 1862.

52. For a list of exemptions, see "An Act to exempt certain persons from enrollment for service in the armies of the Confederate States," April 21, 1862, *ORA*, ser. 4, 1: 1081; See also Memory F. Mitchell, *Legal Aspects of Conscription and Exemption in North Carolina, 1861–1865* (Chapel Hill: University of North Carolina Press, 1965).

53. Petition from Chatham County to H.T. Clark, March 11, 1862, CGP.

54. Citizens of Buncombe to H.T. Clark, May 17, 1862, CGL.

55. *ORA*, October 11, 1862, ser. 4, 2: 160–161.

56. Nancy Williams to H.T. Clark, March 15, 1862, CGP; The Undersigned Ladies of Halifax County to Henry T. Clark, July 1, 1862, CGP; Paul D. Escott, "Poverty and Governmental Aid for the Poor in Confederate North Carolina," *North Carolina Historical Review* 61 (October 1984): 469. For extended discussions of Southern women and the Civil War see Drew Gilpin Faust, *Mothers of Invention: Women of the Slaveholding South in the American Civil War* (Chapel Hill: University of North Carolina Press, 1996); Victoria E. Bynum, *Unruly Women: The Politics of Social and Sexual Control in the Old South* (Chapel Hill: University of North Carolina Press, 1992).

57. *Journal* (Wilmington), July 18, 1861.

58. Proclamation by the Governor, November 7, 1861, CGL. "Linseys" refers to coarse linen fabric, also known as "linsey-woolsey."

59. Proclamation by the Governor, March 28, 1862, CGL; *Journal* (Wilmington), April 10, 1862.

60. H.T. Clark to Thomas Ruffin, May 19, 1862, Hamilton, *Papers of Thomas Ruffin*, 3: 237; Barrett, *The Civil War in North Carolina*, 28.

61. Francis W. Pickens to H.T. Clark, April 18, 1862, CGP.

62. H.T. Clark to Weldon N. Edwards, April 23, 1862, CGL; "An Ordinance for enabling the governor to regulate the price of provisions and clothing, and to cause them to be seized for public use," April 1862, H.T. Clark Papers, PC.

63. H.T. Clark to James J. Iredell, July 15, 1862, CGL.

64. For a discussion of hardships visited upon North Carolinians in disputed areas of the east, see Alex Christopher Meekins, "Caught Between Scylla and Charybdis: the Civil War in Northeastern North Carolina" (master's thesis, North Carolina State University, 2001).

65. Richard Paxton to H.T. Clark, March 21, 1862, CGP. According to the 1860 Federal Census, Paxton owned at least forty-five slaves and was worth about $65,000.

66. *Ibid.*

67. Governor's Message, November 20, 1860, *Executive and Legislative Documents*, 1860–1861, Document 1, 25; Winthrop D. Jordan, *White Over Black: American Attitudes Toward the Negro, 1550–1812* (Baltimore: Penguin Books, 1969); Freehling, *The South vs. The South*, 20–21.

68. H.T. Clark to Thomas Goode Tucker, March 18, 1862, CGL.

69. *Ibid.*

70. *Standard*, April 2, 1862.

71. *Standard*, May 21, 1862.

72. *Standard*, June 25, 30, 1862; Barrett, *Civil War in North Carolina*, 182.

73. Mobley, *War Governor of the South*, 31–32; Richard E. Yates, "Zebulon B. Vance as War Governor of North Carolina, 1862–1865," *The Journal of Southern History* 3 (February 1937), 43–75.

74. *Standard*, June 4, 1862; Mobley, *War Governor of the South*, 31–32.

75. Baker, "Class Conflict and Political Upheaval: The Transformation of North Carolina Politics during the Civil War," 148–178; McKinney, *Zeb Vance*, 96–109; Kruman, *Parties and Politics in North Carolina*, 230–240; Mobley, *War Governor of the South*, 31–32.

Chapter 6

1. As justice of the peace, Clark married several couples. On August 23, 1864, Clark married a couple "at the Edgecombe House in this place. Mr. C.N. Civalier of Tarboro and Miss Myra E. Lee of Virginia." *Southerner*, August 27, 1864.

2. David Clark to H.T. Clark, August 17, 1862, CGP.

3. Mary P. Clark to Catherine Drane, September 26 [1862], Robert Brent Drane Papers, SHC. Monreath was the home of Clark's cousin, Elizabeth Parker Cheshire, and her husband, Joseph Blount Cheshire. Mary was very close to Elizabeth.

4. Fleming, *Edgecombe County*, 68–74.

5. *Ibid.*, 69–70; Barrett, *Civil War in North Carolina*, 138.

6. "Report of Brig. Gen. Edward E. Potter," July 29, 1863, *ORA*, ser. 1, 27, part II, 964–966; "Report of Maj. Ferris Jacobs, Jr.," July 25, 1863, *ORA*, ser. 1, 27, part II, 968–969; *Standard*, July 24, 1863; Barrett, *Civil War in North Carolina*, 164–165; David A. Norris, "'The Yankees Have Been Here!': The Story of Brig. Gen. Edward E. Potter's Raid on Greenville, Tarboro, and Rocky Mount, July 19–23, 1863," *North Carolina Historical Review* 73 (January 1996), 1–27.

7. "Henry Toole Clark," February 1908, Joseph Blount Cheshire Papers, SHC. "Little Sorrell" was also the name of Confederate General "Stonewall" Jackson's horse.

8. *Ibid.*; David A. Norris, "'The Yankees Have Been Here!,'" 12; *State Journal*, August 5, 1863. "Old Nick" was "Mr. Nick Williams of Yadkin County" who had sent the governor several bottles of his whiskey.

9. *Southerner*, February 17, 1903, February 27, 1908; Turner and Bridgers, *History of Edgecombe County*, 229; David A. Norris, "'The Yankees Have Been Here!,'" 18.

10. E.C. Branson, et al., *County Government and County Affairs in North Carolina: Addresses Before the North Carolina Club at the University of North Carolina, 1917–1918* (Chapel Hill: University of North Carolina, 1918), 20–21; A. Fleming Bell and Warren J. Wicker, eds., *County Government in North Carolina*, 4th ed. (Chapel Hill: University of North Carolina at Chapel Hill, 1999).

11. *Ibid.*

12. "Notice," April 2, 1864, Henry T. Clark Papers, PC; George K. Davis and Gary M. Pecquet, "Interest Rates in the Civil War South," *The Journal of Economic History* 50 (March 1990), 133–148.

13. "Henry Toole Clark," February 1908, Joseph Blount Cheshire Papers, SHC; Mary P. Clark to Catherine Drane, September 26 [1862], Robert Brent Drane Papers, SHC; R.R. Bridgers to H.T. Clark, September 6, 1862, HTCD.

14. According to the Rhode Island Historical Society library in Providence, "Nathan Mathewson in North Carolina, owner of substantial property in Providence, makes disposition of his slaves who are probably in North Carolina." http://www.rihs.org/mssinv/PeopleofColorweb.htm.

15. *New York Times*, September 15, 1863; Pardon Application of Henry T. Clark, Military Collection, Civil War Collection, Petitions for Pardon, 1865–1868, Edgecombe County, State Archives, Division of Archives and History, Raleigh; Daniel W. Hamilton, "The Confederate Sequestration Act," *Civil War History* 52 (December 2006), 373–408.

16. Mary P. Clark to Catherine Drane, September 26 [1862], Robert Brent Drane Papers, SHC. Col. Parker survived the war.

17. Watson, *Edgecombe County*, 73–74.

18. Joe A. Mobley, *James City: A Black Community in North Carolina, 1863–1900* (Raleigh: North Carolina Division of Archives and History, 1981); Fleming, *Edgecombe County*, 74–75; Ira Berlin, *Generations of Captivity: A History of African-American Slaves* (Cambridge: Harvard University Press, 2003).

19. Berlin, *Generations of Captivity*, 263.

20. Dan T. Carter, *When the War Was Over: The Failure of Self-Reconstruction in the South, 1865–1867* (Baton Rouge: Louisiana State University Press, 1985).

21. Karen L. Zipf, "The WHITES shall rule the land or die": Gender, Race, and Class in North Carolina Reconstruction Politics," *The Journal of Southern History* 65 (August 1999), 499–534.

22. John David Smith, *Black Voices from Reconstruction, 1865–1877* (Brookfield, Conn.: Millbrook Press, 1996), 66.

23. [Unknown from Halifax Co., N.C.] to H.T. Clark, June 21, 1868, HTCD.

24. Eric Foner, *A Short History of Reconstruction, 1863–1877* (New York: Harper and Row, 1990), 73–78.

25. Appendix, Records of the Field Offices for the State of North Carolina, Bureau of Refugees, Freedmen, and Abandoned Lands, 1865–1872, National Archives, Washington, D.C.; Labor Contract, January 1867, HTCD.

26. Federal Census of the United States, 1870: Edgecombe County, North Carolina. Chesterfield Clark was forty-nine and the father of two. His wife, Hannah, was likely Gov. Clark's domestic servant.

27. *Ibid*.; Smith, *Black Voices from Reconstruction*.

28. Oscar J. Dunn as cited in Smith, *Black Voices from Reconstruction*, 65.

29. Hans L. Trefousse, *Andrew Johnson: A Biography* (New York: W.W. Norton, 1989); Eric L. McKitrick, *Andrew Johnson and Reconstruction* (New York: Oxford University Press, 1961, reprinted 1988).

30. Andrew Johnson, May 29, 1865, Proclamation of Amnesty and Pardon for the Confederate States, James D. Richardson, ed., *A Compilation of the Messages and Papers of the Presidents, 1789–1897*, 11 vols. (Washington, D.C.: Government Printing Office, 1897), 6: 312.

31. Jonathan T. Dorris, "Pardon Seekers and Brokers: a Sequel of Appomattox, *The Journal of Southern History* 1 (August 1935), 276–292.

32. Carter, *When the War was Over*, 24–25.

33. Free blacks in North Carolina lost the right to vote in 1835.

34. Richard L. Zuber, *North Carolina During Reconstruction* (Raleigh: Division of Archives and History, 1969).

35. *Ibid*.; Watson, *Edgecombe County*, 77; Turner and Bridgers, *History of Edgecombe County*, 263.

36. Allen W. Trelease, "Reconstruction: The Halfway Revolution," in *The North Carolina Experience: An Interpretive and Documentary History*, Lindley S. Butler and Alan D. Watson, eds., (Chapel Hill: University of North Carolina Press, 1984), 286–306.

37. Hill, *The Governors of North Carolina*, 156–157; Richard L. Zuber, *Jonathan Worth: A Biography of a Southern Unionist* (Chapel Hill: University of North Carolina Press, 1965); Jonathan Worth to H.T. Clark, March 19, 1859, and Jonathan Worth to John A. Gilmer, March 20, 1859, Jonathan Worth to Englehard and Price, January 27, 1869, J.G. de Roulhac Hamilton, ed., *The Correspondence of Jonathan Worth* (Raleigh: Edwards and Broughton Printing Co., 1909), 65–67, 1272.

38. Jonathan T. Dorris, "Pardoning Leaders of the Confederacy," *The Mississippi Valley Historical Review* 15 (June 1928), 3–21.

39. Dorris, "Pardon Seekers and Brokers," 283; Carter, *When the War Was Over*.

40. *New York Times*, August 11, 1866; *DNCB*, s.v. "William A. Graham;" McKinney, *Zeb Vance*; Mobley, *War Governor of the South*; Robert K. Ackerman, *Wade Hampton III* (Columbia: University of South Carolina Press, 2007), 93–94, 119; Dorris, "Pardoning Leaders of the Confederacy," 3–21.

41. Case Files of Applications from Former Confederates for Presidential Pardons ("Amnesty Papers") 1865–1867, Records of the Adjutant General's Office, 1780s–1917, National Archives, Washington, D.C., M1003.

42. Dorris, "Pardon Seekers and Brokers," 276; Carter, *When the War was Over*, 50–54.

43. H.T. Clark to Jonathan Worth, May 6, 1867, Hamilton, *The Correspondence of Jonathan Worth*, 944.

44. John Poole to H.T. Clark, February 5, 1866, HTCD.

45. Burgess S. Gaither to Jonathan Worth, January 17, 1866, Benjamin S. Hendrick to Jonathan Worth, January 27, 1866, Jonathan Worth to Col. W.G. Moore, June 9, 1867, Hamilton, *The Correspondence of Jonathan Worth*, 476, 483, 977.

46. H.T. Clark to Jonathan Worth, September 12, 1866, Pardon Application of Henry T. Clark, State Archives, Raleigh.

47. *Ibid*.

48. H.T. Clark to Andrew Johnson, July 17, 1865, Pardon Application of Henry T. Clark, State Archives, Raleigh. Unrepentant letters to the president were not uncommon. Many ex-Confederates were quite brazen in their support for secession while simultaneously seeking pardon.

49. Benjamin S. Hedrick to Jonathan Worth, June 11, 1866, HTCD.

50. Jonathan Worth to H.T. Clark, September 21, 1866, Hamilton, *The Correspondence of Jonathan Worth*, 788–789. The quote, "noblest work of God," is taken from Alexander Pope's *An Essay on Man* (1734).

51. H.T. Clark to Jonathan Worth, May 29, 1867, Pardon Application of Henry T. Clark, State Archives, Raleigh.

52. Pardon Application of Henry T. Clark, State Archives, Raleigh.

53. H.T. Clark to Jonathan Worth, September 12, 1866, Pardon Application of Henry T. Clark, State Archives, Raleigh.
54. Jonathan Worth to Andrew Johnson, March 29, 1867, Hamilton, *The Correspondence of Jonathan Worth*, 927.
55. Jonathan Worth to H.T. Clark, May 24, 1867, HTCD; H.T. Clark to Jonathan Worth, May 29, 1867, Pardon Application of Henry T. Clark, State Archives, Raleigh; *New York Times*, June 4, 5, 8, 1867; *Sentinel* (Raleigh), June 4, 7, 8, 11, 1867. All of the living ex-governors of North Carolina — Graham, Swain, Manly, and Bragg — joined Worth in Raleigh, except for Clark and Vance.
56. Battle, *History of the University of North Carolina*, 760; Pardon Application of Henry T. Clark, State Archives, Raleigh; *New York Times*, June 7, 8, 1867; *Sentinel*, June 4, 7, 8, 11, 1867.
57. *Public Laws of the State of North Carolina, 1866–1867*, 6–7, 221.
58. *Southerner*, ca. 1909.
59. *Journal of the Senate of North Carolina, 1866–1867*; *New York Times*, April 6, 1867.
60. *Journal of the Senate of North Carolina, 1866–1867*, 287.
61. "Report of Charles Manly, Treasurer of the University of North Carolina, 1866," *Executive and Legislative Documents Laid Before the General Assembly of North Carolina, 1866–1867*, Document 22 (Raleigh, 1867), 2; Battle, *History of the University of North Carolina*, 754.
62. H.T. Clark to William A. Graham, October 6, 1867, Williams, Hamilton, Peacock, *The Papers of William A. Graham*, 7: 379; Battle, *History of the University of North Carolina*, 760; H.T. Clark to Jonathan Worth, August 20, 1867, Hamilton, *The Correspondence of Jonathan Worth*, 1038–1039.
63. *Journal of the Senate of North Carolina, 1866–1867*, 24, 91–104.
64. Ibid., 138–144.
65. Zuber, *North Carolina During Reconstruction*, 7–10.
66. Jonathan Worth to H.T. Clark, April 30, 1867, Hamilton, *The Correspondence of Jonathan Worth*, 939.
67. H.T. Clark to Jonathan Worth, May 6, 1867, Hamilton, *The Correspondence of Jonathan Worth*, 944.
68. Zuber, *North Carolina During Reconstruction*; Allen W. Trelease, "Reconstruction: the Halfway Revolution," in *The North Carolina Experience*, 288.
69. Zuber, *North Carolina During Reconstruction*.
70. *Southerner*, March 12, 1868.
71. "Henry Toole Clark," February 1908, Joseph Blount Cheshire Papers, SHC; Zuber, *North Carolina During Reconstruction*. Saunders married Florida Cotton, Clark's niece, in 1863. Florida was the daughter of Clark's sister, Laura Placidia Clark. The couple was married only two years when Florida died suddenly in July 1865, and Saunders never remarried.
72. Turner and Bridgers, *History of Edgecombe County*, 251–252.
73. Ibid., 270.

74. Wheeler, *Reminiscences and Memoirs of North Carolina and Eminent North Carolinians*, 159.
75. H.T. Clark to John H. Wheeler, August 15, 1873, HTCD; Saunders, *The Colonial Records of North Carolina*, 1: viii.
76. "Regulations for the Tournament," December 1869, Henry T. Clark Papers, PC; *Southerner*, December 2, 23, 1869.
77. Jacqueline Drane Nash, *A Goodly Heritage: The Story of Calvary Parish* (Wendell, N.C.: Broadfoot, 1960).
78. Ibid. Cheshire married Clark's first cousin, Elizabeth Parker, and he became the patriarch of a distinguished line of future Joseph Blount Cheshires.
79. Joseph B. Cheshire, *The Church in the Confederate States* (New York: Longmans, Green, and Co., 1912), 274.
80. Will of H.T. Clark, n.d. 1874, State Archives, Raleigh; Business receipts, HTCUNC; *DNCB*, s.v. "Henry Clark Bridgers, "John Luther Bridgers, Jr."
81. H.T. Clark to Haywood Clark, June 9, 1873, HTCUNC; *DNCB*, s.v., "Sewall L. Fremont."
82. *Southerner*, April 17, 1874; *Sentinel*, April 17, 1874; Wheeler, *Reminiscences and Memoirs of North Carolina and Eminent North Carolinians*, 159; Mercer, "The Administration of Governor Henry Toole Clark," 80; R.R. Bridgers to John L. Bridgers, April 18, 1874, John L. Bridgers Papers, Duke University.

Epilogue

1. Escott, "Unwilling Hercules," *The North Carolina Experience*, 267.
2. John H. Wheeler, *Reminiscences and Memoirs of North Carolina and Eminent North Carolinians*, (Columbus, Ohio: Columbus Printing Works, 1884), 159; Barrett, "North Carolina," *The Confederate Governors*, 143; *DNCB*, s.v. "Henry Toole Clark."
3. H.T. Clark to Andrew Johnson, July 17, 1865, Pardon Application, State Archives, Raleigh.
4. Joe A. Mobley, "Zebulon B. Vance: A Confederate Nationalist in the North Carolina Gubernatorial Election of 1864," *North Carolina Historical Review* 77 (October 2000), 433–454; McKinney, *Zeb Vance*, 231–247; David D. Scarboro, "North Carolina and the Confederacy: The Weakness of States' Rights during the Civil War," 134.
5. H.T. Clark to Andrew Johnson, July 17, 1865, Pardon Application, State Archives, Raleigh.
6. Davis, *Look Away: A History of the Confederate States of America*, 2–3.
7. H.T. Clark to Jonathan Worth, September 12, 1866, Pardon Application, State Archives, Raleigh.
8. Barrett, *The Civil War in North Carolina*, 182.
9. H.T. Clark to Jonathan Worth, September 12, 1866, Pardon Application, State Archives, Raleigh.
10. Will of Henry T. Clark, n.d. 1874, State Archives, Raleigh; Business receipts, HTCUNC; *DNCB*, s.v. "Henry Clark Bridgers," "John Luther Bridgers, Jr."

11. *Ibid.*; Haywood Clark to John L. Bridgers, April 1874, John L. Bridgers Papers, Duke University.
12. Will of Mary W. Clark, June 19, 1893, State Archives, Raleigh.
13. McKinney, *Zeb Vance,* 234.

Appendix A

1. Henry had recently left Tarboro for Chapel Hill to take his entrance exams to enter the university.
2. A teacher or instructor.
3. Horace, "Then my exalted head will knock against the stars." The poem from which this phrase originates rejects all the usual avenues to fame and riches. The poet claims to prefer the worry-free life of an Epicurean poet-sage who, in an idealized countryside, has time to enjoy life's little pleasures.
4. William Henry Hodge was from Tarboro and UNC student, Class of 1825.
5. Chapel Hill.
6. Samuel Smith Hinton of Wake County, North Carolina, Class of 1825.
7. Virgil, "Beauty is but skin deep."
8. John Gillies, *History of Ancient Greece, its Colonies and Conquests* (London, 1786). Gillies (1747–1836) was a Scottish historian and classical scholar. His *History of Ancient Greece* was written from a strong Whig bias, but it was valuable at a time when the study of Greek history was in its infancy. This book remains in Gov. Clark's library in Tarboro. *The Travels of Anacharsis the Younger in Greece* (1788) by Jean-Jacques Barthélemy (1716–95). This book is an imaginary travel journal and one of the first historical novels. It was called "the encyclopedia of the new cult of the antique" in the late 18th Century and had an impact on the growth of philhellenism (love of Greek culture) in western Europe and America into the nineteenth century. The book went through many editions.
9. Thomas Wynn Watts of Martin County, Class of 1826.
10. Sam was J.W. Clark's slave.
11. Richard S. Croom of Lenoir County, class of 1826.
12. Old West building, a campus dormitory being built at the time. It remains today serving its original purpose.
13. Perseverance conquers.
14. Horace, "let the plague seize the last" or "the Devil take the hindmost," essentially meaning every man for himself.
15. This passage shows Henry's early interest in politics. Thomas H. Hall (1773–1853) defeated the incumbent Richard Hines (?–1851) in the election. Hall occupied Clark's former seat in the Congress. Sharp and Wilkinson served two one-year terms in the House for Edgecombe County.
16. His grandmother in this instance is Elizabeth Haywood Toole (1758–1832).

Appendix B

1. The "Holy Alliance" generally refers to the 1815 coalition of Russia, Austria, and Prussia (and not Great Britain). Clark is likely referring to the various European alliances against Napoleon during the Napoleonic wars (1803–1815), and more specifically, the "Quadruple Alliance" of March 1813 between Great Britain, Austria, Russia, and Prussia.
2. A reference to the U.S. Congressional abolition of the slave trade in 1808. The British, however, abolished the slave trade in 1807.

Bibliography

A Word on Sources

Piecing together a life from scraps of paper is a challenge, and Governor Clark himself has not been much help. He was a modest man who left few intimate reflections. When he did write, he often commented on how much he hated doing so, and his letters usually tell us more about his business affairs than himself. He wrote with a clear, steady hand that reveals a sharp mind, and it's unfortunate that he didn't write more, not only for the historical record, but for those pearls of wisdom that he occasionally shared with his family (much as his own father had done). The most comprehensive collection of his papers, located in the Special Collections Library at Duke University in Durham, N.C., contains mostly receipts and account slips, although several dozen family letters are included among the notes detailing his plantation expenses, slave hire and real estate transactions. The most interesting items in the collection relate to Clark's slaveowning activities: there are contracts, correspondence to his agent in Alabama, and slave lists. I hope other scholars will explore this underused collection in the future.

Selected items from the Duke collection have been microfilmed and can be found in several university libraries, including the University of North Carolina at Chapel Hill, though items concerning his slave interests are generally absent from the microfilm record. The Clark family have been outstanding alumni of the University of North Carolina, and the archives in the Wilson Library at Chapel Hill have a few items from the governor's life as a student and businessman, such as some school books and a small account ledger. Official records of his governorship, pardon information, and some personal items are found in the State Archives in Raleigh. Interesting among these items are copies of three letters from his wife, Mary, just before their marriage, and Clark's scrapbook of news clippings, census records, military lists, and government proclamations. The scrapbook contains items that demanded the attention of a governor, and he used it as a diary or "daybook" to reference facts, figures, names, dates, and developments occurring during his tenure as chief executive, and later as a concerned observer of the war after 1862.

Other miscellaneous artifacts are located in Tarboro at the Blount-Bridgers House museum, where several books from the Clark library still reside in the governor's former desk secretary — all of which visitors can see today. The museum also has sixteen original letters from James West Clark to his young son, which I've edited and printed here because I think they are worthy of a larger reading public. There are also a few family items owned by Clark's great grandson, Henry Toole Clark, Jr., and his wife, Blanche, of Chapel Hill, including Christopher Clark's bible, which lists some very helpful marriage and birth dates, and an original oil painting of the governor.

Bibliography

Ironically, there are more records of other families in his collection than of his own. Clark displayed an obsession, if not a madness, for genealogy. His papers at Duke and an oversized file in the state archives at Raleigh brim with arcane bits of trivia, exuberant family trees, indenture contracts, and souvenirs from North Carolina's earliest settlers. In fact, these items were intended to inaugurate a larger, state-owned genealogical repository, which Clark was to direct. The work he did as a genealogist is impressive in its own right and I hope others will take some time to fully catalogue and make more available this extraordinary resource.

Where holes in the record exist (and there are many), I have used newspapers, family sources and stories, and secondary texts to tell Clark's story. Although he never committed to paper his more intimate thoughts, or left us extensive social or political commentary, his actions as a Democratic Party leader and war governor were reported (though not always widely), and correspondences from others to him help us to draw reasonable conclusions. Original spellings are retained when quoting from primary sources, but in several cases spellings and phrasings have been edited for modern readability and context. The use of [sic] was avoided. I have chosen to quote extensively at times, since no other source on Clark is readily available. For this reason I hope that readers will forgive my frequent use of block quotations.

Secondary sources on Clark and his hometown include Turner and Bridgers' *History of Edgecombe County* (1920). Although this book is the most detailed source of the area's early history, it suffers from significant biases and should be supplemented by Monika S. Fleming's *Edgecombe County: Along the Tar River* (2003) and Alan D. Watson's *Edgecombe County: A Brief History* (1979).

John Barrett's *The Civil War in North Carolina* (1963) still remains the best, most comprehensive military source available for students of the Civil War in North Carolina, and I relied on it heavily to construct the larger war narrative. William R. Trotter's trilogy *The Civil War in North Carolina* (1991)—"Ironclads and Columbiads, the Coast"; "Silk Flags and Cold Steel, The Piedmont;" and "Bushwhackers: The Mountains"—is a highly readable popular history of the war, but with a mildly pro-Confederate view. Joe A. Mobley's *Zeb Vance: War Governor of the South* (2005) is a useful and well-written sequel to my account of Clark's administration.

Lorri Glover's *Southern Sons* (2007) and Bertram Wyatt-Brown's *Southern Honor* (1983) provide enlightening analysis of the Old South's social and cultural values. Dan T. Carter's *When the War was Over* (1985) offers the best discussion of the South's reaction to defeat in the two years immediately following the Civil War. Elizabeth Fox and Eugene D. Genovese's massive tome *The Mind of the Master Class* (2005) should answer any further questions about the planters.

Readers interested in the history of slavery should consult Ira Berlin's *Many Thousands Gone: The First Two Centuries of Slavery in North America* (1998); Walter Johnson's *Soul by Soul: Life Inside the Antebellum Slave Market* (2001); and Jonathan Martin's *Divided Mastery: Slave Hiring in the American South* (2004). The legacy of Clark's (and his contemporaries') conservative racial views have been addressed with stunning clarity in Jason Sokol's *There Goes My Everything: White Southerners in the Age of Civil Rights, 1945–1975* (2006).

For a larger treatment of the times in which Clark lived, readers should see Daniel W. Howe's *What Hath God Wrought: The Transformation of America, 1815–1848* (2007); William W. Freehling's *The Road to Disunion* (two volumes, 1991, 2007); David Potter's *The Impending Crisis, 1848–1861* (1977); and Eric Foner's *Reconstruction: America's Unfinished Revolution* (2002).

Bibliography

Primary Sources

MANUSCRIPTS

DUKE UNIVERSITY LIBRARY, DURHAM, N.C., SPECIAL COLLECTIONS
  Henry Toole Clark Papers
  John L. Bridgers Papers

EDGECOMBE COUNTY COURT HOUSE, TARBORO, N.C.
  Edgecombe County Deed Books

NORTH CAROLINA OFFICE OF ARCHIVES AND HISTORY, RALEIGH, STATE ARCHIVES
  County Records
    Record of Wills, Edgecombe County, 1810–1885, microfilm.
    Will of Henry Toole Clark, April 23, 1874, Edgecombe County Original Wills
  Governor's Office
    Governor's Letter Books
    Governor's Papers
  Miscellaneous Papers
    Miscellaneous Papers, 1861–1912
  Petitions for Pardon
    Civil War Collection, 1865–1868
  Private Collections
    Henry Toole Clark Papers
    Miscellaneous Papers

PRINCETON UNIVERSITY, PRINCETON, NEW JERSEY, MUDD MANUSCRIPT LIBRARY
  Undergraduate Alumni Files, James West Clark

UNIVERSITY OF NORTH CAROLINA, CHAPEL HILL, DAVIS LIBRARY
  Henry Toole Clark Papers, microfilm

UNIVERSITY OF NORTH CAROLINA, CHAPEL HILL, SOUTHERN HISTORICAL COLLECTION, WILSON LIBRARY
  Diary of Thomas Bragg
  Robert Brent Drane Papers
  Francis M. Parker Papers
  David Schenck Papers
  John Francis Speight Papers

NORTH CAROLINA STATE LAWS AND REPORTS

Documents of the Convention of 1861–1862
Executive and Legislative Documents, 1860–1861, 1866–1867
Journal of the House of Commons of North Carolina, 1860–1861
Journal of the Senate of North Carolina, 1850–1851, 1852, 1854–1855, 1858–1859, 1861, 1866–1867
North Carolina Constitutional Convention of 1835, http://docsouth.unc.edu/nc/conv1835/menu.html
Ordinances of the State Convention, 1861–1864
Public and Private Laws of North Carolina, 1861, 1862–1863, 1865–1866, 1866–1867

FEDERAL RECORDS

Second Census of the United States, 1800: Bertie County, North Carolina, Population Schedule. National Archives, Washington, D.C. Microfilm, State Archives, Office of Archives and History, Raleigh.
Third Census (1810), Fourth Census (1820), Fifth Census (1830), Sixth Census (1840), Seventh Census (1850), Eighth Census (1860), and Ninth Census (1870) of the United States: Edgecombe County, North Carolina, Population Schedule. National Archives, Washington, D.C. Microfilm, State Archives, Office of Archives and History, Raleigh.
Records of the Field Offices for the State of North Carolina, Bureau of Refugees, Freedmen, and Abandoned Lands, 1865–1872, National Archives, Washington, D.C.

Newspapers

Daily Progress (New Bern)
Free Press (Tarboro)
Journal (Livingston, Alabama)
Journal (Wilmington)
The New York Times
North Carolina Standard (Raleigh)
Register (Raleigh)
Sentinel (Raleigh)
Southerner (Tarboro)
State Journal (Raleigh)
Sumter County Whig (Livingston, Alabama)
Times (London, U.K.)
Tri-Weekly Standard (Raleigh)
Voice of Sumter (Sumter County, Alabama)

Documents and Diaries

Alumni Directory of the University of North Carolina at Chapel Hill. Chapel Hill: Alumni Office, 1954.

Cappon, Lester J., ed. *The Adams-Jefferson Letters: The Complete Correspondence Between Thomas Jefferson, Abigail and John Adams*, Chapel Hill: University of North Carolina Press, 1987.

Cheney, John L., ed. *North Carolina Government 1585–1974: A Narrative and Statistical History*. Raleigh: North Carolina Department of the Secretary of State, 1981.

Clark, Walter, ed. *Histories of the Several Regiments and Battalions from North Carolina in the Great War, 1861–1865*. 5 vols. Raleigh: State of North Carolina, 1901.

Crabtree, Beth, and James W. Patton, eds. *Journal of a Secesh Lady: The Diary of Catherine Ann Devereux Edmondston, 1860–1866*. Raleigh: Office of Archives and History, 1979.

Crow, Terrel Armisted, and Mary Moulton Barden, eds. *Live Your Own Life: The Family Papers of Mary Bayard Clarke, 1854–1886*. Columbia: University of South Carolina Press, 2003.

Hamilton, J.G. de Roulhac, ed. *The Correspondence of Jonathan Worth*. Raleigh: Edwards and Broughton Printing Co., 1909.

_____. *The Papers of Thomas Ruffin*. 4 vols. Raleigh: North Carolina Historical Commission, 1920.

Official Records of the Union and Confederate Navies in the War of the Rebellion. 31 vols. Washington, D.C.: Government Printing Office, 1894–1927.

Poteat, R. Matthew, ed. "Dear Mother: The Papers of Sergeant William D. Bishop, Co. L 22nd North Carolina Troops." Raleigh: unpublished manuscript, State Archives, Office of Archives and History, Raleigh, 2003.

Raper, Horace, and Thornton W. Mitchell, eds. *The Papers of William Woods Holden*. 1 vol. to date. Raleigh: Office of Archives and History, 2000.

Richardson, James D., ed. *A Compilation of the Messages and Papers of the Presidents, 1789–1897*, 11 vols. Washington, D.C.: Government Printing Office, 1897.

Ruffin, Edmund. *The Farmer's Register*. Vols. VI and VII. 1838, 1839.

Shanks, Henry Thomas, ed. *The Papers of Willie Person Mangum*. 5 vols. Raleigh: Office of Archives and History, 1952.

Tolbert, Noble J., ed. *The Papers of John W. Ellis*. 2 vols. Raleigh: Office of Archives and History, 1964.

The War of the Rebellion: A Compilation of the Official Records of the Union and Confederate Armies. 128 vols. Washington, D.C.: Government Printing Office, 1880–1891.

Wilentz, Sean, ed., "Jackson Addresses the People of South Carolina, December 10, 1832," in *Major Problems in the Early Republic 1787–1848*. Lexington, Mass.: D.C. Heath, 1992.

Williams, Max R., J. G. de Roulhac Hamilton, and Mary R. Peacock, eds. *The Papers of William Alexander Graham*. 8 vols. Raleigh: Office of Archives and History, 1957–1992.

Secondary Sources

Books

Ackerman, Robert K. *Wade Hampton III*. Columbia: University of South Carolina Press, 2007.

Ashe, Samuel A., Stephen B. Weeks, and Charles L. Van Noppen, eds. *Biographical History of North Carolina*, 8 vols. Greensboro: Charles L. Van Noppen, 1905–1917.

Baldwin, Joseph G. *The Flush Times of Alabama and Mississippi*. New York: Sagamore Press, 1957.

Barney, William L. *The Road to Secession: A New Perspective On the Old South*. New York: Praeger, 1972.

Barrett, John G. *The Civil War in North Carolina*. Chapel Hill: University of North Carolina Press, 1963.

Bibliography

Battle, Kemp P. *History of the University of North Carolina: From its Beginning to the Death of President Swain, 1789–1868*. 2 vols. Raleigh: Edwards and Broughton, 1908–1912.

Bell, A. Fleming, and Warren J. Wicker, eds. *County Government in North Carolina*. 4th ed. Chapel Hill: University of North Carolina, 1999.

Bensel, Richard Franklin. *Yankee Leviathan: The Origins of Central State Authority in America, 1859–1877*. Cambridge, Mass.: Cambridge University Press, 1990.

Beringer, Richard E., Herman Hattaway, et al. *Why The South Lost the Civil War*. Athens: University of Georgia Press, 1986.

Berlin, Ira. *Generations of Captivity: A History of African-American Slaves*. Cambridge, Mass.: Harvard University Press, 2003.

Blackett, R.J. *Divided Hearts: Britain and the American Civil War*. Baton Rouge: Lousiana State University Press, 2001.

Blundell, Bezer. *The Contributions of John Lewis Peyton to the History of Virginia and of the Civil War in America, 1861–65*. London: John Wilson, 1868.

Bonham, Milledge L., Jr. *British Consuls in the Confederacy*. New York: Columbia University Press. 1911.

Boritt, Gabor S., ed. *Why The Confederacy Lost*. New York: Oxford University Press, 1992.

Branson, E.C., et al. *County Government and County Affairs in North Carolina: Addresses Before the North Carolina Club at the University of North Carolina, 1917–1918*. Chapel Hill: University of North Carolina, 1918.

Brown, Louis A. *The Salisbury Prison: A Case Study of Confederate Military Prisons 1861–1865*. Wendell, N.C.: Avera Press, 1980.

Browning, Jr., Robert M. *From Cape Charles to Cape Fear: The North Atlantic Blockading Squadron During The Civil War*. Tuscaloosa: University of Alabama Press, 1993.

Butler, Lindley S. *Pirates, Privateers, and Rebel Raiders of the Carolina Coast*. Chapel Hill: University of North Carolina Press, 2000.

Butler, Lindley S., and Alan Watson, eds. *The North Carolina Experience: An Interpretive and Documentary History*. Chapel Hill: University of North Carolina Press, 1984.

Bynum, Victoria E. *Unruly Women: The Politics of Social and Sexual Control in the Old South*. Chapel Hill: University of North Carolina Press, 1992.

Carter, Dan T. *When the War Was Over: The Failure of Self-Reconstruction in the South, 1865–1867*. Baton Rouge: Louisiana State University Press, 1985.

Chambers, William N., and Walter Dean Burnham, eds. *The American Party Systems: Stages of Political Development*. New York: Oxford University Press, 1967.

Cheshire, Joseph Blount. *The Church in the Confederate States*. New York: Longmans, Green, and Co., 1912.

_____. *Nonnulla: Memories, Stories, Traditions, More or Less Authentic*. Chapel Hill: University of North Carolina Press, 1930.

Clark, Robert L., ed. *A History of Public Sector Pensions in the United States*. Philadelphia: University of Pennsylvania Press, 2000.

Coulter, E. Merton. *College Life in the Old South*. Athens: University of Georgia Press, 1928.

_____. *The Confederate States of America 1861–1865*. Baton Rouge: Louisiana State University Press, 1950.

Crawford, Martin. *Ashe County's Civil War: Community and Society in the Appalachian South*. Charlottesville: University of Virginia Press, 2001.

Davis, William C. *Look Away: A History of the Confederate States of America*. New York: Free Press, 2002.

Donald, David, ed. *Why the North Won the Civil War*. Baton Rouge: Louisiana State University Press, 1960.

Durrill, Wayne K. *War of Another Kind: A Southern Community in the Great Rebellion*. Oxford: Oxford University Press, 1990.

Escott, Paul D. *After Secession: Jefferson Davis and the Failure of Confederate Nationalism*. Baton Rouge: Louisiana State University Press, 1978.

_____. *Many Excellent People: Power and Privilege in North Carolina, 1850–1900*. Chapel Hill: University of North Carolina Press, 1985.

Faust, Drew Gilpin. *The Creation of Confederate Nationalism: Ideology and Identity in the Civil War South*. Baton Rouge: Louisiana State University Press, 1988.

_____. *Mothers of Invention: Women of the Slaveholding South in the American Civil War*. Chapel Hill: University of North Carolina Press, 1996.

Faust, Patricia L., et al., eds. *Historical Times Illustrated Encyclopedia of the Civil War*. New York: Harper and Row, 1986.

Fleming, Monika S. *Edgecombe County: Along the Tar River*. Making of America Series. Charleston, S.C.: Arcadia Publishing, 2003.

Foner, Eric. *A Short History of Reconstruction, 1863–1877*. New York: Harper and Row, 1990.

Freehling, William W. *Prelude to Civil War: The Nullification Controversy in South Carolina, 1816–1836*. New York: Harper and Row, 1966.

_____. *The South vs. The South: How Anti-Confederate Southerners Shaped the Course of the Civil War*. New York: Oxford University Press, 2001.

Gallagher, Gary W. *The Confederate War*. Cambridge: Harvard University Press, 1997.

Genovese, Eugene D. *The Slaveholders' Dilemma: Freedom and Progress in Southern Conservative Thought, 1820–1860*. Columbia: University of South Carolina Press, 1992.

Glover, Lorri. *Southern Sons: Becoming Men in the New Nation*. Baltimore: Johns Hopkins University Press, 2007.

Gohdes, Clarence. *Scuppernong: North Carolina's Grape and Its Wines*. Durham, N.C.: Duke University Press, 1982.

Harris, William C. *North Carolina and the Coming of the Civil War*. Raleigh: Office of Archives and History, 1988.

_____. *William Woods Holden: Firebrand of North Carolina Politics*. Baton Rouge: Louisiana State University Press, 1987.

Harsh, Joseph L. *Confederate Tide Rising: Robert E. Lee and the Making of Southern Strategy, 1861–1862*. Kent, Ohio: Kent State University Press, 1998.

Hesseltine, William B. *Civil War Prisons: A Study in War Psychology*. New York: Frederick Unger Publishing, 1930.

Hill, Louis B. *State Socialism in the Confederate States of America*. Charlottesville, Va.: Historical Publishing Co., 1936.

Hill, Michael, ed. *The Governors of North Carolina*. Raleigh: Office of Archives and History, 2007.

Holt, Michael F. *The Fate of Their County: Politicians, Slavery Extension, and the Coming of the Civil War*. New York: Hill and Wang, 2004.

_____. *The Rise and Fall of the American Whig Party: Jacksonian Politics and the Onset of the Civil War*. New York: Oxford University Press, 1999.

Hume, Albert Luther. *A Compilation of the History of Dyer County*. Dyersburg, Tenn.: the complier, 1960.

Inscoe, John C., and Gordon B. McKinney. *The Heart of Confederate Appalachia: Western North Carolina in the Civil War*. Chapel Hill: University of North Carolina Press, 2000.

Johnson, Walter. *Soul by Soul: Life Inside the Antebellum Slave Market*. Cambridge, Mass.: Harvard University Press, 1999.

Jomini, Antoine Henri. *The Art of War*, trans. G.H. Mendell and W.P. Craighill. Westport, Conn.: Greenwood, 1971.

Jordan, Winthrop D. *White Over Black: American Attitudes Toward the Negro, 1550–1812*. Baltimore: Penguin Books, 1969.

Kruman, Marc W. *Parties and Politics in North Carolina, 1836–1865*. Baton Rouge: Louisiana State University Press, 1983.

Kurlansky, Mark. *Salt: A World History*. New York: Walker and Co., 2002.

Lefler, Hugh T., and Albert R. Newsome. *North Carolina: A History of a Southern State*. Chapel Hill: University of North Carolina Press, 1973.

Lefler, Hugh T., and William S. Powell. *Colonial North Carolina: A History*. New York: Charles Scribner and Sons, 1973.

Lightner, David L. *Slavery and the Commerce Power: How the Struggle Against the Interstate Slave Trade Led to the Civil War*. New Haven, Conn.: Yale University Press, 2006.

Lonn, Ella. *Desertion During the Civil War*. Gloucester, Mass.: Peter Smith, 1966.

_____. *Salt as a Factor in the Confederacy*. Tuscaloosa: University of Alabama Press, 1965.

Manarin, Louis H., and Weymouth T. Jordan, Jr., comps. *North Carolina Troops, 1861–1865: A Roster*. 15 vols. to date. Raleigh: Office of Archives and History, 1979.

McCoy, Drew R. *The Elusive Republic: Political Economy in Jeffersonian America*. Chapel Hill: University of North Carolina Press, 1980.

McKinney, Gordon B. *Zeb Vance: North Carolina's Civil War Governor and Gilded Age Political Leader*. Chapel Hill: University of North Carolina Press, 2004.

Bibliography

McKitrick, Eric L. *Andrew Johnson and Reconstruction.* New York: Oxford University Press, 1961, reprinted 1988.

Mitchell, Memory F. *Legal Aspects of Conscription and Exemption in North Carolina, 1861–1865.* Chapel Hill: University of North Carolina Press, 1965.

Mobley, Joe A. *James City: A Black Community in North Carolina, 1863–1900.* Raleigh: North Carolina Division of Archives and History, 1981.

_____. *"War Governor of the South": North Carolina's Zeb Vance in the Confederacy.* Gainesville: University Press of Florida, 2005.

Moore, Albert Burton. *Conscription and Conflict in the Confederacy.* New York: Macmillan Co., 1924.

Morgan, Edmund S. *American Slavery, American Freedom: The Ordeal of Colonial Virginia.* New York: Norton, 1975.

Murray, Elizabeth Reid. *Wake: Capital County of North Carolina.* 1 vol. to date. Raleigh: Capital County Publishing Co., 1983.

Musicant, Ivan. *Divided Waters: The Naval History of the Civil War.* New York: Harper Collins, 1995.

Nash, Jacqueline Drane. *A Goodly Heritage: The Story of Calvary Parish.* Wendell, N.C.: Broadfoot, 1960.

Nelson, William H. *The American Tory.* Oxford: Oxford University Press, 1961.

Owsley, Frank L. *King Cotton Diplomacy: Foreign Relations of the Confederate States of America.* Chicago: University of Chicago Press, 1959.

_____. *State Rights in the Confederacy.* Chicago, Ill.: University of Chicago Press, 1925.

Page, David. *Ship Versus Shore: Civil War Engagements Along Southern Shores and Rivers.* Nashville: Rutledge Hill Press, 1994.

Peyton, John L. *The American Crisis: Pages from the Notebook of a State Agent During the Civil War.* 2 vols. London: Saunders, Otley, and Co., 1867.

Potter, David. *Lincoln and His Party in the Secession Crisis.* New Haven, Conn.: Yale University Press, 1942.

Powell, William S. *North Carolina: A History.* Chapel Hill: University of North Carolina Press, 1988.

_____, ed. *Dictionary of North Carolina Biography.* 6 vols. Chapel Hill: University of North Carolina Press, 1979–1996.

Rable, George C. *The Confederate Republic: A Revolution Against Politics.* Chapel Hill: University of North Carolina Press, 1994.

Ramsdell, Charles W. *Behind the Lines in the Southern Confederacy.* Baton Rouge: Louisiana State University Press, 1944.

Reid, Brian Holden. *Robert E. Lee: Icon for a Nation.* London: Orion Publishing, 2005.

Ringold, May Spencer. *The Role of the State Legislatures in the Confederacy.* Athens: University of Georgia Press, 1966.

Robinson, William Morrison. *The Confederate Privateers.* New Haven: Yale University Press, 1928.

Sanders, John L. "The Constitution of North Carolina," *The North Carolina Encyclopedia*, November 2007, http://statelibrary.dcr.state.nc.us/nc/stgovt/Preconst.htm.

Sitterson, J. Carlyle. *The Secession Movement in North Carolina.* Chapel Hill: University of North Carolina Press, 1939.

Smith, John David. *Black Voices from Reconstruction, 1865–1877.* Brookfield, Conn.: Millbrook Press, 1996.

Spratt, Robert D. *A History of the Town of Livingston, Alabama.* Livingston: University of West Alabama, Livingston Press, 1928; reprint, 1997.

Tatum, Georgia Lee. *Disloyalty in the Confederacy.* Chapel Hill: University of North Carolina Press, 1934.

Taylor, Joe Gray. *Eating, Drinking, and Visiting in the South: An Informal History.* Baton Rouge: Louisiana State University Press, 1982.

Thomas, Emory M. *The Confederacy as a Revolutionary Experience.* Englewood Cliffs, N.J.: Prentice-Hall, 1971.

Tindall, George Brown, and David E. Shi. *America: A Narrative History.* Sixth edition, vol. 1. New York: W.W. Norton and Co., 2004.

Trefousse, Hans L. *Andrew Johnson: A Biography.* New York: W.W. Norton and Co., 1989.

Trotter, William R. *Ironclads and Columbiads: The Civil War in North Carolina, The Coast.* Winston-Salem, N.C.: Blair Publishing, 1989.

Tucker, Glen. *Zeb Vance: Champion of Personal Freedom.* New York: Bobbs-Merrill Co., 1965.

Turner, Herbert Snipes. *The Dreamer: Archibald DeBow Murphey, 1777–1832.* Verona, Va.: McClure Press, 1971.

Turner, J. Kelly, and John L. Bridgers, Jr. *History of Edgecombe County, North Carolina*. Raleigh: Edwards and Broughton, 1920.
Vandiver, Frank E. *Their Tattered Flags: The Epic of the Confederacy*. New York: Harpers Magazine Press, 1970.
von Clausewitz, Carl. *On War*. Edited and translated by Michael Howard and Peter Paret. Princeton, N.J.: Princeton University Press, 1976.
Watson, Alan D. *Edgecombe County: A Brief History*. Raleigh: Office of Archives and History, 1979.
Watson, Harry L. *Liberty and Power: the Politics of Jacksonian America*. New York: Noonday Press, 1990.
Wiley, Bell Irvin. *The Life of Johnny Reb: The Common Soldier of the Confederacy*. Indianapolis: Bobbs-Merrill, 1943.
Wise, Stephen R. *Lifeline of the Confederacy: Blockade Running During the Civil War*. Columbia: University of South Carolina Press, 1988.
Wooster, Ralph A. *Politicians, Planters, and Plain Folk: Courthouse and Statehouse in the Upper South, 1850–1860*. Knoxville: University of Tennessee Press, 1975.
_____. *The Secession Conventions of the South*. Princeton, N.J.: Princeton University Press, 1962.
Wyatt-Brown, Bertram. *Southern Honor: Ethics and Behavior in the Old South*. New York: Oxford University Press, 1982.
Yearns, W. Buck, ed. *The Confederate Governors*. Athens: University of Georgia Press, 1985.
_____, and John G. Barrett, eds. *North Carolina Civil War Documentary*. Chapel Hill: University of North Carolina Press, 1980.
Zuber, Richard L. *North Carolina During Reconstruction*. Raleigh: Division of Archives and History, 1969.
_____. *Jonathan Worth: A Biography of a Southern Unionist*. Chapel Hill: University of North Carolina Press, 1965.

Articles

Auman, William T. "Neighbor against Neighbor: The Inner Civil War in the Randolph Area of Confederate North Carolina." *The North Carolina Historical Review* 61 (January 1984), 59–92.
_____, and David D. Scarboro, "The Heroes of America in Civil War North Carolina." *The North Carolina Historical Review* 58 (October 1981), 327–363.
Baker, Robin E. "Class Conflict and Political Upheaval: The Transformation of North Carolina Politics During the Civil War." *The North Carolina Historical Review* 69 (April 1992), 148–178.
Bardolph, Richard. "Inconstant Rebels: Desertion of North Carolina Troops in the Civil War." *The North Carolina Historical Review* 41 (April 1964), 163–189.
Butts, Donald C. "The 'Irrepressible Conflict': Slave Taxation and North Carolina's Gubernatorial Election of 1860." *The North Carolina Historical Review* 58 (January 1981), 44–67.
Davis, George K., and Gary M. Pecquet. "Interest Rates in the Civil War South." *The Journal of Economic History* 50 (March 1990), 133–148.
Dorris, Jonathan T. "Pardon Seekers and Brokers: A Sequel of Appomattox." *The Journal of Southern History* 1 (August 1935), 276–292.
_____. "Pardoning Leaders of the Confederacy." *The Mississippi Valley Historical Review* 15 (June 1928), 3–21.
Escott, Paul D. "Poverty and Governmental Aid for the Poor in Confederate North Carolina." *The North Carolina Historical Review* 61 (October 1984).
_____, and Jeffery J. Crow. "The Social Order and Violent Disorder: An Analysis of North Carolina in the Revolution and the Civil War." *Journal of Southern History* 52 (August 1986), 373–402.
Ewan, Christopher. "The Emancipation Proclamation and British Public Opinion," *The Historian* 67 (Spring 2005), 1–19.
Flippin, Percy Scott, ed. "The Hershel V. Johnson Correspondence." *The North Carolina Historical Review* 4 (April 1927), 182–201.
Hamilton, Daniel W. "The Confederate Sequestration Act." *Civil War History* 52 (December 2006), 373–408.
Hoffmann, William S. "John Branch and the Origins of the Whig Party in North Carolina." *The North Carolina Historical Review* 35 (July 1958), 299–315.
Margo, Robert A., and Georgia C. Villaflor. "The Growth of Wages in Antebellum America: New Evidence." *The Journal of Economic History* 47, No. 4 (December 1987), 873–895.
McGee, David H. "A Revolution in Raleigh: the Early Transformation of a Confederate State Capital,

1861," in *Inside the Confederate Government: Essays in Honor of Emory Thomas*, ed. Lesley J. Gordon and John C. Inscoe. Baton Rouge: Louisiana State University Press, 2005.

Meekins, Alex Christopher. "Unionism and the Arcane Origin of 'Buffalo.'" *The North Carolina Historical Review* 85 (July 2008), 282–316.

Merrill, James M. "The Hatteras Expedition, August, 1861." *The North Carolina Historical Review* 29 (April 1952), 201–219.

Mobley, Joe A. "Zebulon B. Vance: A Confederate Nationalist in the North Carolina Gubernatorial Election of 1864." *The North Carolina Historical Review* 77 (October 2000), 433–454.

Norris, David A. "'The Yankees Have Been Here!': The Story of Brig. Gen. Edward E. Potter's Raid on Greenville, Tarboro, and Rocky Mount, July 19–23, 1863." *The North Carolina Historical Review* 73 (January 1996), 1–27.

O'Brien, Gail. "Power and Influence in Mecklenburg County, 1850–1880." *The North Carolina Historical Review* 54 (April 1977), 120–144.

Owsley, Frank L. "Local Defense and the Overthrow of the Confederacy." *Mississippi Valley Historical Review* 11 (March 1925), 489–525.

Poteat, R. Matthew. "A Modest Estimate of His Own Abilities": Governor Henry Toole Clark and the Early Civil War Leadership of North Carolina." *The North Carolina Historical Review* 84 (January and April 2007), 1–36, 128–155.

Ramsdell, Charles W. "Review of State Rights in the Confederacy." *Mississippi Valley Historical Review* 14 (June 1927), 107–110.

Reid, Richard. "A Test Case of Crying Evil: Desertion Among North Carolina Troops During the Civil War." *The North Carolina Historical Review* 58 (July 1981), 234–262.

Robinson, William Morrison, Jr. "Admiralty in 1861: The Confederate States District Court for the Division of Pamlico of the District of North Carolina." *The North Carolina Historical Review* 17 (April 1940), 132–138.

Scarboro, David D. "North Carolina and the Confederacy: The Weakness of States' Rights During the Civil War." *The North Carolina Historical Review* 56 (April 1979), 133–149.

Spraggins, Tinsley Lee. "Mobilization of Negro Labor for the Department of Virginia and North Carolina." *The North Carolina Historical Review* 24 (April 1947), 160–197.

Story, Ronald. "Harvard Students, the Boston Elite, and the New England Preparatory System, 1800–1876." *History of Education Quarterly* 15 (Autumn 1975), 281–298.

Vandiver, Frank E. "Makeshifts of Confederate Ordnance." *Journal of Southern History* 17 (May 1951), 180–193.

Walton, Brian G. "Elections to the United States Senate in North Carolina, 1835–1861." *The North Carolina Historical Review* 53 (April 1976), 168–92.

Watson, Alan D. "Battling 'Old Rip'": Internal Improvements and the Role of State Government in Antebellum North Carolina." *The North Carolina Historical Review* 77 (April 2000), 179–204.

Yates, Richard E. "Zebulon B. Vance as War Governor of North Carolina, 1862–1865," *The Journal of Southern History* 3 (February 1937), 43–75.

Zipf, Karen L. "The whites shall rule the land or die": Gender, Race, and Class in North Carolina Reconstruction Politics." *The Journal of Southern History* 65 (August 1999), 499–534.

THESES AND DISSERTATIONS

Kerridge, Ronald David. "Answering 'The Trumpet to Discord': Southerners at the College of New Jersey 1820–1860, and Their Careers." Senior thesis, Princeton University, 1984.

Meekins, Alex Christopher. "Caught Between Scylla and Charybdis: the Civil War in Northeastern North Carolina." Master's thesis, North Carolina State University, 2001.

Mercer, Gary. "The Administration of Governor Henry Toole Clark, 1861–1862." Master's thesis, East Carolina University, 1965.

Poteat, R. Matthew. "To the Last Man and the Last Dollar: Governor Henry Toole Clark and Civil War North Carolina, July 1861 to September 1862." Master's thesis, North Carolina State University, 2005.

Powell, Michael Albert. "Confederate Federalism: A View from the Governors." Ph.D. dissertation, University of Maryland, College Park, 2004.

Smith, Louis Roycraft. "A History of Sumter County, Alabama, through 1886." Ph.D. dissertation, University of Alabama, Tuscaloosa, 1988.

Index

Page numbers in *italics* indicate illustrations.

Abolitionists 29, 54, 62–63, 147
Adams, John 16
African Americans *see* Freedmen, Slavery
Alabama 7, 12, 39–47, 49–51, 61, *174*
Alamance County, N.C. 77
CSS Albemarle 121
Albemarle Sound 15, 18–19, 22, 93, 97–98
Ambrose, Henry 107–108
American Party 68
American Revolution 19
American Whig Society 20
Anderson, Joseph 94
Antietam Campaign 99, 111, 125
Appomattox, Battle of 8, 125
Ashe, Thomas S. 138
Ashe, William S. 87–88, 185n74
Ashe County, N.C. 109
Asheville, N.C. 113
Atkinson, William 115

Bank of the United States 53
Barringer, Daniel M. 80
Bath, N.C. 15
Beaufort, N.C. 90, 99
Beaufort County, N.C. 95, 108
Bell, John 68, 182n97
Benjamin, Judah P. 78–79, 95, 109
Bentonville, Battle of 125
Bermuda 84
Berrien, John M. 26
Bertie County, N.C. 17–20, 22–23, 76
Blockade runners 10, 87, 100–101, 104, 186n42
Blount-Bridgers House 59, *193*
Borrits, William 20
Bourne, Maria Toole Clark 59, 151
Bowes, Michael 106
Bragg, Thomas 73, 80, 191n55
Branch, John 24–26
Breckinridge, John C. 68, 182n97

Bridgers, Henry Clark 149
Bridgers, John L. 62, 149, 151
Bridgers, Laura Clark 59, 141, 148, 151, 153, 158
Bridgers, Robert Rufus 51, 125, 144
Buchanan, James 57, 68
Bull Run, Battle of *see* Manassas, Battle of
Bull Run Creek, Va. 81
Bunch, Robert 101–102, 112, 186n51
Buncombe County, N.C. 113, 117
Burgwyn, Henry King 77
Burke, Thomas 73
Burns, Otway 22
Burnside, Ambrose 99, 105, 112
Butler, Benjamin 92, 96
Butler, William 57

Calhoun, Floride 25
Calhoun, John C. 24–25, 52, 147
Calvary Episcopal Church 63, 141, *142–143*, 144, 151
Cape Fear Academy 142
Cape Fear region 15, 87, 91, 94
Carrie Sanford 101–102
Cass, Lewis 57
Causey, Joshua 113
Charleston, S.C. 46, 68, 73, 84–86, 101, 112
Charlestown, S.C. *see* Charleston, S.C.
Chatham County, N.C. 115, 113
Chatham Salt Mining and Manufacturing Co. 115
Cheshire, Elizabeth Parker 189n3, 191n78
Cheshire, Joseph Blount 141–142, 189n3, 191n78
Cheshire, Joseph Blount, Jr. 142, 178n2, 186n42
Choctaw Indians 41
Chowan River 17–18
Chowanoke Indians 15

Clark, Arabella (daughter of HTC and Mary) *see* Smith, Arabella Clark
Clark, Arabella Toole (wife of JW Clark) 21–22, 25–26, 28, 162–163, 178n1, 181n60
Clark, Christopher 6, 15–20, 26, 38, 193
Clark, David 119
Clark, Elizabeth (daughter of Christopher Clark and Elizabeth) 18
Clark, Elizabeth (wife of Christopher Clark) 18
Clark, Hannah Turner 18, 38
Clark, Haywood 59, 142–143, 151, 174
Clark, Henry Irwin 59, 151
Clark, Henry Selby 55
Clark, Henry Toole: appearance *31*, 38; birth and childhood 28–29; businessman 6–7, 15, 22–23, 27, 38, 43, 58, 60–62, 124–126, 142, 150–151; Calvary Episcopal Church 63, 141; Confederate prison 10, 70, 76–79; conscription 8, 11, 83, 99, 110–113; contracts for weapons 86; defense of the state 81, 90–91, 93–103, 108–110, 112–114, 116–117, 148, 150; Democratic Party 7, 22, 52–57, 63–64, 119; disaffection 10, 94–95, 100, 104, 106–114, 119; elevation to governorship 5, 70, 73–76; failure as political leader 8–13, 70, 89, 95–96, 99, 101–104, 113, 116–117, 120, 145–143, 150; and freedmen 126–129; genealogy 139–140, 194; gunpowder manufacture 10, 106; illness and death 144; impressments of arms, supplies, and slaves 11, 87–88, 104, 115, 119; marriage and family 12–13, 58–60, 119–120, 124–125,

203

Index

139–144, 150–151; Military Board 79–80, 91; in New York City 37; political philosophy 7–9, 11–13, 52–54, 57, 62, 64–70, 87–88, 137–139, 145–147, 150–151, 166–168; political activity after governorship 124, 130–131, 134–139, 189n1; presidential pardon 129–134, 146–147; raises and equips troops 8, 10, 70, 83–90, 99; relations with the Confederacy 11–12, 70, 77–79, 81, 85–88, 90, 93–104, 106, 109–113, 117, 145–148; salt works 10, 104–106; sends troops to Confederacy 5, 12, 70, 87, 89–90, 93, 96, 109–112, 114, 155–156; slave-hire business 38–52, 61; slave ownership 6–8, 11, 23, 38, 51–54, 61–62, 65–68, 70, 116; Speaker of the Senate 5, 7, 9, 67, 70–71, 75, 169, 183n8; State Senator 7–9, 63–67, 71, 130–131, 134–136; status in society 5–8, 12–13, 15, 30, 37, 57–58; University of North Carolina 29–37, 80, 153–165, 192n1; Union raids on Tarboro 120–124; Whig party 52–53

Clark, James West: 6, 15, 20–29, *21*, 32, 35–39, 43, 58, 141, 146; letters to HTC 32–37, 153–65

Clark, Laura (daughter of HTC and Mary) *see* Bridgers, Laura Clark

Clark, Laura Placidia (daughter of JW Clark and Arabella) 22, 158, 191n71

Clark, Maria (daughter of JW Clark and Arabella) 22

Clark, Maria Toole (daughter of HTC and Mary) *see* Bourne, Maria T.

Clark, Mary (daughter of Christopher Clark and Elizabeth) *see* West, Mary Clark

Clark, Mary (daughter of JW Clark and Arabella) 22, 157

Clark, Mary Parker (daughter of HTC and Mary) 59

Clark, Mary Weeks Parker (wife of HTC) 12, 58–59, 76, 120–121, 125, 150–151

Clark, Sarah 18

Clark-Cotton House *27*

Clark family slaves: as investments 6–7, 19–20, 38–39; list of individual slaves *42;* slave-hires 40–47, 49–52, 61

Clarke, Mary Bayard Devereux 96

Clarke, William J. 99

Clingman, Thomas L. 69

Compromise of 1850 63

Conetoe Plantation 22, 26–27

Confederacy *see* Confederate States of America

Confederate Army 70, 82, 92–93, 98–99, 108–113, 105, 109, 111, 115, 119–125, 188n35

Confederate Navy 93

Confederate Party 117–118

Confederate privateers 91–93

Confederate States of America 1, 68, 151; Congress 11, 77, 87, 95, 110–111, 113, 125; "Cotton Diplomacy" 101; government 1, 9, 70, 79, 82, 84–90, 93, 96, 98, 100–102, 106, 110, 112, 114, 117, 119, 145, 150, 186n51; neglects defense of North Carolina 9, 11–12, 81, 89–90, 92–94, 96–100, 102–103, 106, 112, 117, 148, 150; War Department 77, 87, 90, 93, 96–7, 99, 109, 113, 148

Conscription (Confederate) 8, 11, 82, 110–113; disaffection 111, exemption from 113–114; substitution 113

Conscription (State) 83, 111, disaffection 107

Conservative Party 8, 10, 117, 119, 137–138

Conventions *see* North Carolina Conventions

Constitutional Union Party 68

Craven, Braxton 78

Croom, Richard S. 161, 192n11

Currituck County, N.C. 105

Currituck Sound, N.C. 93

Daniel's Schoolhouse 122

Dancy, John 62

Dancy, William 54, 63–64, 182n72

Davidson County, N.C. 76, 107, 187n18

Davis, Jefferson 11, 81–82, 94, 108, 111, 148; and arms 87–88; HTC urges him to defend N.C. 97–98; proclamations 96–97

Democrat-Republicans *see* Democrats

Democratic Party 6–7, 10–11, 22–25, 33, 53–55, 57, 63, 119, 146

Democrats 8–10, 25, 53–57, 63–68, 70, 80, 117, 119, 130; Conservative Party 132, 137; "Jacksonian Democrats" 23, 71, 129; "Jeffersonian Democrats" 23–4, 57, 63; suffrage 65–66

Dialectic Society 32–33, 134

Donnell, Richard 55

Douglas, Stephen A. 68, 182n97

Draft *see* Conscription

Duckenfield, William 19

Duke University *see* Trinity College

Dyer County, Tenn. 22, 26–28, 45–6

Eaton, John 24–25

Eaton, Peggy 24–25

Edenton, N.C. 15–6, 19–20, 115

Edgecombe Agricultural Society 23, 62

Edgecombe County, N.C. 6, 21–22, 24, 38, 53–57, 61–70, 75, 110, 120, 124, 126, 130; antebellum prosperity 61–62, 126, 130

"Edgecombe Democracy" 6, 63, 130

Edmondston, Catherine Anne Devereux 94

Edwards, Weldon N. 57, 114–115

Ellis, John W. 9, 67, 79, 82, 91; illness and death 1, 5, 73, 75–76; views on slavery 116

Ellis, Mary 76

Elmwood *17–18*, 20, 22, 179n6

Emancipation 126–128

Emancipation Proclamation 108

Emmons, Ebenezer 105

England 15, 19; arms from 84–86, 100, 145

Episcopal Church (American) 141

Estvan, Bela 86

Fanning, David 73

Fayetteville, N.C. 82–83

Federalists 23–24

First North Carolina Union Vol. 108

Forsyth County, N.C. 187n19

Fort, Lewis 22

Fort Branch, N.C. 121–122

Fort Caswell 91, 186n53

Fort Clark 91–92, 186n53

Fort Hatteras 91–93, 186n53

Fort Johnston 91, 186n53

Fort Macon 90–91, 99, 102, 186n53

Fort Ocracoke 91–92, 186n53

Fort Oregon 91–92, 186n53

Fort Sumter 8, 69, 80–82, 106

Foster, Charles Henry 94

Foster, John 121

Fourteenth Amendment 8, 72, 134–136, 138

Franklin County, N.C. 120

Free Press 61, 139

"Free Suffrage" 65

Freedmen 126–130, 135–138

Freedmen's Bureau 127–128

Freemont, Sewall L. 143

Froelich, Louis 86

Gadd, Robert 112

General Washington 16, 19

Georgia 20, 22, 39, 68–69, 120, 165

Goldsboro, N.C. 46, 86, 99

Goldsborough, Louis M. 94

Gorgas, Josiah 106

Granville, John Carteret, Lord 16

Graham, John W. 95

Graham, William A. 84, 95–96, 117, 130–131, 135, 139, 191n55

Grayson, William J. 30

Great Britain: American Revolution

204

Index

19; British citizen drafted 112; fails to recognize Confederacy 101–102; HTC's praise for "English Character" 166–168, 192n1; shipping 101; and slavery 39, 168, 192n2; and War of 1812 28; weapons from 84, 86, 100, 145; *see also:* England
Greene County, Ala. 41, 47
Guilford County, N.C. 187n19
Guion, Haywood 80

Hair, James (slave agent) 47–51, *48*, 61–62
Hair, Sam 47
Halifax County, N.C. 114
Hall, Edward D. 96
Hall, Samuel 68
Hamilton, N.C. 121
Hampton, Wade 131
Hampton Roads, Va. 92
Hargrave, Catherine 58
Hargrave, Franklin 58
Harrison, William Henry 181n32, 183n1
Harvey Birch 84–85
Hatteras Inlet 91–98, 102, 108, 148
Hawkins, Rush 94
Haywood, Elizabeth *see* Toole, Elizabeth Haywood
Haywood, William 22
Haywood, William H., Jr. 37
Haywood family 22
Helton, John 107
"Highland Brigade" *see* Thomas's Legion
Hill, Daniel H. 94, 108
Hill, John 68
Hilma *59*, 60–61, 120–122, *122*, *124*, *148*, *149*, 151, *175*
Hodge, William Henry 36, 154–155, 160–163, 165, 192n4
Holden, William W. 57, 63, 130–132, 136; criticism of HTC 79, 80–81, 117; early support of Vance 117–118; as Governor 129–130, 138; opposes HTC pardon 131–133
Howard, George 54, 130
Huger, Benjamin 93, 98, 102
Hunter, Robert M. 101
Hyde County, N.C. 104–106, 108

Internal Improvements 23–24; HTC's views on 7, 64–65
Iredell, James 16

Jackson, Andrew 6, 21, 24–26, 52–53, 55–56, 181n32
Jackson County, N.C. 109
"Jacksonian Democracy" 53, 71
Jamestown, Va. 15
Jamesville, N.C. 65
Jefferson, Thomas 11, 16, 57, 147

Johnson, Andrew 128–129; presidential pardons 128–134, 146–147, 190n48; reconstruction plans 8, 127–131, 135
Johnson, Jacob 134
Johnston, Joseph E. 125
Johnston, William 117–118
Johnston, Col. William 77–78
Jones, Willie 11

Kinston, N.C. 112, 120
Kirk-Holden War 138
Know-Nothing Party *see* American Party
Ku Klux Klan 138

Lafayette, Marquis de 30–31
Laurel Valley 109
Leach, James Madison 133, 135
Lee, Robert E. 86–87, 99, 100, 121
Lewis (slave) 43–44, 52, 61
Lincoln, Abraham 5, 8, 68, 77, 81–82, 108, 129
Livingstone, Ala. 41, 43–49

Macon, Nathaniel 11
Madison County, N.C. 109
Manassas, Battle of 81
Mangum, Willie P. 53, 55, 73
Manly, Charles 63–64, 80, 191n55
Martin, Alexander 73
Martin, James G. 10, 83, 88, 100, 121, 186n42
Martin, Josiah 19
Martin, William F. 92
Mathewson, John 125
Mathewson, Nathan 125
McClellan, George B. 97
McKay, James 57
McRae, Donald 101–102, 186n48
Mexican-American War 7, 56–57
Military Board (N.C.) 79–80, 91, 95
Militia (N.C.) 78, 81–83, 99, 103, 107–112, 120
Mitchell, Bill ix
Monreath 120, 150, 189n3
Moore, James H. 106–107
Moore's Creek Bridge, Battle of 19
Mordecai, George W. 105
Morehead City, N.C. 99, 105
"Mosquito Fleet" 91–93, 103
Murphey, Archibald D. 131

C.S.S. *Nashville* 84–85
Nashville, Tenn. 46, 62, 182n69
Nashville Convention 62–63
Ned (slave) 50, 61
Neville's Church 183n24
New Bern, N.C. 102, 105, 112, 120–122; Admiralty Court 91–92; Union capture of 99–100
Ninth New York Zouaves 94
Norcom, James 20, 179n10

Norfleet 36, 157
Norfleet, Robert 60
Norfleet, William 57
Norfolk, Va. 92–93, 97–98
North Carolina: antebellum society 6–7, 13; coastal defense 81–82, 90–103; creation of colony 15–16; lack of industry 81, 83, 100, 104, 106; local government 124, 137; readmission to the Union 138; secession 68–69, 183n103
North Carolina Constitution: 5, 10, 22, 66, 70–75, 124, 177n1; Amendments of 1835 71–72; Constitution of 1868 8, 124, 137; suffrage requirements 65–66, 71–72, 136; succession to governorship 5, 10, 70, 72–75; and weak executive 10, 65, 72, 150
North Carolina Convention (1835) 71–72
North Carolina Convention (1861–1862) 68–69, 82–83, 95–96, 99, 108–109, 114–116, 130, 141, 146, 183n103
North Carolina Convention (1865) 129–131, 136
North Carolina Convention (1868) 136–137
North Carolina General Assembly 6, 19, 63–64, 66, 68, 72, 74, 107; abolished 135; funding for defense 82, 90, 93, 100, 105–106; post-war 134, 138; power to elect the governor 70–71, 73–75; secession 68, 82
North Carolina Historical Society 139
North Carolina House of Commons 21, 24, 64–66, 68, 71, 83, 87, 134, 136–137, 177n1
North Carolina House of Representatives *see* North Carolina House of Commons
North Carolina Railroad 64
North Carolina Senate 24, *71–72*
North Carolina Standard 75, 117, 132, 139

Ocracoke Inlet 91, 185n5
O'Neal, Margaret "Peggy" *see* Eaton, Peggy
Oregon Inlet 91–92

Pamlico Sound 93, 97–98, 121
Parker, Daniel E. 27–28, 45–46, 49
Parker, Francis Marion 125
Parker, Haywood 41, 47
Parker, Mary Toole 22
Parker, Mary Weeks *see* Clark, Mary W. Parker
Parker, Theophilus 22, 41, 58, 165
Parker family 141

Index

Partisan Rangers 112
"Petticoat Affair" 24–25, 52
Pettigrew, William 108
Petway, William D. 64
Peyton, John Lewis 84–86
Philanthropic Society 32–33
Pickens, Francis W. 114
Planters 6–7, 12–13, 30–32, 40, 64, 66; and the Freedman's Bureau 128
Plymouth, N.C. 120–121
Polk, James K. 37, 57
Poole, John 130, 132
Porter, David 93
Portsmouth Island, N.C. 92
Portugal 16–17
Potter, Edward E. 121
Princeton University 20–21

Quaker Belt 10, 106, 111, 187n19
Quakers 105–106

Raleigh, N.C. 21, 46, 57, 62, 69, 82–84, 96, 99, 118–119; and Clark 37, 150; funeral of Gov. Ellis 76–77; POWs arrive 77; recruits arrive 70; Union capture of 125; visit of Lafayette 31; visit of Pres. Johnson 134, 191n55
Randolph, George 86–87, 111–112, 114
Randolph County, N.C. 187n19
Rayner, Kenneth 76, 183n18
Reconstruction 8, 12, 135–138
Reid, David 64–65, 73
Republican Party 68, 129–130, 135, 137–139
Richmond 69, 77, 86, 97
Roanoke Island 19, 93, 97–99, *98*, 102, 105, 148
Rocky Mount, N.C. 22, 46, 120
Rocky Mount Mills 120–121, 127, 182n80
Ruffin, Thomas 96

St. James Episcopal Church *47*
Salisbury, N.C. 77–78, 89
Salisbury Prison 77–79, 183n28
Sally 26
Salmon Creek 17–19
Salt 10, 104–106, 115
Saltville, Va. 104–105
Sam (slave) 161
Saunders, William L. 138–139, 191n71
Schenck, David 95
Secession 6–8, 10, 68–69, 80, 82, 84, 106, 108–109, 130, 145, 150, 183n103, 190n48
Secessionists 80, 82, 107–108, 117, 129, 130, 133, 183n103, 183n18
Seventh North Carolina 96
Seward, William H. 134
Sherman, William T. 125
Sickles, Daniel E. 130, 134, 136

Slavery: abolition of 51, 126, 130; economic importance 6–7, 38–41, 65–67, 116, 126; effects of emancipation 126–128, 130; impressments into Confederate service 115, 119; as political issue 56, 62–64, 68; slave-hire 38–41, 43–47, 49, 50–52; slave unrest and insurrection 43–44, 50, 108, 115–116; slave trade 39–40, 168, 192n2; white southerners views of 30, 62, 66–68, 116
Smith, Arabella Clark 59, 151
Snap Dragon 22
Solomon (slave) 45, 61
Sothel, Seth 17, 179n6
South Carolina 15, 52–53, 68, 101, 114, 116, 165
"Southern Rights" 54, 62–63, 68–69
Southerner see *Free Press*
Southwick 86
Speight, James P. 75
State Journal 75, 80, 83
"States Rights" 24, 53
Stringham, Silas 92
Stuart Buchanan and Co. 105
Substitution 113
Sumter County, Ala. 40–43, 48–49

Tar River 21–23, 64, 121–122, 182n80
Tarboro, N.C. *27, 56, 175*; Clark family 5, 7, 12, 21–22, 26–29, 31, 39, 41, 43, 45–47, 51, 58, 60–61, 118–120, 124, 130, 141; location and prominence 21–22, 46, 65, 120, 126, 182n80; in politics 137, 182n97; raided by Union troops 120–122, 124, 126, 130, 137, 139, 141–144, 182n80; tournament (1869) 139–140
Tarboro Academy 29, 53, 183n18, 192n1
Tarboro Male Academy see Tarboro Academy
Tarborough Academy see Tarboro Academy
Taylor, Marble Nash 94
Tennessee: base for Union raids 109–110; Clark Family business in 7, 22, 26–28, 38, 45
Third Georgia 93, 98
Third New York 121
Thirteenth Amendment 129–130
Thirtieth North Carolina 125
Thirty-first North Carolina (militia) 98
Thomas, William George 86
Thomas, William Holland 109–110
Thomas's Legion 109–110
Timberlake, John 24
Todd, David 77
Toole, Arabella see Clark, Arabella Toole

Toole, Elizabeth Haywood 21, 158, 163, 165, 192n16
Toole, Henry Irwin (cousin of HTC) 54–55, 146
Toole, Henry Irwin (grandfather of HTC) 21–22, 181n37
Toole, Mary see Mary Toole Parker
Toole family 21–22, 141
Transit 91
Trinity College 78
Tucker, Thomas Goode 116
Turner, James 73
Turner, Josiah 74–75, 138
Turner, Thomas 18
Twenty-first North Carolina (militia) 53
Twenty-fourth Massachusetts 108
Twenty-fourth North Carolina 99

Union Army see United States Army
Union Navy see United States Navy
United Daughters of the Confederacy 151
United States Army: in eastern N.C. 92–99, 115, 120–122; at Hatteras 94; at Roanoke Island 105, 126
United States Congress 6, 24, 53, 57, 62–63, 128–129, 130–132, 135–138, 146, 180n5, 192n15
United States Navy 92, 114; southern blockade 82, 84–85, 91, 93, 100–102, 114–115
United States Navy Department 6, 21, 24, 26, 146
University of North Carolina–Chapel Hill 23, 28–37, *35*, 130, 134–135, 153–165, 176–178
University of Virginia 29, 32

Van Buren, Martin 25, 52
Vance, Robert B. 109
Vance, Zebulon B. 1, 104, 106, 138, 191n55; *Advance* 100, 186n42; capture 125; compared to HTC 5, 9–12, 147, 150–151; 1862 gubernatorial election 117–121; pardon 131–132
Virginia 12, 15–16, 18, 99–100; secession 81–82; source of slaves 40; Union troops in N.C. 92–93, "Virginia-first" policy 9, 96–97, 102–103, 148
Virginia Convention 69

Walker, Leroy P. 77–78, 93, 96, 183n28
Walnut Creek Plantation 22, 26–28, 58
War of 1812 22, 24, 28, 90
Washington, D.C. 24–27, 94, 130–131, 133–135, 141, 146

Index

Washington, George 23, 34
Washington, N.C. 64, 95, 108, 110, 121, 177n3
Washington County, N.C. 107–108, 177n3
Waterhouse, George 106
West, George 20
West, Mary Clark 18, 20
Wheeler, John H. 139
Whigs 7, 23, 52–57, 67; challenge HTC's governorship 70, 74; Conservative Party 8, 10, 117, 137; Constitutional Union Party 68; early support of HTC 9, 70; HTC appointees to Military Board 80; slavery 53–54, 63–64, 68; suffrage requirements 65–6
Whitaker, Spier 107
William 16, 19
Williams, Robert, Jr. 163
Wilmington, N.C. 46, 57, 99, 101–102; arrival of arms 85–86; fortification 90; HTC's children 142, 151; salt operation 105

Wilmington and Weldon Railroad 46, 99, 120–121, 143, 151
Winslow 91, 185n5, 185n6
Winslow, Warren 73, 80
Wilmot Proviso 57, 63
Wilson, Louis D. 56, 56–57
Woodfin, N.W. 105
Worth, John M. 105
Worth, Jonathan 130–136, 131n55

Yancey, William Lowndes 69
Yancy (slave) 50–51